TWELFTH NIGHT

Arden Early Modern Drama Guides

Series Editors:
Andrew Hiscock
University of Wales, Bangor, UK and Lisa Hopkins,
Sheffield Hallam University, UK

Arden Early Modern Drama Guides offers practical and accessible introductions to the critical and performative contexts of key Elizabethan and Jacobean plays. Each guide introduces the text's critical and performance history but also provides students with an invaluable insight into the landscape of current scholarly research through a keynote essay on the state of the art and newly commissioned essays of fresh research from different critical perspectives.

A Midsummer Night's Dream edited by Regina Buccola
Doctor Faustus edited by Sarah Munson Deats
King Lear edited by Andrew Hiscock and Lisa Hopkins
1 Henry IV edited by Stephen Longstaffe
'Tis Pity She's a Whore edited by Lisa Hopkins
Women Beware Women edited by Andrew Hiscock
Volpone edited by Matthew Steggle
The Duchess of Malfi edited by Christina Luckyj
The Alchemist edited by Erin Julian and Helen Ostovich
The Jew of Malta edited by Robert A Logan
Macbeth edited by John Drakakis and Dale Townshend
Richard III edited by Annaliese Connolly
Twelfth Night edited by Alison Findlay and Liz Oakley-Brown

Further titles in preparation

BLOOMSBURY
LONDON • NEW DELHI • NEW YORK • SYDNEY

Bloomsbury Arden

An imprint of Bloomsbury Publishing Plc

50 Bedford Square	1385 Broadway
London	New York
WC1B 3DP	NY 10018
UK	USA

www.bloomsbury.com

Bloomsbury is a registered trademark of Bloomsbury Publishing Plc

First published 2014

© Alison Findlay, Liz Oakley-Brown and contributors 2014

Alison Findlay, Liz Oakley-Brown and contributors have asserted their rights under the Copyright, Designs and Patents Act, 1988, to be identified as Authors of this work.

British Library Cataloguing-in-Publication Data
A catalogue record for this book is available from the British Library.

ISBN: HB: 978-1-4411-2878-2
PB: 978-1-4725-0329-9
ePDF: 978-1-4725-0331-2
ePub: 978-1-4725-0330-5

Library of Congress Cataloging-in-Publication Data
Twelfth night : a critical reader / edited by Alison Findlay and Liz Oakley-Brown.
pages cm. -- (Arden early modern drama guides)
Includes bibliographical references and index.
ISBN 978-1-4411-2878-2 (HB) -- ISBN 978-1-4725-0329-9 (pbk.) -- ISBN 978-1-4725-0330-5 (e-Pub) -- ISBN 978-1-4725-0331-2 (e-PDF)
1. Shakespeare, William, 1564-1616. Twelfth night. 2. Shakespeare, William, 1564-1616--Dramatic production. 3. Shakespeare, William, 1564-1616--Study and teaching. I. Findlay, Alison, 1963- II. Oakley-Brown, Liz.
PR2837.T933 2013
822.3'3--dc23
2013021390

Typeset by Fakenham Prepress Solutions, Fakenham, Norfolk NR21 8NN
Printed and bound in India

CONTENTS

LIST OF ILLUSTRATIONS

ACKNOWLEDGEMENTS

For their help with planning and overseeing publication of this book, we wish to thank the Series Editors, Professors Andrew Hiscock (Bangor University) and Lisa Hopkins (Sheffield Hallam University) and Margaret Bartley at Arden Shakespeare. We offer very heartfelt thanks to all of our authors for their individual contributions to the volume. We recognise the considerable pressure colleagues are currently working under and are delighted to include essays from such an outstanding team of international scholars. We also wish to thank Eleanor Findlay and Emily Hayton for their willingness to share their thoughts about watching the Stratford Festival production and performing in the 2012 Schools Shakespeare *Twelfth Night*. We thank John Shepherd for his permission to reproduce the photograph of the Bingo Dragon Theatre Company production, and all involved in that production, especially its remarkable Malvolio. Our students at Lancaster University have been and continue to be an inspiring group of individuals with whom we develop our ideas in teaching. We dedicate this book to them.

Alison Findlay and Liz Oakley-Brown
Lancaster University, 2013

SERIES INTRODUCTION

The drama of Shakespeare and his contemporaries has remained at the very heart of English curricula internationally and the pedagogic needs surrounding this body of literature have grown increasingly complex as more sophisticated resources become available to scholars, tutors and students. This series aims to offer a clear picture of the critical and performative contexts of a range of chosen texts. In addition, each volume furnishes readers with invaluable insights into the landscape of current scholarly research as well as including new pieces of research by leading critics.

This series is designed to respond to the clearly identified needs of scholars, tutors and students for volumes which will bridge the gap between accounts of previous critical developments and performance history and an acquaintance with new research initiatives related to the chosen plays. Thus, our ambition is to offer innovative and challenging guides that will provide practical, accessible and thought-provoking analyses of early modern drama. Each volume is organized according to a progressive reading strategy involving introductory discussion, critical review and cutting-edge scholarly debate. It has been an enormous pleasure to work with so many dedicated scholars of early modern drama and we are sure that this series will encourage you to read 400-year-old playtexts with fresh eyes.

Andrew Hiscock and Lisa Hopkins

TIMELINE

1537	*Gl'Ingannati* (*The Deceived Ones*) published in Italy
1547?	*Gl'Inganni* (*The Deceived*) published in Italy
1560	Laurent Joubert, *Treatise on Laughter*
1569	Heliodorus's *Aethiopica* translated into English by Thomas Underdowne
1581	Barnabe Riche, *Farewell to Militarie Profession*
1584	Reginald Scot, *The Discovery of Witchcraft*
1589	John Bucke, *Instructions for the Use of the Rosarie*
1590	Philip Sidney's *Arcadia*
1591–1609	Henslowe's diary, a manuscript notebook of 238 folios
1595	Plautus's *Menaecmi: A Pleasant and Fine Conceited Comaedie* translated into English by William Warner
1595	Edward Bunny, *A Survey of the Popes Supremacie*
1596–7	Expedition of the Dutch explorer Willem Barentsz to seek the North East Passage
1598	Emanuel Forde, *Parismus, the Renowned Prince of Bohemia*
c. 1598	Nicholas Hilliard, *Treatise Concerning the Arte of Limning*
1601	*Twelfth Night* is possibly the play performed at court on 6 January 1601
1602	John Manningham records being present at a performance on Candlemas (2 February)
1612	Thomas Heywood, *An Apology for Actors*
1618	*The King's Men* perform *Twelfth Night* at court
1623	*The King's Men* perform the play (as *Malvolio*) at Court; *Twelfth Night* first published in the First Folio

1661	Samuel Pepys's first record of seeing the play on 11 September
1703	William Burnaby's adaptation *Love Betray'd; or, the Agreable Disapointment*
1741	Drury Lane revival of *Twelfth Night*
1820	Frederick Reynolds's musical production containing 'Songs, Glees and Choruses', some of which were from other Shakespearean dramatic and non-dramatic texts
1868	John Manningham's diary discovered
1910	First extant film of *Twelfth Night* (dir. Charles Kent)
1912	Harley Granville-Barker's production
1916	A. C. Bradley, 'Feste the Jester'
1946	W. H. Auden, *Lectures on Shakespeare*
1954	First full-length study of the play (Leslie Hotson, *The First Night of Twelfth Night* [London: Rupert Hart-Davis, 1954])
1996	Trevor Nunn's film of *Twelfth Night*
2002	Tim Carroll's 'original practices' production at the Inns of Court (February) and the Globe (May)
2004	Katharine Davies, *The Madness of Love* (originally titled *A Good Voyage*)
2012	The Reclaim Shakespeare Company launched its website and manifesto 'BP or not BP'; Tim Carroll's 2002 production revived at the Globe
2012	*What You Will: A Fly on the Wall, Behind the Scenes, Documentary Tragi-Comical Road Movie* (dir. Simon Reade)

NOTES ON CONTRIBUTORS

Linda Anderson is Professor of English at Virginia Tech and the author, most recently, of *A Place in the Story: Servants and Service in Shakespeare's Plays* (University of Delaware Press, 2005).

William C. Carroll is Professor of English at Boston University. Among his publications are *The Great Feast of Language in Love's Labour's Lost* (Princeton University Press, 1976), *The Metamorphoses of Shakespearean Comedy* (Princeton University Press, 1985) and *Fat King, Lean Beggar: Representations of Poverty in the Age of Shakespeare* (Cornell University Press, 1996). He has also published the following editions: Thomas Middleton, *Women Beware Women* (New Mermaids Series), *Macbeth: Texts and Contexts* (Bedford Shakespeare Series), *The Two Gentlemen of Verona* (Arden Third Series), *Love's Labour's Lost* (New Cambridge Shakespeare) and, most recently, *Thomas Middleton: Four Plays* (Methuen, 2012). He is Co-General Editor of the New Mermaid Drama Series.

Keir Elam is Professor of English Literature at the University of Bologna, where he is resident member of the Institute for Advanced Studies and referee for the Humanities in the University Research Observatory. His volumes include *Semiotics of Theatre and Drama* (Routledge, 1988, 2002), *Shakespeare's Universe of Discourse: Language-Games in the Comedies* (Cambridge University Press, 1984) and the Arden *Twelfth Night* (3rd series). He has also published numerous articles on Shakespeare and early modern drama, Beckett and contemporary European theatre. He is general editor of the bilingual Shakespeare series for the publisher Rizzoli and is currently working on a volume for Arden Shakespeare, *Shakespeare's Pictures*.

Alison Findlay is Professor of Renaissance Drama and Director
of the Shakespeare Programme at Lancaster University. Most
recently she has completed *Women in Shakespeare* for the
Shakespeare Dictionary Series published by Arden (Bloomsbury
Press, 2010) and *Much Ado About Nothing: A Guide to the Text and
Play in Performance* (Palgrave Macmillan, 2011). Recent essays on
Shakespeare include pieces on *Henry IV* (2010), *Much Ado About
Nothing* (2010 and 2012) and *The Comedy of Errors* (2012).

Peter Kirwan is Lecturer in Shakespeare and Early Modern
Drama at the University of Nottingham. His primary research
interests are plays of disputed authorship, early modern drama
in contemporary performance and Shakespeare in digital media.
His recent publications include articles for *Shakespeare Quarterly*,
Philological Quarterly, *Literature Compass* and several book
collections, and he is an Associate Editor for the forthcoming
Collaborative Plays by Shakespeare and Others (Macmillan/RSC).
He is also a Trustee of the British Shakespeare Association.

Randall Martin is Professor of English at the University of New
Brunswick. He has recently co-edited *Shakespeare/Adaptation/
Modern Drama: Essays in Honour of Jill L. Levenson* (University
of Toronto Press, 2011) with Katherine Scheil. He is currently
writing a book on Shakespeare and St Paul.

Liz Oakley-Brown is Senior Lecturer in Shakespeare and
Renaissance Writing at Lancaster University. Her publica-
tions include *Ovid and the Cultural Politics of Translation in
Early Modern England* (Ashgate, 2006) and the edited collection
*Shakespeare and the Translation of Identity in Early Modern
England* (Continuum, 2011). She is currently completing the
monograph *Thomas Churchyard: Travel, Translation and Tudor
Identities*.

Tiffany Stern is Professor of Early Modern Drama at
Oxford University and author of *Rehearsal from Shakespeare to
Sheridan* (Oxford University Press, 2000), *Making Shakespeare*
(Routledge, 2004), *Shakespeare in Parts* (with Simon Palfrey,

Oxford University Press, 2007) and *Documents of Performance in Early Modern England* (Cambridge University Press, 2009). She has co-edited a collection of essays with Farah Karim-Cooper, *Shakespeare's Theatres and the Effects of Performance* (2013), and has edited *King Leir* (Nick Hern, 2002), Sheridan's *The Rivals* (Methuen, 2004), Farquhar's *Recruiting Officer* (Methuen, 2011) and Brome's *Jovial Crew* (forthcoming).

Andrew Stott is Professor of English and Dean of Undergraduate Education at the University at Buffalo, SUNY. He is the author of *Comedy* (Routledge, 2005; revised and enlarged 2014), *The Pantomime Life of Joseph Grimaldi* (Canongate, 2009), and *The Vampyre Family: Passion, Envy and the Curse of Byron* (Canongate, 2013).

R. S. White is Australian Professorial Fellow and Winthrop Professor of English at the University of Western Australia. He has published books and articles on Shakespeare and has edited *Twelfth Night: Contemporary Critical Essays* (Palgrave Macmillan, 1996). Among his other works are *Pacifism in English Literature: Minstrels of Peace* (Palgrave Macmillan, 2008) and *John Keats: A Literary Life* (Palgrave Macmillan, 2010), which has been reissued in paperback. He is a past President of the Australian and New Zealand Shakespeare Association and a fellow of the Australian Humanities Academy.

Introduction

ALISON FINDLAY AND LIZ OAKLEY-BROWN

What You Will? Politics, Patronage and Performance

The completion of *Twelfth Night: A Critical Reader* coincides
with major productions of the play by theatrical institutions in
the UK and Canada whose remit is to promote the work of the
Bard. London's Globe Theatre and Stratford's Royal Shakespeare
Company both included *Twelfth Night* in their 2012 seasons while
the 2011 Stratford Ontario Shakespeare Festival's production
was released on DVD.[1] In time, the Globe's return to Tim
Carroll's 2002 'original practices' staging,[2] the RSC's *Twelfth
Night* (directed by David Farr as part of their Shipwreck Trilogy)[3]
and Des McAnuff's Stratford Festival production will take their
place in the catalogue of theatrical revivals of what is generally
viewed as Shakespeare's 'most popular' play.[4] For now, our
discussion of the these recent *Twelfth Night*s will serve as an introduction to the essays collected here – R. S. White's 'The Critical
Backstory', Linda Anderson's 'Performance History' and William
C. Carroll's 'The State of The Art', followed by essays pointing
to 'New Directions' in analyses by Keir Elam, Randall Martin,
Andrew Stott and Tiffany Stern, and Peter Kirwan's review of
learning and teaching resources. Our preamble considers some
of the ways in which *Twelfth Night* speaks to its own period of
production and to twenty-first-century English political and
pedagogical discourses in striking ways.

Scholars have comprehensively discussed the ways in which
the title of *Twelfth Night, Or What You Will* foregrounds equivo-
cation. To be sure, the coordinating conjunction 'or' presents an
immediate interpretative challenge. Furthermore, *Twelfth Night*'s

first word is a subordinate conjunction introducing Orsino's well-known conditional clause: 'If music be the food of love' (1.1.1).[5] Uncertainty, then, characterizes *Twelfth Night* at the outset and, like Malvolio's scrutiny of the letter in 2.5, generations of actors, critics, readers and audiences have searched for meaning.[6] Since the publication of Gary Taylor's *Reinventing Shakespeare: A Cultural History from the Restoration to the Present*,[7] the socio-historical context in which Shakespeare's texts are reproduced has provided ballast for interpretation. In the final section of *Twelfth Night: A Critical Guide*, Peter Kirwan points out that

> [I]n 2012 the Royal Shakespeare Company performed the play in repertory with *The Comedy of Errors* and *The Tempest* as 'Shakespeare's Shipwreck Trilogy', placing emphasis on the staging of encounters with new/undiscovered spaces. However, later in the same year, the all-male Propeller Theatre toured the play with *The Taming of the Shrew*, placing clear focus on gender issues. The play, as with its protean central characters, shifts identity according to the context in which it is encountered.[8]

Kirwan is mainly interested in how *Twelfth Night*'s proximity to other plays in the Shakespearean canon influences our understanding of the text, but his observations above draw attention to recent theoretical and popular interest in corporeality and spatiality.

Carroll's discussion of the critical appropriation of *Twelfth Night* since 2000[9] shows how Stephen Greenblatt's highly influential essay 'Fiction and Friction'[10] has inspired a range of critical writing on embodiment. With Viola/Cesario's enigmatic statement 'I am not what I am' (3.1.22) in mind, Carroll's essay shows how, in R. W. Maslen's words, *Twelfth Night* 'makes it possible to believe that there is no such thing as a stable normality where gender is concerned, either in Elizabethan times or in our own.'[11] From somatic to phenomenological debates, it seems that study of *Twelfth Night* is now synonymous with the 'body boom' that Keir Elam described nearly two decades ago in his essay 'In What Chapter of His Bosom? Reading Shakespeare's Bodies.'[12] Here, Elam argues that

> the early modern body boom has run parallel with the analogous foregrounding of bodily discourse not only in other critical domains such as cultural studies and post-modernist theory, but also in 'popular' culture, with its increasingly dominant workout ethic and Cindy Crawford corporeal self-cultivation imperative.[13]

The 'exemplary and [...] aristocratic early modern body' that Elam takes as his case study is that of Duke Orsino, the Shakespearean character who makes himself 'subject and object of the comedy's opening speech.'[14] For Elam, Orsino's calls for 'excess [...] that surfeiting, / The appetite may sicken, and so die' (1.1.2–3) enmesh him in a 'narcissistic preoccupation' with 'alimentary and sexual [...] drives.'[15] It is this propensity for material and carnal self-love which characterizes Illyrian, and perhaps Anglo-American, culture. Age seems to have only marginally withered the nineties celebrities invoked in 'In What Chapter of His Bosom?' (Arnold Schwarzenegger and Cindy Crawford), allowing us to serendipitously update Elam's original thesis to accommodate current preoccupations with youthfulness.

In the Globe's 2012 production, popular and critical attention focused on Mark Rylance, the theatre's inaugural artistic director (1995–2005), reprising his 2002 role as Olivia. The media looked forward to his 'return to Shakespeare's Globe as Lady Olivia',[16] and 'his hilarious kabuki-inspired' dramatization of the woman's part.[17] Of course, Rylance is known for his interest in 'original practices' and, as Maev Kennedy reported, the 2012 production 'reunite[ed] Rylance's "original practices" group, which created *Twelfth Night* 10 years ago, part of Rylance's championing of attempts to get as close as possible to Tudor staging, costumes, music and acting styles on the Globe stage.'[18] However, the term 'original practices' is somewhat misleading, particularly in terms of recent all-male productions. Stanley Wells' article 'Boys Should Be Girls: Shakespeare's Female Roles and the Boy Players'[19] draws on David Kathman's research on the age of apprentices in order to argue that that the leading female roles, even those of mature characters like Volumnia, Cleopatra and Juliet's nurse, would not have been played by adult male actors but boys, aged from about ten to the late teens. What, then, are the gender politics at stake in the Globe's *Twelfth Night*?

Appraising the 2002 performance, James C. Bulman writes:

> realign Time was clearly catching up with this Olivia: her costume and make-up spoke to her advancing years and her lack of female attractiveness. Actor Mark Rylance delivered his lines in a pinched, feminized voice, stammering at key moments, and glided when he walked as if on casters.[20]

Inevitably, time was advancing even further in terms of Rylance's 2012 performance, and even the actor himself 'joked that he would have a facelift to return as Olivia, adding: "I hope I'll still have some beauty." '[21] Though some might take the view that 'It is wonderful to see this sad but also absurd figure waking to the wonder of love',[22] certain ideologies regarding romantic love and youth prevail. In the words of one reviewer, Rylance's

> performance requires a double suspension of disbelief – not only is he a man, but he is also middle-aged. Yet this only adds to the comedy. His ageing Olivia delivers her first lines with such frigid stateliness, in full mourning dress, that it is all the funnier when she throws herself headlong at the startled Viola.[23]

Other commentators, though, 'really resented Olivia being played as an out-and-out comedy character.'[24] Malvolio's description of Viola/Cesario, 'Not yet old enough for a man, nor young enough for a boy' (1.5.152–3), bespeaks early modern England's interests in the fluid relationship between age and gender. Yet Elam's discussion in this volume also shows how 'Olivia is, both wittingly and unwittingly, at the centre of the play's optical discourse' and the ways in which her 'self-portrait' game in 1.5 also foregrounds the period's ambitions to capture bodies in time. When Illyria's Countess comments

> 'such a one I was this present', which is to say, this is what I looked like at the time the portrait was painted (that is, in this very instant) [...] Olivia is rather cryptically evoking the inscription frequently found in Renaissance portraits, including Hilliard's miniatures: *ætatis suæ* (of her or his age), accompanied by the effective age of the sitter and the date of composition. She is thereby playing [...] on her double presence as painter and subject of her self-portrait, since the composing and viewing of the picture coincide in the real time of performance.[25]

In the Globe's 2012 staging, the real time of performance, which highlights the fifty-something actor playing Olivia, engages with contemporary culture's specific anxieties. Produced in a climate preoccupied with the preservation of the maturing body, discourses of women's ageing subjectivities arguably take centre stage.

If *Twelfth Night* holds gender and embodiment up for scrutiny, it also questions the material spaces in which bodies are produced. Accordingly, critics have responded to Viola's enquiry 'What country friends is this?' (1.2.1) in a variety of ways. For instance, while Illyria 'was an ancient region of the Balkan peninsula', Keir Elam proposes that 'the play's economy of space feeds into its poetics of place.'[26] Moreover, taking his cue from the play's resistance to Viola's enquiry 'since the captain's response – "This is Illyria, lady" (1.2.2) – only raises further questions', Elam describes Shakespeare's island as a 'no-place that could be any place.'[27] In a 2011 essay, Nathalie Rivère de Carles argues that it is the 'land of the exotic.'[28] However, in the last five years or so, *Twelfth Night*'s dramatization of seascapes as well as landscapes has been examined. For instance, Steve Mentz's *At The Bottom Of Shakespeare's Ocean*, part of Continuum's *Shakespeare Now* series, situates his reading of the comedy amidst Hugues Maret's 1766 essay on the medicinal and divisive effects of fresh and sea water.[29] Maret's post-Cartesian treatise shows how the body's immersion in the sea causes a 'prodigious upheaval' as 'the soul [...] lets the reins of government of the body over which it presides drop, so to speak.'[30] For Mentz:

> In *Twelfth Night*, the ocean creates something like the same consequences [...] The play's central narrative, in which two bodies with 'one face, one voice, one habit' (5.1.200) are thrown into the surf and 'two persons' (5.1.200) emerge, provides a prehistory of Maret's understanding of the destabilizing force of salt water. The twins get reborn in the stormy sea.[31]

Randall Martin's essay in *Twelfth Night: A Critical Guide* engages with the burgeoning critical interest in early modern maritime space. However, as the Globe's 2012 outdoors run came to a close,[32] the Reclaim Shakespeare Company's intervention during the RSC's season drew attention to seafaring and theatre sponsorship, and Charlie Cooper's article for the *Independent* published on 3 October 2012 reported on the means by which the RSC had been 'hit by [a] string of theatrical protests over sponsorship deal with British oil giant':

> It is a Saturday night in Stratford-upon-Avon and theatre-goers are settling into their seats for an evening with the world's greatest playwright.
>   Duly the actors appear on stage – but this isn't Shakespeare as we know it. Parading in a green and yellow ruff, a character called BP is taken down a peg by the Bard's famous clown, Feste: 'For some are born green, some achieve greenness, and some purchase a semblance of greenness by sponsoring cultural events.'

The performance, an unscheduled prelude to last weekend's Royal Shakespeare Company (RSC) production of *Twelfth Night*, was the latest in a string of protests about BP's sponsorship of the World Shakespeare Festival that have divided theatregoers. [...]

At the end of each intervention, activists call on audience members to tear the BP logo off their copy of the evening's programme.

BP was widely criticised for safety failures after the Deepwater Horizon oil spill, which devastated coastal communities and wildlife in the Gulf of Mexico in 2010. In Shakespeare-inspired speeches, campaigners also condemn BP's controversial $2.5bn tar sand extraction project in Canada and a recent abortive plan to begin oil exploration in the Arctic.[33]

This was the Reclaim Shakespeare Company's third intervention on the RSC's stage. On 29 September 2012, their 'guerrilla Shakespeare'[34] took the form of 'three actor-vists' who performed a short *Twelfth Night*-inspired piece:

The script
Character 1 – BP:
    If oil be the fuel for us, drill on;
    Give us excess of it, that, surfeiting,
    The planet may sicken, and so die.
    Let's drill again! And cast a dying pall,
    O'er the tar sands of sweet Canada,
    The Arctic and the Gulf of Mexico,
    Stealing and screwing over.
Character 2 – RSC:
    British Petrolio! By the roses of the spring,
    by branding, sponsorship and everything,
    I love thee so, that, discarding my pride,
    nor wit nor reason can my passion hide.
    For I do love thee for thy patronage

With adorations, fertile tears, with groans
that thunder love, with sighs of fire …
Character 3 – Feste:
[Interrupts RSC]
If this were played upon a stage now,
I would condemn't as an improbable fiction!
Alas, poor RSC, how hath BP baffled thee?
Thou hast made contract of eternal bond
With a notable pirate, a deepwater thief!
Art thou mad, to profit from such a dissembler?
For some are born green, some achieve greenness,
And some purchase a semblance of greenness by
sponsoring cultural events …
I prithee, RSC, direct thy feet
Where thou and BP henceforth may never meet!
Character 2 – RSC:
Enough! No more!
Oil's not as sweet now as it was before.
BP, thou villain! How was I beguiled?
Disguise, I see thou art a wickedness,
Wherein the oily enemy does much.
[Points at BP] You spread a green and yellow melancholy,
Sitting without conscience in your offices,
Smiling at grief.
I would I were well rid of this knavery.
Out damned logo! [rips logo from programme][35]

The Reclaim Shakespeare Company's adaptation of Shakespeare's comedy seems allied with *Twelfth Night*'s obvious interest in the land-dwelling dynamics of power, class and service.[36] In this context, however, the animation of Shakespearean tropes concerned with mastery and subjection is bound up with authority, sponsorship and popular theatre.

Yet we might also look to the play's – and the Reclaim Shakespeare Company's – brief but telling invocation of piracy to see how ideological tensions concerned with trade are realized.

According to Claire Jowitt, Antonio's declaration in 2.1 that he has 'many enemies in Orsino's court' (2.1.41), 3.3.26–37 makes plain 'the cause of the animosity.'[37] In this episode

> Antonio describes [...] a type of trade dispute common between rival city states or countries, since in the aftermath of the battle reparation has been made by his (unnamed) compatriots for traffic's sake' with the Illyrians. Despite Antonio's side's victory it seems that the Illyrians are the more powerful nation, since in order to resume trade relations they have to be appeased with reparation. Only Antonio resists. The David and Goliath nature of the relationship between Antonio's city state and Illyria is further revealed in the Duke's reaction to meeting Antonio in [5.1.48–74].[38]

Historically, early modern Illyria 'was known for its notorious behaviour, drinking and piracy.'[39] The Reclaim Shakespeare Company's appropriation of Orsino's address to Antonio ('Notable pirate! Thou deepwater thief!' [5.1.65]) revivifies *Twelfth Night*'s engagement with questions of legitimate and illegitimate trade. Like the antagonism between Orsino and Antonio, the 'actor-vists'' interventions remind us that Shakespeare not only interrogates whose 'will' is being served (or served up) but also probes the significance of commerce and material acquisition.

Although this appearance on the Stratford stage made the *Independent*'s headlines, the Reclaim Shakespeare Company had already offered a prelude to *Twelfth Night*'s Press Night on 24 April 2012. By contrast with the later performance, the earlier protest took the form of an *a capella* duet. As stated on their website, *bp OR NOT bp*,

> One of the singers, Andrew Shilston, said 'These days it's hard to connect to the horror of what's being done – possibly in our name – by oil companies. Human lives, countless species and entire ecosystems are being systematically

crushed by them. BP is leading the charge but attempting
to hide behind a fig leaf of sponsorship.'[40]

The lyrical remonstration begins:

> When I hear that BP story
> Green and yellow melancholy
> Deepwater despair [...][41]

The Reclaim Shakespeare Company's intervention which begins
with Viola/Cesario's hepatic figuration of unrequited desire[42]
as 'green and yellow melancholy' (2.4.113), bespeaks the power
of lyrical performance.[43] The Company's performers remarked
that song was a more affective and thus more effective form of
political intervention: 'a lot of words in protest can sound angry'
but 'there's something about music that touches the heart',[44] an
observation that Shakespeare's Illyria and the script of *Twelfth
Night* certainly bears out.

Play On: Music

While signalling provisionality, Orsino's opening lines 'If music
be the food of love, play on' are also an overture to the feast of
songs, tunes and musical metaphors indicated by the script, as
Tiffany Stern's essay in this volume discusses.[45] Orsino's court
resonates with music and, if Leslie Hotson is correct in proposing
that *Twelfth Night* was indeed the play performed at court on 6
January 1601, then Virginio Orsino's account demonstrates how
the play picked up on the day's musical celebrations, as well as
offering a compliment to Orsino, Duke of Bracchiano, Queen
Elizabeth's principal guest at the performance. Hotson showed
that Lord Hunsdon made elaborate arrangements for festivities to
honour not only the Italian Duke, but also the Russian Ambassador
and Dukes from Germany and Bourbon and Navarre:

To Confer with my Lord Admirall and the Master of the

Revells for takeing order generally with the players to make
choyse of play that shalbe best furnished with great apparell,
have greate variety and change of Music and daunces, and
of a Subject that shall be most pleasing to her Maiestie.[46]

Virginio Orsino's letter to his wife recounts that first 'we heard a
wondrous music' in the chapel to which he had walked with the
Queen and the Ambassador, Grigori Mikulin. The latter reported
that 'in the Chapel they began to play on the organ, and on wind
instruments, with much other music and song. The officers said
"They are singing the psalms of David"'. This was followed by
a dinner-time performance by the Children of the Chapel Royal,
prepared especially for the occasion. The Lord Chamberlain's
memorandum notes '*The Children of the Chappell to come before
the Queene at Dinner with a Caroll*', thus continuing a courtly
Twelfth Night tradition. Performances by the Choristers of the
Chapel Royal and by members of the theatre company were
augmented by other music. Hunsdon was 'To appoint Musicke
severally for the Queene and some for the play in the Hall.
And Hales to have one place expresly to shew his own voyce'.[47]
Robert Hales was the royal singer and lutenist with an unbroken
record of annual payments of £40 from 1583 until his death in
1615.[48] While the Queen dined in state, Virginio Orsino was
taken to a separate hall 'where there was prepared for me a most
notable banquet, at the end of which appeared a good music.'
Music echoed throughout the palace. Shortly after he retired to
a lodging appointed so 'to rest myself', the chief courtiers paid
him visits and 'then there was music, of some instruments to
my belief never heard in Italy, but miraculous ones; so that with
good entertainment we came to the hour of supper.'[49] Richard
Crewdston suggests that the instruments would probably have
been the stringed bandora and opharion developed in England
in the latter part of the sixteenth century.[50] The performers
appointed to 'play on' with such incidental music were '*the
Musitions of the City*' who were 'to be ready to attend.' Finally,
after supper, Orsino was ushered in to a hall to greet the ladies

of the court and then accompanied the Queen to the evening's performances:

> Her Majesty mounted the stairs, amid such sounding of trumpets that methought I was on the field of war, and entered a public hall, where all round were rising steps with ladies, and divers consorts of music. As soon as her Majesty was set at her place many ladies and knights began a Great Ball. When this came to an end, there was acted a mingled comedy, with pieces of music and dances, and this too I am keeping to tell by word of mouth.[51]

Orsino's account makes it clear that the play followed the festive dancing by the men and women of the court. His dramatic counterpart's opening lines, 'If music be the food of love', would have invited members of the consort appointed to accompany the performance to 'play on', thus blending the day's festivities with the fictional romance, and blending the Orsinos who played the male leads in Court and on stage. The real-life Orsino's reference to the play as '*una commedia mescolata*' draws attention to its varied tone, mingling melancholy and mirth.[52] Virginio Orsino had had his own sea of troubles, being orphaned at the age of thirteen, like Viola, and more recently suffering an ignominious defeat when he tried to recapture the island of Chios from the Turks in 1599.

If the '*commedia mescolata*' was *Twelfth Night* (frustratingly, Orsino's letter reserves the name as well as the details for later), then his description is the first criticism to identify an atmospheric instability in the play. The fine balance of melancholy and mirth has frequently been betrayed in subsequent interpretations. This volume's essays by R. S. White and William C. Carroll on the play's critical history show how readers have often been biased in favour of its farcical and festive elements or its darker cruelty. White cites Charles Lamb's essay on Malvolio as a tragic victim and Carroll identifies a strand of post-millennial readings of Malvolio as a scapegoat. Linda Anderson's survey of performance history notes the tendency of modern productions to over-play the comedy of the romantic complications caused by cross-dressing in order to compensate for a sympathetic treatment of Malvolio. In the RSC's 1987 production, for example, the Greek island holiday humour was brazenly upstaged by the tragedy of Antony Sher's Malvolio, physically chained to a stake in a materialization of Sir Toby's sadistic promise to 'have the bear again, and [...] fool him black and blue' (2.5.8–9). Perhaps the predominance of music in *Twelfth Night* is a feature designed to hold the play's extremes in harmony. In 1601, the Lord Chamberlain's prescription of a 'choyse of play' that would 'have greate variety and change of Music' seems to hint again at the mixture of tone noted by Virginio Orsino, its connoisseur spectator.

Four centuries later, the 'greate variety and change of Music' in Des McAnuff's *Twelfth Night* at Stratford, Ontario served exactly this affective purpose: conjuring and modulating between emotional states and perspectives. Filmed live at the Festival Theatre in 2011, this *Twelfth Night* could have been subtitled 'Play On' instead of 'What You Will' since, as with the performance of 1601, the play was embedded in a culture of music, the score composed by McAnuff and Michael Roth. Each scriptural hint or snatch of a line was a cue for music. Feste, an itinerant guitarist played by Ben Carlson, dominated the stage, accompanied by a band of players who adapted to perform everything from rock to acoustic folk ballads, the traditional Elizabethan catch 'Hold thy peace' and Elton-John style sensitivity in singing round a piano at Orsino's court. Andrew Stott's essay discusses how Feste, as a provider of explicit nostalgia, is first and foremost a professional entertainer who must be paid, and McAnuff's production gave Ben Carlson maximum opportunity to characterize Feste as a performer who 'offers specialist entertainment of which old songs are just a part, along with ventriloquism, mock-Latin disquisitions, and dexterous riddles.'[53]

The production took its cue from Keir Elam's view that Feste is 'the most astute commentator on the play of which he is part.'[54] It opened with a rock evocation of the threatening world of the storm, shipwreck and Viola's rescue, modulated into Orsino's court with a group singing 'Play On', effectively the theme of the production. Incidental music gave an echo to the seat where love was throned in cases, like the end of Act 1 Scene 4 where Antonio's passion for Sebastian, 'I do adore thee so / That danger will seem sport and I will go' (2.1.43–4), was accompanied by swelling music and the actor singing the refrain 'If music be the food of love, play on', which was taken up by a chorus of voices. Olivia's passion for Cesario in 3.1 was signalled by incidental music and the same refrain.

Comic variations on the 'play on' theme were provided by refer-ences to sports games. Sir Toby and Sir Andrew were engaged in a round of golf for Act 1 Scene 3 and Viola as Cesario nervously learned how to wield a baseball bat, guided sensually by Orsino in 1.4. She countered his comments 'they shall belie thy happy years / That say thou art a man' (1.4.30–1) by hitting a powerful shot which cracked an off-stage window. Sir Andrew and Sir Toby appeared in cricket whites for the non-duel scene, and Sebastian's entrance delicately tipped the balance to bring out the danger, if not malice, in sport. The tragic potential of the Malvolio plot was pre-empted by its badminton court setting. Malvolio appeared as a ridiculously outdated Elizabethan lover attempting to reach Olivia across, under and over the net. In the prison scene, Feste's 'Hey Robin' was played by the full rock band, enveloping Malvolio, who sang along with the repeated chorus 'She loves another better than me.' Rather than maliciously attacking an isolated victim, the staging thus acknowledged that the darkness of ignorance is a common experience in love. Malvolio's pain of unrequited love was spotlit, centre-stage in a glass-box prison, where he clutched the letter as he sang. The real note of regret in the conclusion was Malvolio's failure to remember or participate in the emotionally expressive worlds of love and music that he had glimpsed in madness. He was not as tragic a figure as the school-master Mr Boase in Katharine Davies's novel adaptation *The Madness of Love* (as discussed in Anderson's essay), but he reacted with a similar retreat into himself. Having firmly snecked up his own emotions, Malvolio, played by Tom Rooney, returned to the stage in the role of a mean-spirited Puritan. A single spot on his silent, suit-clad figure at the end of the production reminded spectators of the Lenten world beyond the theatre.

The simultaneous pain and pleasure of being in love was reflected through modulations in music. The production gestured towards the possibility, examined in Tiffany Stern's chapter, that the songs given to Feste in the Folio text might have been sung by Viola/Cesario in an earlier version, since the character promises to speak to Orsino 'in many kinds of music' (1.2.55).[55] At the Festival Theatre, Act 2 Scene 4 opened with Viola sitting on the piano, singing the second verse of 'O Mistress Mine' with Orsino's courtiers, and repeating the last line 'Youth's a stuff will not endure' alone. While Feste sang 'Come away death' on a darkened stage, Orsino and Cesario sat close together, tentatively putting their arms out to touch each other during the first verse. Olivia, as the object of Orsino's unrequited affection and as an awakened, desiring subject, entered too, sitting at the front of the stage to view herself in a mirror and make up the triangle of melancholy but deliciously impassioned lovers. The growing tides of emotion in Viola's 'willow cabin' speech (1.5.268) and in Olivia's feelings for Cesario (1.5.300–3) were signalled by swelling incidental music.

The music was far from simply sentimental, however. The sexist culture of many love lyrics, and Olivia's resistance to such masculine (self) blazoning, was neatly illustrated in an interlude that opened the second half. Feste and all the other male musicians took turns to sing Marlowe's 'Come Live With Me and Be My Love', culminating in a chorus line with numerous phallic guitar necks thrust flamboyantly towards Olivia. She and her ladies took centre stage behind the microphone to respond with 'The Nymph's Reply', warning that 'All these in me no means can move / To come to thee and be thy Love.'[56] Carroll's essay in this volume remarks how queer theory, particularly Judith Butler's work on the performativity of gender, has influenced analyses of gender and transvestism since the millennium.[57] Other than a very pointed referencing of Antonio's homoerotic desire for Sebastian, the production did little to challenge heteronormativity. By foregrounding musical performance, however, the 2011 production effectively gestured towards the performative nature of gender and class.

Play on Perspective

In addition to its many references to music, *Twelfth Night* is 'probably Shakespeare's most intensely visual play' with a dazzling display of optical illusions and allusions to the processes of visual perception, as Keir Elam's essay argues. In Debra Hanson's design for the Stratford Festival production, the possibilities of mistaking were materialized by the framing device of a huge, splintered mirror which hung at the back of the thrust stage. This was not obvious until after the shipwreck overture, in which the only illuminated object was a model white ship on a perfectly round white globe, amidst the blue darkness of the storm. Viola entered in a rowing boat through the huge hole at the heart of the mirror, as if to signal gaping absence, not just as an emotional loss, but a crisis forcing her to re-evaluate her identity. The play's opening line 'What country, friends, is this?', spoken from the boat, exemplified the beginning of a journey of discovery and self-discovery through the play, as Randall Martin's essay in our volume explores. Referring back to classical and biblical traditions of sea travel as 'both fatally risky and metaphysically transgressive', Martin demonstrates the importance of shipwreck and miraculous self-preservation as a means for spiritual and social resurrection.[58] After the storm, characters in the Festival Theatre production entered and exited through the broken glass, inevitably seeing the world around them imperfectly.

The range of critical responses surveyed in White's and Carroll's essays testify to the script's ability to accommodate diametrically opposed viewpoints. Carroll sees multiplicity and indeterminacy as characteristics of the play. Its 'visual and verbal dialectic between concealment and revelation'[59] was played out to the full in the Festival Theatre's staging of Act 2 Scene 5, where the broken mirror framed Malvolio picking up the letter which supposedly revealed Olivia's feelings, and Sir Toby, Sir Andrew and Fabian darted backwards and forwards across the edges of the stage, visibly prominent to the audience in their anxiety to remain hidden from Malvolio. His delusions of grandeur were played centre stage, directly in front of the gap in the mirror, as if to signal the emptiness of his fantasies.

Religious perspectives, especially the diametric opposition of Puritan and Catholic viewpoints in Illyria, have, as Carroll points out, been a topic of much recent scholarship. Religious extremes are located in Olivia's household, of course, and McAnuff's production successfully set the formality of that environment against Orsino's narcissistic, decadent court of leisured pleasure. Olivia's ostentatious mourning at a tombstone (which replaced the model white ship) was an overtly Catholic form of speaking to the dead because pictures of her father and brother were displayed there. When Feste gently mocked her for clinging to her rosary and the past, the production played out Penuel's view that *Twelfth Night* is a response to 'changes in mourning rituals that accompanied the decline of English Catholicism.'[60] The play's mourning for lost fathers and lost tradition is a feature that links it thematically as well as chronologically to *Hamlet*, of course. This intertextual mode of reading *Twelfth Night* was undertaken in an excellent but little-known comparative analysis of two productions: *Hamlet, / La Nuit Des Rois: La Scene et Ses Miroirs*.[61] Feste's parody of a catechism reminds Olivia that she is only looking through a glass darkly, as St Paul puts it, and that her personal darkness of ignorance needs to be enlightened.

The difficulties of seeing clearly are followed up when Feste catechizes the enclosed Puritan, Malvolio, for being buried in ignorance and 'more puzzled than the Egyptians in their fog' (4.1.43). The equivocal nature of Feste's words is evident because this biblical allusion was used by both Catholics and Protestants in the 1590s. In the dedication of his *Instructions for the Use of the Rosarie* (1589) to Lady Anne Hungerford, for example,

John Bucke thanks God who has 'brought me out of that dark Egiptiacal England, (the verie sea of heresie) and placed me under so good and gracious a ladie, in whome I dailie behold manie examples of true Religion.'[62] Meanwhile, the Protestant Edward Bunny complained that princes were too often bound by 'that yoke of more than Egyptiacal bondage which the pope laid vpon them.'[63] *Twelfth Night* critiques religious extremism *per se*. Dean and Hunt note that Feste's 'Master Parson' role dramatizes contemporary parodies of Catholic priests,[64] a feature repeated in Des McAnuff's 2011 production. Ben Carlson's Feste played a comic Sir Topas whose performance of 'I am gone sir, and anon, sir' was a parody of death-metal style music that comically subverted the authority of his condemnation of Malvolio.

The difficulties of perception dramatized in *Twelfth Night* lead Elam to describe it as a large-scale 'iconotext', a mixed-media artefact that 'strategically places the verbal and the visual', in 'an often difficult and dangerous intercourse.'[65] Doubling is a crucial aspect of the play's disorienting practice: through allusions to pictures and in the 'obsessive doubling' of the bodies and identities of the twins, Sebastian and Viola. Both sorts of doubling involve nostalgia, an aspect of the play examined by Penuel who reads 'chronological repetition' in Viola's imitation of her brother as a perpetuation of her father's name.[66] Feste's reference to the 'picture of we three', which interpellates each spectator as the third fool alongside Feste and Sir Toby, may continue a tradition of commemorating fools of the past. In Robert Wilson's *Three Lords and Ladies of London* (1590), for example, Simplicity shows the ignorant Will, Wit and Wealth a picture of the famous fool Tarlton and delivers a eulogy, concluding 'there will neuer come his like while the earth can corne. O passing fine *Tarlton* I would thou hadst lived yet' (C1v). Will, Wit and Wealth's refusal to follow Tarlton's example and serve as apprentices to trade, preferring to serve the Lords Pleasure, Policy and Pomp, is demonstrably foolish. The exchange applauds the kind of freedom-in-service enjoyed by Feste and the wisdom of the supposed fool which his own role advertises in *Twelfth Night*. His joke probably invokes memories of the picture and trinity of fools in Wilson's play. Feste's reference to 'the picture of we three' may be another commemoration of a lost father, in this case, Tarlton as a professional father-figure.

The doubling of identities and substitutions which centre on the 'illusion' of Cesario look back to *The Comedy of Errors* and forward to the dark comedy of *Measure for Measure* and to the romance of *The Winter's Tale*. In Des McAnuff's staging of the end of Act 2 Scene 5, Cesario and Sebastian crossed the stage simultaneously, without seeing each other but giving the audience a foretaste of the 'natural perspective that is and is not' when they meet in Act 5. Such tricks made spectators aware that they too view events, as Hermia says 'with parted eye, / When every thing seems double' (*Dream* 4.1.186–7). The Stratford Festival production's eclectic costuming, which combined magnificent Victorian dress for Olivia and her gentlewomen with a modern kitchen and takeaway pizza for Act 2 Scene 3, highlighted nineteenth-century traditions of service that are so often lost in modern revivals, as Linda Anderson observes. The dominant presence of Feste (whose name Orsino was repeatedly unable to remember, resorting to 'fellow') offered a Foucauldian critique of the largely middle-class, middle-aged audience of the Festival Theatre, raising an awareness of themselves as 'other Victorians' in their nostalgia for the Illyria depicted on stage.

What's to Come is Still Unsure (2.3.48)

If the play is, at one level, about learning to look afresh, then Peter Kirwan's essay in our volume draws attention to a range of perspectives on *Twelfth Night* offered by resources for teaching. The Latinate definition of education as a 'drawing out' of potential, promoted most famously by Muriel Spark's Miss Jean Brodie,[67] suggests that given the right circumstances, all spectators, readers and listeners of whatever age can learn like the youthful protagonists. Kirwan comments that 'Viola and Sebastian's protean adaptability emerges when the correct circumstances

and environment tease it out of them.' The Festival Theatre
production offered such an environment to younger spectators
as well as using nostalgia to educate its more mature, traditional
audience members in self-awareness. For young spectators whose
encounters with Shakespeare echo Viola's bemused words 'What
country friends is this?', the production offered a contemporary
point of entry by witty use of the familiar, including the pizza
in Act 2 Scene 3, a detail perhaps inspired by Filter Theatre's
2007 *Twelfth Night* where pizzas were distributed to members
of the audience. Individuals from the Filter audiences were then
invited on stage to participate in a tequila drinking competition
and to throw felt balls from the auditorium to stick on a velcro
hat worn by Sir Andrew.[68] In the Festival Theatre production,
Malvolio's killjoy, paternal attempts to restore order in the kitchen
were mischievously undercut by a perfectly timed toaster which
'popped' in response to his angry reprimand 'Is there no respect
of place, persons or time in you?' causing smothered giggles
on stage and effectively speaking for the irrepressible spirit of
youthful festivity. Viola's address to the guitar-playing Feste,
'dost thou live by thy Fender?', was likewise deemed witty by a
teenage spectator. The production's use of music was a language
that allowed access the more contemplative, melancholy aspects
of the play too:

> I think music amplifies the emotions of the characters and
> projects them out to the audience so the audience can feel
> part of the play and understand more of what the characters
> are feeling.[69]

Primarily visual points of access to *Twelfth Night* for younger
readers are provided by the BBC Children's Shakespeare and by
the *Manga Shakespeare* (a Japanese-style graphic novel series),
illustrated by Nana Li and with a script edited by Richard
Appiganesi.[70] Some of the editing makes the script exceed-
ingly sense-less (to quote Sir Toby). Indeed, cutting out the
senseless clauses of Sir Andrew's letter and declaring it comes

from 'a clotpoll' does a disservice to Shakespeare's sense, as does cutting the concluding line to Olivia's couplet 'Do not extort thy reason from this clause.' Insensitive editing of Shakespeare's metaphorical language makes it, too, more difficult to understand, as in Act 2 Scene 4, where a shortened version of Viola's line about the music to 'it gives echo to [the seat where] where love is throned' makes Shakespeare's image more obscure. Cutting the words 'like patience on a monument' makes nonsense of the lovely image conjured by Viola's imagination,[71] selling short the very stylish artwork in which the image is realized.

At many points, however, the *Manga Shakespeare Twelfth Night* makes excellent use of a combination of word and image. The book opens with a picture of the twins mirrored side by side – Viola thinking 'Disguise, I see thou art a wickedness', Sebastian wondering 'If it be thus to dream, still let me sleep' – with the caption 'One face, one voice, one habit – and two persons' (though Viola is not cross-dressed in the image). The subsequent pages use a visual *dramatis personae* to introduce the other protagonists, each with a tagline from the text. Orsino, tagged with the line 'if music be the food of love', is a typically effete Manga hero, appearing painfully slim with a long fringe and fur-collared leather coat and, in the narrative, speaking from a lonely gothic castle with a windswept balcony. Cesario flies from the wintry castle in a bi-plane to gain entry to Olivia's more traditional Tudor summer palace. (The blurb on the back of the book claims it is 'Christmas in Illyria', but this is not borne out by anything between the covers). Following class hierarchy, the *dramatis personae* pictures pair Orsino with the disdainful but classically beautiful blonde Olivia, whose tagline is 'we will draw the curtain and show you the picture.' In the narrative, Olivia speaks this line from a full-page portrait of a diva goddess with huge eyes. The graphic novel, expanding on the script, wittily juxtaposes this with her playful inventory, drawn as a series of black-edged labels depicting her body parts, just as in the French blazon tradition. Another very effective combination of script and pictures occurs in Viola's soliloquy 'Disguise, I see thou art a wickedness.' Though the script is pared down to a minimum, the novel portrays the images of time and the Gordian knot very effectively in a picture with cogs and rope tying the three protagonists together and Viola's final resignatory couplet depicted by a *chibi* – a childlike version of her in a scholar's cap puzzling over the sum '1 + 1 + 1 = 2?.'[72]

In the comic plot, the edited text does not fight shy of Elizabethan language in the dialogues between Sir Toby, Maria and Sir Andrew. Act 1 Scene 3 is complete with references to 'cutting a caper', the galliard and the 'accost' jokes, which are made accessible through the depicted reactions of a pert Maria, who is firmly in control of the fools in hand (also pouring water from the fountain over the drunken Sir Toby). Malvolio's dream of rising to be 'Count' is visualized in a circus fantasy as a magician's (self)-delusional trick, drawing an implicit parallel between him and Feste, whose wit and knowledge does not really come through in the novel. Feste's doubling as Sir Thopas in the madhouse scene, for example, is not given enough space to make it open to any formal capacity. Maria appears besides the tall Malvolio in the *dramatis personae*, setting up a parallel between his failure and the woman's successful ascent to dominate a series of men who are senior in physical and social terms. The *dramatis personae* concludes with the paired figures of the older Sea Captain and younger Antonio (as a Johnny Depp-style pirate), with Feste and Fabian and, in a final image, the servants Curio and Valentine and the priest who prays for 'a contract of eternal bond of love.' The oppositions between competing desires and, implicitly, between different types of gender style are highlighted by this page. It is followed by a double-page colour picture of the shipwreck parting the twins, who reach out their hands to each other from opposite sides of the book.

Teenagers' sense of self-estrangement and confusion over the performance of gender identities in the twenty-first century is well served by the manga style, in which highly cultivated forms of powerful femininity are set alongside traditional images of portly, older men and much younger masculine figures that are, often unpredictably, violent, sensitive, excessively loyal and extremely vulnerable. Security is provided in the form of *chibi* child-like caricatures (a feature of manga texts), who speak their passions far more egotistically and directly on behalf of the protagonists at key points in the narrative. Feste's child alter-ego is caught raiding the pantry in Act 1 Scene 3; those of Maria and her co-conspirators and Malvolio himself are conjured up mischief-making in the letter plot. Olivia's and Viola's both emerge in Act 3 Scene 4 in the desperate moments of rejection (for Olivia) and need for escape and self-preservation for Viola. The retreat to a childish self at moments of crisis highlights the difficulties of reconfiguring an identity within an adult landscape in social and sexual terms for the text's adolescent readers.

Kirwan's essay for this collection comments that pedagogic approaches which 'involve performance are now *de rigueur* particularly at school level.'[73] The pioneering work of Rex Gibson's Shakespeare in Schools project to encourage creative approaches has finally been taken up by the RSC in its highly publicized 'Stand Up for Shakespeare' campaign.[74] This has, however, been focused on secondary school teaching, and the prescription of Shakespeare within the National Curriculum by central government. The Royal Shakespeare Company, it might be argued, is thus fulfilling its role as the institution charged with the duty of disseminating government policy.[75] Rex Gibson's transformative effect on a generation of primary school teachers, who in turn encourage their pupils to 'stand up' for a very different kind of Shakespeare and teaching agenda, appears to have been forgotten by the Bard's flagship theatre company. However, primary practice is alive and well in the Shakespeare Schools Festival initiative, which invites classes of primary and secondary pupils to stage thirty-minute adaptations of the plays, using scripts prepared by the Schools Festival.[76] In 2012 an adaptation of *Twelfth Night* was one of the choices offered to schools. The recollections of one primary school performer, playing Viola, offer ample testament to the effect of standing up for a Shakespeare who stands simply for pleasure and fun:

I would never have thought of Shakespeare as one of my favourite things to act or watch on a stage but since I saw *Much Ado About Nothing* and was in *Twelfth Night* I can't get enough of it! When I got into the role [of Viola] I felt all the confusion the she was feeling and when I went off the stage I was itching to go back on. I felt amazing saying the lines; I have practised them many times before so it felt different saying them for the last time.[77]

Even amidst this excitement, a strong sense of the play's preoccupation with imminent loss comes across. This may be incidental, of course, but ten-year-old Emily's words undoubtedly capture the intense vivacity that live performance holds for young actors, and how fleetingly fragile such moments are. Pleasure must be paid for, Feste reminds us, and there is no doubt that the survival of *Twelfth Night* as a regularly performed text will depend largely upon government bodies, notably the Department of Education, and upon national institutions like the Royal Shakespeare Company, the National Theatre and the Globe, which are funded by Arts Council subsidies and the sponsorship of corporate powers. Nevertheless, our reference to companies like Filter Theatre (whose *Twelfth Night* was welcomed as part of the Royal Shakespeare Theatre's Global Shakespeare Festival) and to those 'happenings' staged by the Reclaim Shakespeare Company demonstrate that grass-roots reworkings of *Twelfth Night* continue to flourish. *What You Will: A Fly on the Wall, Behind the Scenes, Documentary Tragi-Comical Road Movie* (2012), co-produced by Filter Theatre and the RSC, wryly dramatizes the relationship between small and large institutional companies. One of the artistic directors of 'Sea in a Sieve', the satiric pseudonym for Filter in the film, is harangued by his actress wife for preferring small-scale touring as the best way to make Shakespeare's text come alive rather than pursuing more lucrative television or film work. The other artistic director (who plays Malvolio and treats one fellow actor cruelly) is tricked by her fake phone call from the RSC, inviting him to join the company.

Our introduction has offered analysis of recent representations of *Twelfth Night* by major theatre companies. At the same time, our sense of the value of local, micro-productions in the Shakespeare ecology is marked by our wish to set down on record political appropriations designed to 'reclaim Shakespeare' from corporate ownership, and to note the work of small-scale practitioners such as Bingo-Dragon, a not-for-profit company led by some of our own Lancaster graduates, whose 2012 production of *Twelfth Night* is depicted below.

1 Twelfth Night, *Bingo Dragon Theatre Company, 2012, http://www. bingodragon.co.uk/ (photograph: John Shepherd, http://www.j-photo. co.uk/)*

The Shakespeare Schools Festival and the initiatives emerging through the British Shakespeare Association's new journal *Teaching Shakespeare* point to the regenerative energies at work as young people and teachers at all levels engage with the text. In times of financial hardship, Feste's line 'What's to come is still unsure' is readily understood in pessimistic terms. Nevertheless, it is that very uncertainty which inspires us to remake *Twelfth Night* again and again. The new millennium is a big place, and since 'what's to come' is still unsure, the play's own poised indeterminacy offers us the excitement of both opportunity and risk.

CHAPTER ONE

The Critical Backstory

R. S. WHITE

We do not know exactly when, where or why *Twelfe Night, Or What You Will*, as the First Folio title reads, was first performed. Dating early modern plays is a specialized enclave of the Shakespeare industry and it is still not a precise science because of the more relaxed attitudes to record-keeping in early modern times. However, the margin for error is not so wide for this play as some others, and the consensus emerging from the labours of modern editors has narrowed down the parameters to 1600 or 1601. This lets us know approximately where it comes in relation to Shakespeare's adjacent output, standing as it does on a threshold a year or so after *As You Like It* and therefore the last of the plays clearly intended as romantic comedies. Those using the comic form which followed, *All's Well That Ends Well* and *Measure for Measure*, are considered 'dark' or 'problem comedies' because the generic closure of comedy seems inadequate to resolve the anxieties and tensions raised in the actions. *Twelfth Night* has come to be regarded as a kind of farewell to the 'witty conceited' plays about courting couples that had, alongside chronicle histories, been Shakespeare's main outputs in the 1590s. Meanwhile, *Hamlet* is placed on the same millennial cusp (1600–1601), followed by the satirical and bitter tragedy *Troilus and Cressida*, tempting us to construct a mythology that Shakespeare was turning his attention towards darker matters, but equally plausibly as a response to changing theatrical fashion.

The 'where' of the first performance is even more shrouded in mystery since we have no evidence whether *Twelfth Night* was intended for the public stage or an indoor theatre such as an Inn of Court (where professional lawyers were trained in London). 'Why?' was provisionally answered in 1662 with the suggestion that the odd title of the play suggests it was written for a performance on Twelfth Night (5 or 6 January), perhaps as an entertainment to cheer people up in the cold winter months, although the play itself may be set in summer if its references to 'midsummer madness' (3.4.53) and Feste's 'let summer bear it out' (1.5.17) are read literally.[1] If so, and it is far from settled, this would suggest a private performance, since the outdoor theatres would have been 'dark' in midwinter. On the other hand, the subtitle, *Or What You Will*, as throwaway as *As You Like It*, gives nothing away, and allows Shakespeare and the Lord Chamberlain's Men (soon to become the King's Men on James I's accession to the throne in 1603–4) considerable leeway to adapt the play to any occasion or conditions of performance they liked. Bernard Shaw, in his tongue-in-cheek, debunking vein of anti-bardolatry, suggests that both 'what you will' and 'as you like it' show Shakespeare disclaiming the kind of 'romantic nonsense' which he found to be 'the only thing that paid in the theatre' and which he could write with a 'cheap' facility.[2]

The text of the play leaves all these questions open. It was not published in Shakespeare's lifetime in a quarto version, as some of his other plays were, whether 'authorized' or not, but instead was published first in the wonderful First Folio, Shakespeare's 'collected works' edited after his death in 1623 by his friends and collaborators, John Heminges and Henry Condell. In some ways this makes editing the play easier since there is only one text to worry about, but in other ways it does not help us to solve some of the intricate problems in the text and plot, many of which continue to defy us. To give just a couple of small examples, we do not know whether Orsino is a duke or a count, and while Valentine says Orsino has known the disguised Viola 'but three days' (1.4.3), yet Antonio later says he has come to Illyria 'Today […] and for three months before', which is confirmed immediately by Orsino, though there is no indication this length of time has passed (5.1.89 and 94).[3]

The first hard evidence of an early performance comes in a report from one of the very few contemporary eyewitness accounts of a play by Shakespeare. John Manningham, a law student at London's Middle Temple Inn of Court, kept a diary which was discovered as late as 1868 by John P. Collier. In his diary, Manningham records being present at a performance on Candlemas (2 February) in 1602:

> At our feast wee had a play called ~~Mid~~ 'Twelve night, or What You Will'; much like the *Commedy of Errores*, or *Menechmi* in Plautus, but most like and neere to that in Italian called *Inganni*. A good practise in it to make the Steward beleeve his Lady Widdowe was in love with him, by counterfeyting a letter as from his Lady in generall termes, telling him what shee liked best in him, and prescribing his gesture in smiling, his apparraile, &c., and then when he came to practise making him believe they tooke him to be mad.[4]

Manningham's words have been pored over by scholars for what can be gleaned about the reception of plays in Shakespeare's time. These days it is not assumed that the Middle Temple performance was the play's first, though there is one recent dissenter from the Middle Temple itself, Anthony Arlidge.[5] The statement does show that Manningham knew about some of Shakespeare's other plays, such as presumably *A Midsummer Night's Dream*, judging from his false start in writing 'Mid' and crossing it out, and also *The Comedy of Errors* which came to his mind because of the common motif of twins, and which also led him to posit sources, Plautus's *Menaecmi* for both *Errors* and for *Twelfth Night*, and *Gl'Inganni*, which appeared from different Italian authors in the sixteenth century. In themselves, these references are revealing not just for their factual identification of sources but also because they demonstrate an Elizabethan humanist's understanding of literary imitation, whereby a writer would choose a model from classical literature and rewrite it in his own fashion.

As to deducing much else from Manningham's words, there is an error in describing Olivia as a widow, but at least it seems that he recalled as the most memorable incident the gulling of Olivia's steward, Malvolio, and the way that the character is taken to be mad when he appears smiling and cross-gartered. Many audiences since then would agree that this is the most memorable section in performance, since it is undoubtedly a theatrically funny episode, but it may be surprising that there is less attention paid to the plot strand which we would think of as the central one, the romantic triangle concerning Viola, Orsino and Olivia, resolved by the sighting of Viola's twin Sebastian. Of this story, Manningham picked out only the use of twins for comment. Although we cannot read much into such an oversight, it at least inadvertently suggests some of the general changes in critical approach which have happened over the four centuries since Shakespeare's death. For example, we may have moved away from a belief in the visual primacy of plays as performed on stage, ephemeral as such events may be, and give priority instead to the written script in which we can find themes, ambiguities and serious, latent issues.

How far back does a 'backstory' go? These days it is considered possible to argue that a text in some sense exists before it is actually written down or performed, due to the multitude of cultural mediations involving intertextual sources and references that are pulled into unity by the author. Roland Barthes' wake over 'the death of the author' depends on such assumptions, and it ends with the famous statement 'the birth of the reader must be at the cost of the death of the Author':[6] enter the critic to the process of constant reconstruction. Some have even ventured to suggest that works written later can be paradoxical 'sources' for our modern 'readings', since understandings of a play by Shakespeare are inescapably informed by all that we have read or heard about it. In this postmodern construction, Samuel Taylor Coleridge, Johann Wolfgang von Goethe, T. S. Eliot, Jacques Derrida and Kenneth Branagh can all take their places in some postmodern pantheon as 'sources' for Shakespeare insofar as his works exist in today's world. However, to stick to the more traditional way of conceiving sources and influences, *Twelfth Night* gives us a model example of the way in which Shakespeare's creativity drew from many diverse works. Manningham pointed to classical and Italian sources, but closer to England Shakespeare definitely read and drew upon Barnaby Rich's story 'Apolonius and Silla' in *Barnaby Riche's Farewell to Militarie Profession* (1581, reprinted in 1591). Through this list and more, Geoffrey Bullough undertakes the 'formidable task' of assessing Shakespeare's indebtedness.[7] However, these precursors are all quite unsentimental and farcical, and we must acknowledge that Shakespeare himself was the inventor of the genre itself, dramatized romantic comedy, forging romance as the popular medium of his time into shapely plays about courtship. In this he clearly drew upon Philip Sidney's *Arcadia* (1590, which is not mentioned by Bullough), since in other works he shows signs of having read it attentively, and the figure of the man disguised as woman (if not woman as a man) is the main sexual catalyst in Sidney's important prose romance. Furthermore, as if to defy all source hunters, Malvolio stands splendidly alone and aloof as Shakespeare's complete invention, though perhaps a satire of some 'real-life', puritanical court official known to Shakespeare who opposed the 'cakes and ale' of popular theatre.

There were some signs during Shakespeare's writing career of the beginning of a transition from 'performance' to 'reading' since, as his plays became more famous in production, so pirated 'Quarto' editions were published to cash in on their success. This was not, however, the case for *Twelfth Night*, a fact which might paradoxically point to the play's success in performance since the Company would have held tightly to the script. Even the actors in its very first performance, whenever and wherever it may have happened, would not have held a reading copy of the play in its entirety, since the practice was to give each actor only the script for the scenes in which he himself (and they were all men) appeared, with cues to bring him on- and off-stage.[8] There were practical reasons for this, such as economizing on paper, fear of industrial espionage in allowing a script to fall into the hands of another company or a publisher, the sheer amount of memorizing required already by actors in a repertoire consisting of several plays simultaneously running, and the lack of necessity for them to know much outside their own lines anyway. Actors must have been trained to listen keenly to what other characters were saying in order to build up a picture of their roles in the scenes in which they appear, just as Shakespeare's fictional characters listen acutely to each other in sustaining plausible conversations.[9] If not the actors, then the first recorded *readers* of *Twelfth Night* were Heminges and Condell. They made one firm assumption – that '*Twelfe-night, or, what you will*' belonged within the group of plays they unambiguously nominated as Comedies, not Histories or Tragedies. This may be so self-evident that it does not seem significant in itself, but it runs parallel to Manningham's assessment of the theatrical genre and does not on the face of it suggest the darker linings found in the play by twentieth-century critics after the invention in 1896 by F. S. Boas of a hybrid group which he called 'Problem Plays.'[10]

Seventeenth and Eighteenth Centuries

We know that *Twelfth Night* was performed at court in 1618 and 1623, which suggests the play was successful in Shakespeare's time and beyond. In the latter case, the Master of the Revels used a different title, confirming Manningham's opinion of the central interest: 'At Candlemas *Malvolio* was acted by the King's Servants.' Candlemas was not Twelfth Night but 2 February, and if Shakespeare intended his enigmatic title to signal misrule and revelry he could even have chosen the later date, which has traditionally been associated with the end of winter and beginning of spring. From 1642 to 1660 theatres were closed during the Commonwealth period. When they re-opened upon the Restoration of the monarchy in 1660, *Twelfth Night* seems to have been revived infrequently, and at least one keen theatre-goer of the time did not warm to it. Samuel Pepys saw it three times: on 11 September 1661 he records

Walking through Lincoln's Inn Fields observed at the
Opera a new play 'Twelfth Night', was acted there, and
the King there; so I, against my own mind and resolution,
could not forbear to go in, which did make the play seem a
burthen to me, and I took no pleasure at all in it.[11]

It may have been the occasion rather than the play that irked
Pepys, but on 6 January 1662–3 he leaves nothing open to doubt:

After dinner to the Duke's House, and there saw 'Twelfth
Night' acted well, though it be but a silly play, and not
related at all to the name or day.

Again, on 20 January 1668, he writes:

to the Duke of York's house and saw 'Twelfth Night', as it is
now revived; but I think, one of the weakest plays that ever
I saw on the stage.

Taste had shifted towards revivals of Jonsonian satire and
citizen comedy and away from sentimental, romantic comedy by
Shakespeare.

Pepys could not have been alone in his lack of enjoyment
since the play was not staged in its own form from 1669 to 1741.
Despite the opportunities given by the appearance of women
playing female roles on the stage for the first time in England,
Restoration audiences were not enamoured of Shakespeare's mode
of sentimental, woman-centred romantic comedy, preferring
instead their own brand of abrasively witty, aristocratic and social
comedy. The re-opened stages catered for exclusive coteries of
aristocrats, but by the early eighteenth century a new class was
frequenting theatres, which in turn had to be much larger to cater
for the swelling middle-class audiences. Drury Lane in 1794
seated 3,611, indicating a change towards middle-brow audiences
with a preference for the sentimental.[12] Still *Twelfth Night* did
not thrive, however, not re-appearing in the form Shakespeare

wrote it until Garrick and Charles Macklin revived it at the
Drury Lane Theatre in 1741. Fiona Ritchie points out that this
production was billed as 'Never Acted there before' and 'Written
by Shakespear', and that Viola was played by Hannah Pritchard,
since by now such roles were universally played by women. 'A
run of six nights followed, and the play was acted twice more that
season', so it was clearly a successful revival of a play that had
fallen out of the repertory.[13] During that hiatus, it was known only
in an unsuccessful, rewritten forms, such as the one by William
Burnaby, *Love Betray'd; or, the Agreeable Disappointment* (1703),
'which flopped at Lincoln's Inn Fields.'[14]

Samuel Johnson in many ways epitomized the kind of
neo-classical criticism dominant in the eighteenth century.
Although he resisted the temptation to rewrite plays, yet in many
cases while editing the plays he reproved Shakespeare for lack of
literary decorum. In his notes to *Twelfth Night* he even ridiculed
Shakespeare for anachronisms and 'mistakes' that we (perhaps to
our discredit) barely notice today, such as referring to the 'bed
of Ware in England' and the bells of St Bennet in London in a
play set far away in Illyria on the Adriatic coast (sometimes called
'Sclavonia' in early modern times).[15] He criticizes the language
of some parts of the play for coming 'so near profaneness', and
sardonically views Viola as an 'excellent schemer' whose 'design'
to win the affections of Orsino and 'supplant the lady' Olivia
is unseemly. Johnson notes anachronisms such as Malvolio's
'wind up my watch', commenting 'In our author's time watches
were very uncommon. When Guy Faux was taken, it was urged
as a circumstance of suspicion that a watch was found upon
him'. Meanwhile, his overall summary of the play struck the
Romantic generation that followed as sanctimonious and irrel-
evant, although it reveals his formally decorous, ethically based
and judgmental approach to literature:

> This play is in the graver part elegant and easy, and in
> some of the lighter scenes exquisitely humorous [...] The
> soliloquy of Malvolio is truly comick; he is betrayed to

ridicule merely by his pride. The marriage of Olivia, and the succeeding perplexity, though well enough contrived to divert on the stage, wants credibility, and fails to produce the proper instruction required in the drama, as it exhibits no just picture of life.

No wonder that John Keats, in one of his volumes of Shakespeare which contained Johnson's notes, scribbled over one such endnote, writing in admonition 'come not near our fairy queen.'[16]

Romantics (1789–1836)

The Romantic age ushered in a different set of priorities, with writers pinning their colours to the imagination rather than reason, and showing a willingness to embrace the apparent waywardness of Shakespeare's freedom from formal rules. At this time also we find European commentators contributing their thoughts on Shakespeare. A. W. von Schlegel, whose *Lectures on Dramatic Art and Literature* were written from 1808–11, was amongst the first of the great German critics. Although he was sidetracked by the then-current belief that *Twelfth Night* was Shakespeare's last play, his description of its merits include both structural and imaginative qualities. He notes 'the entertainment of an intrigue, contrived with great ingenuity [...] a rich fund of comic characters and situations, and the beauteous colours of an ethereal poetry.' Extending equal attention to plot, character and poetry, he focuses on love as the central subject, 'more as an affair of the imagination than the heart' and almost 'arbitrary' in its workings.[17] Schlegel calls the various liaisons 'ideal follies' rather than true emotional states, anticipating some modern critics like G. K. Hunter, for example, who speaks of 'poetical delusions' that seem to present happiness as 'illogical and chancy' to characters who are compelled to be 'disguised, obsessed and frustrated.'[18] Just as the German critics created the reading of Hamlet as consistently 'the melancholy prince', so Schlegel set *Twelfth Night* on its way towards becoming regarded later as a play of 'melancholy mood.'

William Hazlitt remarked that Shakespeare was a greater poet than wit: 'his imagination was the leading and master-quality of his mind, which was always ready to soar into its native element: the ludicrous was only secondary and subordinate.' Hazlitt deemed *Twelfth Night* to be representative of this kind of imaginative, romantic comedy, thematically centred on 'the disguises of self-love' and on the triumph of 'the natural' over the 'artificial' and affected. It was, Hazlitt claimed, 'full of sweetness and pleasantry. It is perhaps too good-natured for comedy. It has little satire, and no spleen'. Hazlitt was among the first to emphasize the musicality of Shakespeare's verse and its effect in the comedies, quoting Orsino to make the point:

Oh! it came o'er the ear like the sweet south
Breathing upon a bank of violets,
Stealing and giving odour.

Consistent with his approach through the play's poetry, Hazlitt appreciates Shakespeare's heroines in the comedies as the embodiment of the 'sympathy' that he saw as a Shakespearean signature: 'the difference between Shakspeare's [sic] comic heroines and those of a later period may be referred to the same distinction between natural and artificial life, between the world of fancy and the world of fashion.' The melancholy, musing Olivia becomes a kind of touchstone of sensibility: 'The heroine of romance and poetry sits secluded in the bowers of fancy, sole queen and arbitress of all hearts', though Viola's confession of her hidden love is credited as 'the great and secret charm of TWELFTH NIGHT.'[19]

Hazlitt's contemporary, Charles Lamb, was more concerned with Malvolio than the female characters. *Twelfth Night* was the first Shakespearean production Lamb had seen, in 1790 when he was sixteen, and he recalled the performance at Drury Lane in his essay 'On Some of the Old Actors.' Barrymore played Orsino with a 'full Shakspearian sound' and Mrs Jordan presented Viola 'with her steady melting eye', but it was Bensley's performance of Malvolio that made Lamb appreciate how the character was popularly 'misunderstood.' Bensley was associated with roles of 'heroic conceptions' like Hotspur ranting with the voice of a trumpet and a gait which was 'uncouth and stiff.' Nevertheless, Malvolio was not, Lamb remarked, innately ludicrous:

> He becomes comic but by accident. He is cold, austere, repelling; but dignified, consistent, and his misfortune is to be 'misplaced in Illyria', opposed to its 'levities' [...] His dialect on all occasions is that of a gentleman, and a man of education. We must not confound him with the eternal old, low steward of comedy. He is master of the household to a great Princess; a dignity probably conferred upon him for other respects than age or length of service [...] His rebuke to the knight, and his sottish revellers, is sensible and spirited; and when we take into consideration the unprotected condition of his mistress, and the strict regard with which her state of real or dissembled mourning would draw the eyes of the world upon her house-affairs, Malvolio might feel the honour of the family in some sort in his keeping [...]

Lamb is reminding us not only of class considerations but also the dramatic context. Olivia is reclusively in mourning and the trick played on Malvolio strikes Lamb as both dramatically unprepared and also unfair to his character. He remarks 'Even in his abused state of chains and darkness, a sort of greatness seems never to desert him'. In Bensley's performance of the part with 'an air of Spanish loftiness', Lamb notes, 'you had no room for laughter! [...]. – but in truth you rather admired than pitied the lunacy while it lasted.' Lamb concludes that he can never again see the role 'without a kind of tragic interest.'[20] On the stage, it was not until 1884 in Henry Irving's production that Malvolio was presented fully as a tragic 'hero', but after Lamb's comments (as with Shylock after Kean's acting), Malvolio could never be dismissed lightly. He has amply had his 'revenge' on the whole pack of his detractors as if to prove Feste's adage that 'the whirligig of time brings in his revenges' (5.1.375–6).

Victorian (1837–1901)

The appearance in 1818 of Thomas and Henrietta Bowdler's *The Family Shakespeare* was as much symptom as cause of a new kind of moralistic approach which does not so much look back to Johnson as forward to Victorian sensibilities. It also gave the language a new word, 'bowdlerize', meaning to censor whatever should seem too sexually offensive or explicit for 'family reading.' Such a project may have appeared to the Bowdlers advisable after the popularization of Shakespeare as a writer for children in Charles and Mary Lamb's *Tales from Shakespeare* (1807).

The title of Anna Jameson's book published in 1832, *Characteristics of Women: Moral, Poetical, and Historical*, reveals its perspective.[21] Although essentially a comparison between fictional characters from Shakespeare's plays, the generalizing phrase 'Characteristics of Women' suggests that for Jameson literature illuminates life, and perhaps *is* a part of life, existing on the same level of reality. She clearly believes in an essential-izing set of 'feminine' traits though they are different in each heroine. Viola in particular is 'deep learned in the lore of love', precociously understanding more about the emotional life than other heroines. 'Moral' suggests that Shakespeare's plays are pre-eminently educative for young ladies of Jameson's day, and here Viola's love-lore, however 'true', poses a threat to her feminine decorum which acts as a cautionary tale 'for the especial profit of well-bred young ladies.'[22] Viola's salvation is that she does not reveal except to the audience her innate knowledge of the heart. Although 'she should be touched by a passion made up of pity, admiration, gratitude, and tenderness', yet 'she never told her love.' Furthermore, Viola never forgets she is playing a role in disguise, 'and is guarded by the strictest delicacy', rather uncom-fortable in the pragmatic necessity to conceal 'her feminine nature' in the guise of a pageboy. Meanwhile, 'Poetical' in Jameson's title shows that her main interest is as a reader rather than a theatre-goer, while 'Historical' aligns the plays with the most popular kind of literature of the day, the novel. Shakespeare's heroines are constantly provided with a conjectural, ambient life, an imputed past and often complex inner lives, all to be found in a novelistic presentation of character. Olivia is characterized as bolder and more capricious than Viola, 'facts' which are explained from her 'history': 'She has never in her life been opposed; the first contradiction, therefore, rouses all the woman in her, and turns a caprice into a headlong passion' as she struggles to maintain a 'dignified elegance of […] deportment' under strong emotional pressure.

Mary Cowden Clarke, a distinguished writer and the first woman to edit Shakespeare's plays (1859–60), took Jameson's novelistic and moralistic leads further in a series of fifteen fictional recreations entitled *The Girlhood of Shakespeare's Heroines* (1850–2). Her intended audience included both girls and their mothers, the innocent and the mature, and her educational purpose was to inculcate moral lessons through the example of Shakespeare's heroines imagined in their fictionalized 'girlhoods.' Unlike the Bowdlers and Jameson, Clarke did not exclude 'distasteful' material but, on the contrary, built in awareness of the current *mores* that led to social problems like prostitution and gender inequities.[23] As a result, Clarke creates almost a pre-Freudian way of seeing the female characters in their maturity as products of childhood experiences, manifesting different degrees of sexual knowledge acquired through earlier experiences. Viola, although prudent and self-repressive, has become knowing as a result, Clarke surmises, of an early encounter with a courtesan in a morally dangerous situation, which Viola resists and learns from. Olivia is seen as having been threatened by close proximity to a child molester and her resistance to seduction leads later to her reluctance to marry a changeable man like Orsino. Her more impulsive attraction to the disguised Viola may be partly a result of the latter's safer androgyny and also due to an aristocratic capriciousness overcoming Olivia's sexual caution and fastidiousness of conduct. The sheer fictiveness of such accounts at first

sight suggests they are worthless as insights into Shakespeare's
plays, and yet they do point to ways in which the dramatist gives
tantalizing hints of a life behind what we see (in the play Viola's
father *did* die when the twins were thirteen and he *did* indeed have
a 'mole upon his brow'). Sometimes Clarke's creative interpretations provide clues to the psychological complexity of the roles,
which can be of use to actors and critics, while directing our
attention firmly to the women as central consciousnesses in the
play, a *datum* of much modern criticism, and to a latent emphasis
on sex in the play to be explored by later critics.

If Viola, Olivia, and Malvolio all had their champions in the
nineteenth century, Feste too acquired a central presence. *Twelfth
Night* has sometimes been seen as enacting a struggle between an
anti-comic Malvolio and comic Feste, with the latter victorious on
behalf of the forces of 'festivity.' This trend seems to have started
in the middle of the nineteenth century. Perhaps because he is
less of a presence in the theatre than Malvolio, Feste was taken
for granted in earlier, stage-centred criticism, as either a merely
charming singer of background songs or even ignored altogether,
but some amongst the Victorians began to see his potential. H.
Ulrici in his book *Shakespeare's Dramatic Art*, published in 1839,
gives a glimpse of the nature of such interest by seeing Feste as a
poet 'in full consciousness' and a foil for Malvolio:

> He does not wish to be more nor less than a fool in the
> great mad-house of the world; on this account he has an
> unconquerable aversion to all starched common sense and
> calculating plans, to that hollow unmeaning gravity which
> cannot understand a joke, because it fancies its proudly-
> adopted dignity thereby injured, and which is never able to
> rise above the petty, selfish interests of its own dear self; this
> accounts for his dislike of Malvolio.[24]

Ulrici and others in the late nineteenth century laid the
foundation for a twentieth-century Feste who is the epitome of
Shakespeare's 'wise fools', more flexible, adaptable and intelligent

than Touchstone, less old, disillusioned and vulnerable than Lear's Fool. His treatment of Malvolio later in the play, which Lamb implicitly and many modern critics regard as cruel, is seen by Victorian commentators like C. W. Hutson and John Weiss as effective in curing Malvolio of excessive pride.[25]

Feste's role was later – in 1916 – to give A. C. Bradley one of his rare opportunities for writing on a comedy, perhaps partly because this character shares some lines and characteristics with the Fool in *King Lear*. He consolidates a trend to see Feste as an authorial spokesman as well as an acute observer of his dramatic society:

> He is as sane as his mistress; his position considered, he cannot be called even eccentric, scarcely even flighty; and he possesses not only the ready wit required by his profession, and an intellectual agility greater than it requires, but also an insight into character and into practical situations so swift and sure that he seems to supply, in fuller measure than any of Shakespeare's other Fools, the poet's own comment on the story.[26]

Bradley anticipates an influential strand of criticism that reads Feste as a knowing, poignant and sympathetic figure ('we cannot but feel very sorry for him', says Bradley) central to the creation of what has become known as an 'autumnal' and even melancholy atmosphere in the play.[27] However, such a 'serious' reading of any comedy as a whole did not appear until the middle of the twentieth century, as critics tended to regard the comedies as a group in an affectionate but uncritical spirit. As late as 1958, L. G. Salingar could pronounce without qualification that *Twelfth Night* 'is the most delightful, harmonious and accomplished of Shakespeare's romantic comedies' and that it 'has a prevailing atmosphere of happiness.'[28]

The Twentieth Century

A seminal production in 1912 directed by Harley Granville-Barker liberated *Twelfth Night* from the elaborate spectacle of

Victorian theatre, presenting it as a simple and undistracting
stage experience in which concentration was focused on the
rhythms of Shakespearean language and on surrounding the
romance with a contrasting, chilly and wintry tone.[29] At the
same time George Bernard Shaw praised an amateur, modest,
goodhearted, theatre-in-the round production of *Twelfth Night*
over the excesses of professional companies in grander theatres.[30]
However, if these breathed new theatrical life into the play, it
took criticism half a century to catch up, since despite Bradley's
lead there persisted a tendency to fear that comedy would be
destroyed by close analytical inspection. Instead, a tendency
towards fond but weightless *belle-lettrisme* dominated in studies
by John Dover Wilson, H. B. Charlton and Morton Luce, the
first Arden editor.

     Gradually, however, attention came to bear on the darker
elements of the play. Music provided a clue to the change of
tone. *Twelfth Night* has always been recognized as the play by
Shakespeare most suffused with generally melancholy music and
song, beginning with Orsino's famous paean to the emotional
power of music, 'If music be the food of love, play on […].' W. H.
Auden commented on the prevalence of songs, quoting several
in full to show how they cast light on character, while Peter Hall
made song central in his 1958 production. Auden also pointed out
the curious fact that this play and *The Merchant of Venice* both
contain characters who ostentatiously dislike music, Malvolio
and Shylock, and he points out that 'the characters who welcome
music in Illyria are more uniformly saddened by it.'[31] Feste and
Fabian are the two minstrels and their songs mainly reflect a
distrust of love rather than celebration, regret over the transience
of youth like falling blossoms. As well as containing music, the
play has also inspired many adaptations – at least eleven operas
and literally hundreds of song-settings.[32] One critic who has
built this aspect of the play into a wider interpretation is Barbara
Everett, in her essay 'Or What You Will': 'The musicality of
Twelfth Night … is a matter of internal harmonies, both technical
or formal and substantial.'[33]

Northrop Frye pioneered a form of literary criticism that dealt seriously with the different genres without prioritizing tragedy by seeing each as deriving from a distinctive, pre-literate mythic basis deriving from Jung's notion of a 'collective unconscious.' Comedy was configured as 'The Mythos of Spring',[34] influenced by classical 'New Comedy' and associated with Plautus and Terence. It enacted a pattern moving from a legalistic and anticomic phase, blocking lovers' desires, through a period of confusion and sexual experimentation often through assumed disguises in a 'green world', to the establishment of a new, harmonious society figured through marriage. For example, *As You Like It* and *Twelfth Night* move from unfulfilled melancholy stasis through sexual confusion to celebratory betrothals. Another part of Frye's theory, again borrowed from cultural anthropology, suggested that characters like Malvolio and Shylock are excluded from the festivities as 'scapegoats', derived from the Greek *pharmaki*. Clifford Leech, one of Frye's colleagues at Toronto, consolidated the trend towards serious readings of the play in his short monograph *Twelfth Night and Shakespearian Comedy*.[35] Leech presented the play in formal terms as the point at which a tragic vision of human transience begins to enter the playwright's comic vision. *Twelfth Night* is seen as a pivotal work, reaffirming all that had come before in Shakespeare's comic output but also opening up the doorway to the next phase, the famous tragedies. From this time on, the darker linings in *Twelfth Night* were inescapable.

Frye's lead stimulated C. L. Barber's study of the comedies based on social anthropology: *Shakespeare's Festive Comedy: A Study of Dramatic Form and its Relation to Social Custom*.[36] Barber described the mythic significance of Shakespearean comedy as the 'saturnalian' spirit which drives social festivity in holiday customs. In dealing with *Twelfth Night* he constructs a theory of comedy as a process 'through release to clarification' analogous to social festivity: 'What ["the merrymakers"] bring about as a "pastime" (III.iv.151), to "gull him into a nayword, and make him a common recreation" (II.iii.145–6), happens unplanned

to others by disguise and mistaken identity [... Sir Toby] is
like Falstaff in maintaining saturnalian paradox and in playing
impromptu the role of lord of misrule [... Malvolio] is like a
Puritan because he is hostile to holiday [...]', and so on.[37] Reversal
of roles in disguising 'a girl as a boy' is another symptom of the
holiday spirit, although Barber expresses this in a pre-feminist
light as a temporary reversal that serves to consolidate a heterosexual norm.[38] This view was to be 'problematized' by the next
generation of critics, but Barber's positive influence is evident
in the fact that a significantly titled book, *The Woman's Part:
Feminist Criticism of Shakespeare*, was later dedicated to him.[39]

Class-based readings took their place amongst the more
analytical approaches to Shakespeare's comedies. Back in 1946 W.
H. Auden had invested *Twelfth Night* with a seriousness that was
different from and less sympathetic than Frye's, stemming from
his political response to the post-war creation of the socialist-
inspired Welfare State in Britain. At least implicitly he anticipated
two approaches which became important later: Marxism and
feminism. Auden began his Lecture on the play provocatively:
'*Twelfth Night* is one of Shakespeare's unpleasant plays. It is not a
comedy for schoolchildren', and he continues:

> The characters in *Twelfth Night* are rich and idle, and their
> society is pervasively melancholic [...] Illyria, in *Twelfth
> Night*, is generally more self-conscious, weary, and less
> productive than the society in *The Merchant of Venice*,
> which is busy making money, trading, and doing business.
> The attitude toward money is also very different in the
> two plays. The characters in *The Merchant of Venice* are
> careless about it, throwing it about freely and generously. In
> contrast, there is cynicism about money in *Twelfth Night*, an
> awareness that services must be paid for, that people can be
> bought, and that money can get you what you want [...] The
> society in *Twelfth Night* is beginning to smell gamey. The
> characters in the play are out for gain, they are generally
> seedy, and they are often malicious [...] Unlike Falstaff,

these people emerge victorious and have their nasty little triumph over life. Falstaff is defeated by life.[40]

No doubt it is Toby Belch and Andrew Aguecheek who were in his mind, and no coincidence that they are both knights. Equally trenchantly, Auden points to the female-centred perspective of the play not in sentimental but argumentative terms, asserting that they 'take the initiative' in an otherwise decadent society in which the men 'appear contemptible.' Auden anticipates some feminist concerns, just as his class interests were developed by Marxists. Elliot Krieger summed up his theme on *Twelfth Night* as 'The morality of indulgence' and he examines issues of class and ideology in the play.[41] Others in the 1970s, without necessarily being Marxists, took a view which was aware of social issues and problems that could turn characters into social symptoms and sometimes casualties, for example, Thomas F. van Laan in *Role-Playing in Shakespeare*,[42] and this socially aware line of critical concentration has continued to prove fertile.[43]

By the mid-1970s there seemed to some, like Alexander Leggatt, to be a new danger facing critics of Shakespeare's comedies.[44] Instead of not being taken seriously they were in danger of being analyzed *too* solemnly in ways that swamp the light tones and laughter with portentous archetypal patterns and thematic preoccupations. Leggatt offers his book as a counterweight, valuing the internal variety of each play, and its differences from others. He too finds uncomfortable patterns in *Twelfth Night* by dwelling upon the prevalence of unfulfilled love and seeing Malvolio as only 'the most vivid image of the trapped, isolated self' which can be observed in other characters.

Historicism, Old and New

L. C. Knights, who fused interests in class and history, should be credited as a forefather of New Historicism, which held sway as a dominant approach in the late twentieth century. There have been others less lucky in their hunches. Leslie Hotson in 1954

published a book-length study, *The First Night of Twelfth Night*.[45]
Hotson was concerned to use historical archival material and
topical allusions as a way 'of conjuring up some of the atmosphere of that first night, of catching a glimpse of its moment
in time.' This 'first night' Hotson locates as 6 January (indeed,
Twelfth Night) 1600–1, and he links this with the visit to London
at around this time of a real-life 'Duke Orsino', an ambassador
from Braciano. He was to be entertained by Queen Elizabeth
at a specially commissioned play, which Hotson deduces was
Shakespeare's *Twelfth Night*. He bases his reconstruction on
a paragraph in the papers of the Duke of Northumberland,
describing entertainment of the Muscovite ambassador and an
Italian nobleman. Hotson's unrestrained delight at his discovery
has been adjudged as misplaced by some later scholars, who have
sought to unpick the links in his chain of reasoning. Another
historically based account came from John W. Draper in his
book *The Twelfth Night of Shakespeare's Audience*.[46] Draper's
belief was that it is impossible to understand a play without
'historical background' concerning how 'Shakespeare's audience
must have experienced and felt it.'[47] He describes *Twelfth Night*
as 'Shakespeare's play of social security',[48] since each character
is in search of financial security, and bodies of knowledge culled
from Elizabethan medical learning and astrology are invoked
to explain incidents. Draper's approach was received as rather
arid: Leech calls its style reminiscent of 'a leading article in *The
Economist*' and laments 'the impression that Professor Draper has
not recently seen the play on the stage.'[49]

New historicists – who flourished during the 1990s – presented
themselves as being considerably more sophisticated than these
older 'historical background' practitioners. They followed the
lead of two scholar–critics in particular, Louis B. Montrose and
Stephen Greenblatt, although the latter has always been uncomfortable with the label. This methodology draws on historical
documents to reveal not just context but more underlying and
sometimes unstated tensions, ideologies and anxieties which are
revealed, mediated and negotiated in literary works. Greenblatt,

in a chapter entitled 'Fiction and Friction', uses early modern medical discourse on sex as his point of entry to the mirror image of the disguised heroine 'herself' as well as her 'natural perspective', the twin brother, in *Twelfth Night*.[50] Greenblatt himself is a perceptive critic and irresistible writer, and he uses the approach to shed new light on some of the 'secrets' about sexual identity in the play. In less-spirited hands, however, new historicism sometimes falls foul of the kinds of charges leveled against Draper, running the risk of turning works of the creative imagination designed for the stage into deadening historical documents exemplifying their society's 'networks of material practices' and 'circulation of energies.'

Psychoanalysis

Amongst the heady pluralism of new approaches driven by literary theory in the 1980s and 1990s was psychoanalytical criticism, which arguably took 'serious' readings of *Twelfth Night* to an extreme by digging well beneath the comic surface. Barbara Freedman, for example, saw *Twelfth Night* through the prism of several psychoanalytical theories on loss and mourning.[51] Her book as a whole explores 'spectator consciousness' in terms of Shakespeare's comedies, which are said to 'reverse the look and entrap the audience' in a 'reciprocal gaze.'[52] Taking a Lacanian analysis as the point of departure, the discussion focuses on traumatic loss and mourning seen in the light, for example, of Freud's famous '*fort-da*' game based on 'repetition as deferral', exemplified in the requests for songs to be repeated in the play. The play's attention to written messages suggests 'a theory of the letter as the signifier of a primal loss', and Freedman examines how

> each of the characters in *Twelfth Night* is faced with the
> threat of abandonment, loss, or disillusion in relationship
> and is indeed *character*-ized by a particular means of
> responding to that threat [...] Viola defers the mourning of

her father and brother only to become the anonymous lover
of the wholly preoccupied Orsino; mourning is replaced by
pining, and desire remains unfulfilled. Sebastian, brother
to Viola, mourns his sister's supposed death, while his
companion, Antonio, pines for Sebastian and faces disillu-
sionment when shut out from the love Sebastian so readily
shares with Olivia.[53]

'The experience of being cut off from one's sustenance also
threatens the subplot characters but with humorous results'
(Feste, Toby, Malvolio), such as the 'false hopes' raised in
Malvolio. Minor characters as much as major ones exercise
individual survival strategies – either parasitism (Toby, Andrew),
or independence (Feste), or delusion (Malvolio). Ruth Nevo draws
on different psychoanalytical models in *Comic Transformations in
Shakespeare* as a way of showing how fantasies, anxieties and
obsessions especially visible in the presentation of sexuality in
Twelfth Night underlie and partially explain the form of comedy
as developed by Shakespeare.[54]

Feminist and Gender Studies

Feminism in some ways had its genesis in Shakespeare studies,
especially in his comedies, where assertive heroines find their
triumph. Germaine Greer's PhD thesis at Cambridge was
entitled *The Ethic of Love and Marriage in Shakespeare's Early
Comedies* and her research fed into her book in the *Past Masters*
series, *Shakespeare*. Greer's version of Shakespeare is of a
thoroughgoing 'radical [who maintains] a contempt for author-
itarianism of any kind and a deep conviction of the equality
of all human beings.'[55] She only fleetingly mentions *Twelfth
Night*, but it clearly lies behind her comments on 'the inconstancy of men' and 'the solidity and truth of women.'[56] More
recently she has published *Shakespeare's Wife*,[57] which has some
direct links with Virginia Woolf's imaginative projection in her
pioneering essay on 'Shakespeare's Sister' in *A Room of One's*

Own (1929). Greer, like some other feminist critics such as Juliet Dusinberre, does not see any anachronism in believing that Shakespeare was capable of voicing women's legitimate grievances and depicting their strengths, particularly against a backdrop of Elizabethan Protestant 'companionate marriage.'[58] Another strand of feminist criticism approving of Shakespeare explored the closeness and complexity of female friendships in his works, such as that which develops between Viola and Olivia.[59]

However, while Shakespeare may have been viewed by some critics as a proto-feminist himself, to many he remained little more than a male living in a patriarchal society, writing scripts for males to act, and underlining rather than undermining male dominance. Kathleen McLuskie wrote on 'The Patriarchal Bard', though she does not include consideration of *Twelfth Night*,[60] while Dympna Callaghan in *Shakespeare Without Women* uses the play as a prime example of the exclusion of the female body in the male impersonations of their personages.[61] Materialist feminists have critiqued Shakespeare as a 'hegemonic instrument' for the promotion of patriarchy, imperialism, racism, cultural elitism and 'a ruling-class view of the world.'[62]

Other feminists did not exercise such resistant readings but instead found in Shakespeare's heroines a potential for new insights. Marianne Novy sees in *Twelfth Night* a paradigm of mutuality between men and women that points to a third way in relationships, without coercive power structures.[63] Catherine Belsey, concentrating on Viola's statements which disrupt sexual difference and transgress conventional boundaries ('As I am a man [...] As I am a woman' (2.2.35–40), 'I am not what I am' (3.1.143) and 'What I am and what I would be are as secret as maidenhood'), also suggests that the fluidity of gender definition in the play offers hope for 'unfixing sexual disposition.'[64] Where earlier critics tended to regard the disguise as a creaky Elizabethan comic convention, feminism has revitalized different issues surrounding the revelation. This is not just an academic or theoretical issue, since Trevor Nunn in his fine filmed adaptation of *Twelfth Night* (1996) built the gender enigmas into his theme.[65] Amongst others who have, from different feminist points of view, seen healthy possibilities of new-found freedom in dismantling rigid gender boundaries in Viola's cross-dressing are, from their different points of view, Jean Howard on crossdressing, Phyllis Rackin on androgyny, Valerie Wayne with a materialist approach, and Penny Gay, who provides evidence from theatrical performances.[66] Alison Findlay finds many original and sharply observed things to say about the female roles in *Twelfth Night*.[67] Feminism has provided a particularly rich mine of insights, and not just into gender issues but *Twelfth Night* as whole.

To twenty-first-century readers and audiences it seems obvious that *Twelfth Night* inevitably raises contemporary issues about gender-identity, since the part of Viola was written for a boy actor playing a young woman who disguises herself as a male, Cesario. He/she becomes the focus on sexual attention from both Olivia and, less overtly, Orsino, whom Viola loves. When the 'knot' is untied by the appearance of a simulacrum, her twin brother Sebastian, historicizing issues surrounding gender and sexual identity have added yet another layer of meaning. For example, Stephen Orgel in *Impersonations: The Performance of Gender in Shakespeare's England* suggests Viola's design to present herself as eunuch and name herself Cesario is enacted in a historical context in which sexual preferences were less categorical and more fluid than is the case nowadays.[68]

Related works on transvestism, such as Marjorie Garber's *Vested Interests: Cross-Dressing and Cultural Anxiety* (1991),[69] extend gender approaches into queer studies. Madhavi Menon's *Shakesqueer* (2011)[70] follows the pioneering lead of critics such as Joseph Pequigney,[71] Kate Chedgzoy[72] and Jonathan Goldberg[73] in readings that foreground issues of bisexuality and homosexuality. In *Shakesqueer*, the essay by Sharon Holland, 'Is There an Audience for My Play?', begins by describing the impact of Tim Carroll's production at Shakespeare's Globe in 2002, which had been dubbed by reviewers 'The Male *Twelfth Night*' because of its all-male cast.[74] We have come full circle, but not to the same place occupied by Elizabethan boy actors.

The main conclusion that emerges from this necessarily selective survey is that *Twelfth Night* has shown itself to be resilient and durable enough to be perennially recontextualized, reflecting changing attitudes amongst critics, theatre practitioners and society at large. Its history up to the end of the twentieth century suggests that it will continue to be reshaped, as Chapters Two and Three confirm, and that it will provide 'what we will' for many more generations.

CHAPTER TWO

Performance and Adaptation

Linda Anderson

'If this were played upon a stage now' (3.4.128)[1]

There can be little doubt that *Twelfth Night* is both an extremely popular and a critically acclaimed play. Ralph Berry maintains that it is 'the most often performed of all Shakespeare's comedies', while Gary Taylor concludes that it was Shakespeare's most popular play, at least at 'the two leading Shakespeare theatres in England and North America [...] at the end of the twentieth century.'[2] Testimony to the play's greatness is also easy to find: 'John Masefield described *Twelfth Night* as 'the greatest English comedy'', director Bill Alexander maintained that it is 'among the most perfect plays ever constructed' and Muriel St Clare Byrne described the play as 'the most exquisite and the most popular of the comedies.'[3] However, even if it is true, as Michael Billington has asserted, that '*Twelfth Night* may be Shakespeare's most perfect comedy', the book he edited about the play certainly demonstrates that there is no consensus about it, even among a small group of English directors all of whom directed the play at the Royal Shakespeare Theatre within a twenty-year span.[4] Productions differ on when and where to set the play, and have added, cut and rearranged scenes. Virtually every major character has been interpreted in varied, even contradictory ways, including changes to the characters' ages and social class, barring Orsino and Olivia, whom the play identifies as aristocrats. Perhaps even more significantly, in most modern productions the tone of the play seems to have shifted over time, from comedy to something, to borrow Charles Lamb's phrase, more like 'a kind of tragic interest.'[5] This essay will briefly discuss the play's theatrical history with emphasis on particularly influential and unusual productions; films, recordings, and other adaptations; the remarkable range of changes to and differing interpretations of *Twelfth Night*; and how many aspects of modern productions are related to issues of service and class.

'The whirligig of time' (5.1.375)

We have very little evidence regarding the play's popularity before the closing of the theatres. Samuel Pepys saw the play at least three times during the 1660s, but he was neither impressed nor entertained: '*Twelfth Night* seemed a 'burthen' to the diarist on September 11, 1661; but that was possibly because he was troubled about having gone to the theatre at all. On January 6, 1662–3, he saw it 'acted well, though it be but a silly play, and not related at all to the name or day.' His last recorded attempt produces no better results. On January 20, 1668–9, 'to the Duke of York's House, and saw Twelfth Night, as it is now revived; but I think one of the weakest plays that I ever saw on the stage.' Yet [John] Downes says the comedy 'had mighty Success by its well Performance'.[6]

Despite Downes' assertion, however, what evidence we have suggests that the play was not popular in the late seventeenth and early eighteenth centuries. Although nine of Shakespeare's plays and adaptations of eight others were fairly regularly performed at Covent Garden and Lincoln's Inn Fields from 1720–1 through 1732–3, for example, *Twelfth Night* is never recorded as having been performed at either theatre during this period.[7] From 1741, however, when actor–manager Charles Macklin revived Shakespeare's original play with himself as Malvolio and Hannah Pritchard as Viola, *Twelfth Night* established itself as one of Shakespeare's most popular works, becoming a 'fixture' at Drury Lane Theatre between 1742 and 1776.[8]

The stage history of *Twelfth Night* in the nineteenth century often seems to consist of ever-increasing numbers of alterations to Shakespeare's text, combined with an enormous agglomeration of stage 'business.' Scenes were rearranged, songs were deleted, 'a 'grand masque' of Juno and Ceres might be added, Feste might be played by a woman.[9] A production at Covent Garden on 25 November 1820 'in addition to a masque with a lady in a shell, boasted 'Songs, Glees, and Choruses, the poetry selected entirely from the Plays, Poems and Sonnets of Shakespeare."[10] As J. L. Styan has put it, 'By the turn of the century, essentially Victorian conventions had been substituted for Elizabethan ones'. As an example, he points out: 'Since it seemed incredible by realistic standards that in *Twelfth Night* Olivia should not see that Sebastian was not Cesario, it became fashionable to play the scene of his return in dim moonlight'.[11] Sets became increasingly elaborate: in Sir Henry Irving's 1884 production,

> the sets, designed by Hawes Craven, smothered the play in a decorative romanticism. Orsino reclined on a velvet couch, tasselled in gold, while behind him in a dim myste-rious alcove, dark with painted glass, minstrels played their seductive melodies. And, in the final scene, the spreading portico of Olivia's house was flanked with branching palms beside a blue sea while guards, pages and courtiers stood picturesquely by. It was difficult for Shakespeare's comedy to survive such overweighted, picture-book literalism.[12]

Herbert Beerbohm Tree's set for his 1901 production may have set some sort of record for realism and awkwardness: a 'real' garden – with grass, plants, and fountains – it occupied the entire stage and could not be struck, and thus was the setting for the entire play.[13] Even when elaborate sets could be struck, so much time was lost making the average ten to twelve changes that the text had to be cut substantially to shorten the running time to a reasonable length.[14]

The unwieldy Victorian sets, however, did not indicate the pervasiveness of a single interpretation: Irving's production, featuring Irving as a tragic Malvolio, was disliked by almost everyone; Tree's more comic production, and his caricatured steward, were far more popular.[15] Furthermore, as the twentieth century dawned, a changing attitude toward Shakespearean production affected *Twelfth Night* as much as any play. William Poel's Elizabethan Stage Society production of 1897 staged the play 'before the Prince of Wales and a distinguished audience' in the Hall of the Middle Temple, 'the location of its first performance on 2 February 1601 before Queen Elizabeth.' Other than the use of actresses and electricity, 'the performance struck the note of authenticity', but reviewers were generally unkind, particularly regarding the quality of the acting.[16] There is general agreement that Harley Granville-Barker's productions at the Savoy Theatre of *The Winter's Tale* and *Twelfth Night* (both 1912) and *A Midsummer Night's Dream* (1914) marked the end of the over-adorned Victorian style of Shakespearean production and were immensely influential for later directors, although not universally acclaimed at the time.[17]

Other memorable and influential twentieth-century productions include Tyrone Guthrie's 1937 staging at the Old Vic, which 'featured a truly stellar cast, including Laurence Olivier as Sir Toby, Jessica Tandy as Viola [and Sebastian], Alec Guinness as Sir Andrew, Marius Goring as Feste, and John Abbott as Malvolio.' This version combined serious interpretations of Feste, Viola and Orsino with highly comic depictions of Sir Toby, Sir Andrew and Maria.[18] John Gielgud's 1955 version won some praise, although Olivier's Malvolio was controversial, and Gielgud himself felt that this production of a 'difficult' play 'did not work.'[19] In Peter Hall's 1958 Stratford production 'the romance was invaded by high-spirited fun and the comedy by a grave melancholy' and John Barton, in his 'legendary' 1969 RSC staging, also managed a 'well-nigh perfect achievement of the balance between comedy and tears.'[20] Peter Gill's RSC production in 1974 emphasized the characters' narcissism and eroticism, but was criticized for sacrificing the play's comedy.[21] John Caird's 1983 *Twelfth Night* for the RSC was notable for its dark atmosphere and extreme violence.[22]

'A natural perspective' (5.1.215)

The first filmed version of *Twelfth Night* was produced by the Vitagraph Company of America and directed by J. Stuart Blackton in 1910, as part of a series of one-reel Shakespearean films; these were among Vitagraph's extensive roster of 'prestige' pictures, 'known not just as entertaining but as pictures simultaneously able to perform a socially edifying function – to inform, educate and inspire.'[23] This film survives only in a damaged print: 'Originally of 970 feet it has dwindled to 743; there is no title; parts are missing at the beginning, the ending, and no doubt elsewhere; and the sequences are not always in the proper order'.[24] Various scenes were intentionally omitted or have been lost to time: among other things, Antonio does not appear, and Malvolio is not imprisoned; on the other hand, scenes are also added, including a reappearance of Viola in her 'woman's weeds.' Viola's emergence from the sea was actually filmed outdoors, on the beach at Bay Shore, Long Island.[25]

Although the Vitagraph film still exists, at least in part, many other filmed productions are either lost or hard to obtain. A 1939 video recording of a London theatrical production starring Peggy Ashcroft as Viola and Michael Redgrave as Sir Andrew is unavailable, as are a 1949 Actors Equity/Philco Television Playhouse production and 1950 and 1957 BBC television productions.[26] The Russian version directed by Yakov Fried for Lenfilm in 1955, although apparently received enthusiastically by critics at the time, now seems largely forgotten and unmourned.[27] Televised productions include a 'Hallmark Hall of Fame' production starring Maurice Evans and Rosemary Harris in 1957; a 1968 American production; a 1974 BBC production; and a 1969 ATV production starring Alec Guinness as Malvolio, Ralph Richardson as Sir Toby Belch and Joan Plowright as Viola.[28] A 1963 East German film version was entitled *Was Ihr Wolt* and set 'against the background of an Epiphany masquerade', and an 1986 Australian film version featured modern dress and a female Fool, for which performance the actress, Kerry Walker, won the Australian Film Institute's Best Supporting Actress award.[29]

More easily available films include the 1980 BBC Shakespeare Plays version, directed by John Gorrie, set in what appears to be seventeenth-century England, the cast including Felicity Kendal as Viola, Robert Hardy as Sir Toby and Trevor Peacock as a Feste who flouts modern trends by being relatively young and quite cheerful. In 1988 Kenneth Branagh and Paul Kafno adapted Branagh's Renaissance Theatre Company production for television. The production featured a minimal set and emphasized the cruel treatment of Malvolio, played by Richard Briers. Trevor Nunn directed a 1996 *Twelfth Night* for Fine Line Features, filming during autumn in Cornwall in what is intended to be the nineteenth century. The production is framed as a story told by Feste (Ben Kingsley), who is relatively old and grim; the movie's trailer sums up the emphasis: 'the sexy comedy where everyone's a fool for love.'[30]

'That is, and is not' (5.1.215)

From the re-opening of the theatres until 1741, it is not certain that *Twelfth Night* was ever performed using Shakespeare's Folio text, although it certainly appeared in a variety of other forms. Even after Shakespeare's play was re-established a wide variety of adaptations and expropriations has continued to flourish, and the following cannot hope to be comprehensive. In addition to Sir William Davenant's revision of the play, William Burnaby's *Love Betrayed; or the Agreeable Disappointment* was produced in London in 1703. Burnaby acknowledges borrowing part of Shakespeare's plot 'and about 50 of the Lines'; in fact, a great deal of the plot is Shakespeare's, although Burnaby combines the characters of Malvolio and Sir Andrew, splits Maria's character in two, adds a few additional characters, and renames all except Viola and Sebastian. His ridiculous changes to the plot included a masque, 'but the House neglect[ed] to have it set to Musick', and the play, by Burnaby's own admission, failed and seems never to have been revived.[31]

Burnaby was by no means the last person to believe that *Twelfth Night* could be improved by adding more music. The play was filmed in 1947 as *Noche de Reyes*, 'a Spanish musicalized version' directed by Luis Lucia; a 1965 East German adaptation, *Nichts Als Sünde*, added not only various kinds of music but ballet.[32] In 1968, *Twelfth Night* inspired two off-Broadway musicals: *Love and Let Love*, which closed within a few weeks, and *Your Own Thing*, which was far more successful, running for 933 performances before touring in the United States and Canada, and winning a New York Critics' Circle Citation for Best Musical. This show was also produced in London and Sydney in 1969, although it was far less successful in London, where it had only 42 performances. The musical bore little resemblance to the original, retaining not much more than the identical twins separated in a shipwreck, with the woman cross-dressing, thereby producing romantic confusion. However, Shakespeare's poetry did inspire two of the musical's songs: 'Come Away, Death' and 'She Never Told Her Love.' The 1972 West German film *Viola and Sebastian*, which features 'beat music and hippie elements', may be similar to the American musical, despite being 'set in rural Schleswig Holstein.'[33] In 1982, Ariane Mnouchkine directed the play (as *Le Nuit des Rois*) for Le Théâtre du Soleil in Paris in a version featuring aspects of kabuki and kathakali, a production which was revived for the 1984 Olympic Arts Festival in Los Angeles. In 1988, Hugh Hefner's Playboy Channel debuted a soft-core pornographic version, directed by Ron Wertheim (who also played Feste), in which the plot was retained, although the language was modernized and vulgarized. Olivia was reimagined as 'a reclusive star *a la* Garbo' and Orsino as 'a bored rock star.'[34] Michael Frayn's *Twelfth Night; or What Will You Have?* was presented by the Exacting Theatre Company at the 1990 Edinburgh International Festival, where it was described by Alfred Weiss as 'a crazy cocktail party filled with Shakespearean quotations, misquotations, puns, allusions, non sequiturs, and confusion.'[35] Eddie Sammons reports that a 1991 American film entitled *Shakespeare's Plan 12 from Outer Space* once existed but cannot now be traced.[36]

No doubt the most successful filmed appropriation of recent years is the Hollywood film *She's the Man* (2006), directed by Andy Fickman and starring Amanda Bynes (Viola) and Channing Tatum (as Duke, the Orsino character). After her soccer team is cut, Viola poses as her absent twin brother, Sebastian, at Illyria School, in order to join the boys' soccer team there. She promptly falls in love with her roommate, Duke, who, however, is in love with Olivia, who is attracted to the putative Sebastian. An additional complication is that the disguised Viola breaks up with Sebastian's girlfriend, Monique, who subsequently learns and reveals Viola's real identity. Like most modern appropriations of *Twelfth Night*, this one concentrates on the main, romantic plot – although, typically, without the deaths mentioned in Shakespeare's play – to the nearly complete elimination of the comic-revenge subplot and its class issues.

Versions of *Twelfth Night*, or at least portions of the play, have also been presented in media other than stage and screen. In the early 1890s, an American company released sets of magic-lantern slides of fifteen of Shakespeare's plays, including *Twelfth Night*, under the title of 'Shakespeare Illustrated.'[37] In the late 1930s Orson Welles released a recording of *Twelfth Night* as part of the 'Mercury Text Records', each of which was accompanied by play-text based on work done by Welles and 'his teacher, mentor, and friend' Roger Hill and published in 1934; Michael Anderegg states that these are the first recordings ever made of complete Shakespearean plays.[38] In 1953, Charles Laughton (as 'Count Orsini') read from *Twelfth Night* in *This Is Charles Laughton*.[39]

In 2004 first-time novelist Katharine Davies published a novel entitled *A Good Voyage* (subsequently reissued as *The Madness of Love*),[40] which is essentially a modernized re-telling of *Twelfth Night*. Melody, a headmistress in the seaside village of Illerwick, is beloved of the wealthy but melancholy musician Leo, but Melody is mourning the suicide of her brother and spurns Leo's attentions.

Enter Valentina, whose twin brother Jonathan has abruptly left her to travel alone to Sri Lanka in search of adventure. Valentina determines to have her own adventure, which begins with her getting her hair cut boyishly short, and develops as she answers Leo's advertisement for a gardener. Valentina, naturally, falls in love with Leo as Melody falls in love with Valentina.

While Davies's main plot adheres closely to Shakespeare's original, the subplot is substantially altered. The Malvolio figure, Mr Boase, is Melody's deputy headmaster, a lonely alcoholic who frequently bullies the children in his charge, and it is the children – who are staging *Twelfth Night* at school, with the main child-characters playing Feste, Maria, and Sir Toby – who take revenge on Boase by tricking him into dressing inappropriately for a party arranged by Leo to impress Melody. Despite the comparative wealth and social prominence of Leo and Melody, the novel places relatively little emphasis on class and makes virtually no mention of service; on the other hand, various minor features of *Twelfth Night* – from the emphasis on the sea and gardens to a forged letter, box hedges and yellow stockings – are cleverly worked into the story and add to the fun for readers familiar with the original.

Excerpts from *Twelfth Night*, both as stand-alone skits or as parts of a larger work, have also been attempted, although not always successfully. 'The Tricking of Malvolio', a half-hour excerpt from *Twelfth Night*, was performed by actor–manager Patrick Kirwan's Idyllic Players in 1912 during an Earls Court exposition called 'Shakespeare's England.' It was not a success.[41] A 1916 newsreel gives a brief look at an open-air performance of *Twelfth Night*.[42] The BBC broadcast two different excerpts of the play with different casts in 1937 and a filmed excerpt of the letter scene was performed by the Young Vic Theatre Company as part of the television series 'The World's a Stage' in 1953.[43] In a fourteen-minute, black-and-white, award-winning documentary *Vizkereszt* produced in Hungary in 1968, a group of rural people come to a production of *Twelfth Night* and skate home afterward.[44]

Bits of *Twelfth Night* have also been put to effective use in other productions. The 1935 British film *The Immortal Gentleman*, which depicts Shakespeare meeting with Ben Jonson and Michael Drayton, shows Shakespeare (Basil Gill) portraying Malvolio, while other actors portray Maria, Feste, Sir Toby and Sir Andrew; the 1972 British documentary *The Phoenix and the Turtle* shows the Century Theatre Company rehearsing *Twelfth Night*.[45] The 2004 film *Wicker Park*, which emphasizes romantic obsession and deception, depicts one of the female characters acting in a production of *Twelfth Night*.[46] Also notable are the use of Feste's final song as a kind of elegy in the 1965 Merchant Ivory film *Shakespeare Wallah* and the interweaving of aspects of the play in 1998's *Shakespeare in Love*, in which the main female character is named Viola, appears dressed as a boy for much of the film, and ends – rather than beginning – as apparently the only survivor of a shipwreck.[47]

'How will this fadge?' (2.2.32)

Although directors often take liberties with Shakespeare's scenic arrangements, *Twelfth Night* may be the Shakespearean play most often rearranged in performance, as if Shakespeare's ordering of scenes were arbitrary and could be easily improved upon. Perhaps the most elaborate changes occurred in the late Victorian period, as Billington notes of one production:

> The American manager and distortionist, Augustin Daly, in 1894 frantically rearranged the text in order to meet the demands of scenic realism. His version at Daly's theatre in London began with the arrival of Sebastian and Antonio, proceeded to the star-entrance of Viola (Ada Rehan) and then went on to play the first and fourth scenes of the first Act, featuring Orsino, so that the seacoast could give way to a fantastically elaborate ducal palace.

Daly also added a scene in which Olivia was serenaded.[48] Other scenes have also been transposed: Walter Hudd's 1947 Stratford production transposed the first act's scenes 3 and 4, and Barton transposed the first two scenes of Act 2 in his 1969 RSC production.[49]

While some Victorian productions did everything possible to increase sympathy for Malvolio, others cut lines, or even cut Malvolio from Act 5, to simplify and soften the play's ending; Berry notes that 'It was customary to interpolate these lines for the Duke (after Malvolio's exit): "And now after twelve nights of tastes and pleasures, / Let me commend you to your dancing measures." A dance followed'.[50] Although William Bridges-Adams, the Stratford-upon-Avon Shakespeare Festival manager between 1919 and 1934, was so disinclined to cut Shakespeare's text that he became known as 'Unabridges-Adams', Billington notes that he 'cut the prison-scene, thereby softening the play's cruelty.' Billington also mentions other

> strange liberties […] taken with the text in between-the-wars productions […]. At London's New Theatre in 1932 […] the director, Robert Atkins, gave the last verse of 'The wind and the rain' to Olivia. Donald Wolfit, in his touring production first seen in 1937, suggested that Malvolio enjoyed a last-minute return to Olivia's favor.[51]

Introductions, often featuring Feste, are also common. One of the most popular may have been Günter Krämer's 1981 production at Stuttgart, in which 'Sir Toby Belch got the audience into a holiday mood before curtain by distributing glasses of white wine from a large vat to the early arrivals and by maintaining a steady stream of comic patter.'[52]

The most common structural change directors make to the play, of course, is the transposition of the first two scenes, so that the play begins with Viola's 'What country, friends, is this?' rather than Orsino's 'If music be the food of love, play on.' This change, which originated at least as early as the nineteenth century, was likely inspired not by thematic considerations, but by the desire to limit the number of scene changes necessary in a period of elaborate backdrops and scenery.[53] Even so, it is a change that has persisted, occurring (among other productions) in Hudd's 1947 production, the 1948 production at the New Theatre, in 1966 at the Birmingham Repertory Theatre, in a 1981 Swedish production, and in two 1987 productions: Branagh's at the Riverside Studios and Declan Donnellan's at the Donmar Warehouse.[54] No longer required because of unwieldy scenery, for some directors this switch seems to have acquired a thematic justification.[55]

Various bits of stage business have been carried down through the generations (although others have fallen out of theatrical favour in recent decades). Viola has been known to arrive in Illyria with luggage that she has somehow saved from the shipwreck.[56] Malvolio sometimes 'returns' the ring to the disguised Viola by dropping it from the tip of his steward's staff.[57] The scene most adorned (or encumbered) by extra-textual accretions, however, is Act 2 Scene 3, often referred to as the 'kitchen scene' ('cakes and ale scene' in British theatrical tradition), although there is no reason to think that Shakespeare expected that it would be staged in Olivia's kitchen. Sir Toby and Sir Andrew have frequently engaged in elaborate pantomimes of extreme inebriation, often involving clay pipes and candles, while Malvolio has appeared wearing his steward's chain over a ridiculous nightgown, with hair-curlers protruding from his nightcap; he has even been known to carry a teddy bear.[58] On at least one occasion, an actor performed a stunt against the wishes of his director: Gielgud reported that, when he directed the play at Stratford in 1955 with Laurence Olivier as Malvolio, 'he insisted on falling backwards off a bench in the garden scene, though I begged him not to do it.'[59] Much more elaborate bits of business were also staged, as at the end of Act 2 Scene 3 of Tree's 1901 *Twelfth Night*, as recounted by Max Beerbohm:

As the two topers reel off to bed, the uncanny dawn peers at them through the windows. The Clown wanders on, humming a snatch of the tune he has sung to them. He looks at the empty bowl of sack and the overturned

tankards, smiles, shrugs his shoulders, yawns, lies down
before the embers of the fire, goes to sleep. Down the stairs,
warily, with a night-cap on his head and a sword in his hand,
comes Malvolio, awakened and fearful of danger. He peers
around, lunging with his sword at the harmless furniture.
One thinks of Don Quixiote [sic] and 'the notable adventure
of the wine-skins.' Satisfied, he retraces his footsteps up the
staircase. A cock crows, and, as the curtain falls, one is aware
of a whole slumbering household, and of the mystery of an
actual dawn.[60]

'What country, friends, is this?' (1.2.1)

Perhaps at least in part because they recognize that audiences
are likely to be unclear about both the location and the culture of
Illyria, contemporary directors have experimented with a wide
array of settings for *Twelfth Night*.[61] At the RSC alone, there has
been considerable variety: Barton and Terry Hands' productions (1969 and 1979 respectively) were performed on 'quite a
bare stage, with fairly minimal scenery', although Barton's set
featured an actual willow cabin, or at least the suggestion of
one; on the other hand, in Peter Gill's 1974 RSC production
'Illyria is set in the effete South of England', while Caird's 1983
production featured 'a very precise rocky, craggy, rough piece
of coast', and Bill Alexander's 1987 RSC production was set in
'a sun-kissed, white-walled, travel-brochure Greek island full
of shadowy ginnels and exotic arches. This was an Illyria that
existed as a real place on the map'.[62] That same year, Branagh set
his production of the play during a snowy Victorian Christmas. In
1988 at the Edinburgh Festival, the Cambridge Touring Theatre
staged *Twelfth Night* as *Miami Vice*, with Orsino and his men as
'machine-gun-toting, cocaine sniffing hoods, less interested in
love than in posing languidly in their pastel suits […] Malvolio as
a British ex-colonel, Fabian as a skinhead, [and] the officers as a
SWAT team'; in 1989 at the Folger Shakespeare Theatre, Michael
Kahn set the play in 'Raj India.'[63]

Although the play's title has suggested to other directors besides Branagh that a Christmas – or immediately post-Christmas – setting is appropriate, the play has also been set during Carnival season; as beginning in winter and moving into spring; and in summer.[64] The classic season for setting the play in recent times, however, is autumn, and 'autumnal' is the adjective most likely to be used – at least in a positive way – in any given review, not only regarding the setting, but the tone.[65]

Directors vary not only the seasons, but also the historical period in which the play is set. Although many productions, such as Caird's 1983 version for the RSC, remain set in the Elizabethan period, Peter Hall's influential 1958 Stratford production was 'costumed in a Cavalier style, that suggested, a shade ominously, Van Dyck.'[66] Robin Phillips's 1988 production for the Stratford Ontario Young Company 'was costumed in the style of the early Romantic period', while Bill Cain's Oregon Shakespearean Festival production of the same year was a 'Victorian music-hall rendition'; a production at the University of Hawaii featured 'vividly colored' Gothic costumes; and various productions have been performed in various styles of modern dress.[67] The extreme lengths to which a director may go were perhaps best indicated in Declan Donnellan's 1987 London production, which 'treated Aguecheek as, in Michael Radcliffe's phrase, 'a tumescent jack-rabbit from the boondocks of Middle America', and gave the saxophone-playing Maria a Brooklyn twang. It had Orsino petting Cesario as heavily and unequivocally as Olivia did. It showed the gay Antonio at the last striking up a liaison with Feste. And, most controversially, it had the midnight revellers singing a drunken, bellowed version of 'My Way' […] For Radcliffe [in *The Observer*], 'This was a *Twelfth Night* for those who have never seen the play before and those who thought they never wanted to see it again'.[68] Although many a Shakespearean play has in recent decades been given a setting designed to surprise, if not shock, perhaps no play has encouraged more experimentation than *Twelfth Night*.

'How have you made division of yourself?' (5.1.220)

Many of the most obvious changes in production and interpretation of *Twelfth Night* since it was first written and performed have been made to the characters, with changes to the servant-characters being some of the most obvious. Malvolio, in particular, has undergone various transformations, frequently with regard to class and service. Although Orsino is the Duke of Illyria and Olivia is a Countess and pursued by two suitors, what limited evidence we have suggests that for seventeenth-century audiences Malvolio was the main attraction: John Manningham's description of the play's performance on Candlemas 1602 centres on Malvolio; Henry Herbert, Master of the Revels, used 'Malvolio' as the title of the play for the performance on Candlemas 1623; and Charles I wrote 'Malvolio' next to the play's title in his copy of the Folio.[69] Whether or not Lamb was correct in seeing Robert Bensley as creating a new, tragic interpretation of Malvolio, it is certainly true that since then Malvolio 'has arrived in many guises.'[70] Samuel Phelps, acting the role in 1857 at Sadler's Wells, adopted the 'bearing and attire' of a Spanish grandee, grave and contemptuous, and so in love with himself as to be essentially impervious to attack.[71] Edward Aveling, in his July 1884 review of Irving's production at the Lyceum in London, indicates that Irving's Malvolio hinted at 'the low birth of the steward', adding that Irving 'intended us to pity Malvolio, to weep for if not with him'; Tree's Malvolio, on the other hand, was a ridiculous caricature, followed by a retinue of four miniature versions of himself.[72]

In the twentieth century, however, the trend toward tragic Malvolios grew stronger, with directors choosing various ways to generate sympathy for Olivia's steward. At Stratford in 1937, John Abbott played a very young Malvolio, apparently genuinely in love with Olivia, which gave his 'final discomfiture [a] touch of tragedy'; Laurence Olivier (Stratford, 1955) made it clear that his Malvolio had worked his way up from lower-class origins; Nicol Williamson's Malvolio (RSC, 1974) was 'founded on a combination of innate loneliness and emotional pain';

and Antony Sher's (RSC, 1987) was apparently driven mad by his mistreatment.[73] More recent Malvolios sometimes depict even more reasons for us to sympathize with them: in the 1988 Stratford Ontario Young Company production, 'Peter Donaldson played Malvolio as a prim Japanese *major domo*', whose social awkwardness was explained by his racial and cultural difference, and whose treatment by his enemies suggested racial prejudice.[74]

Malvolio, however, is hardly the only character who has been interpreted in multiple ways. Orsino has been a 'virile romantic', a bisexual groper of the men around him and Leonardo da Vinci.[75] Olivia has been portrayed as a mature, dignified woman and a giggling coquette; she may be either a vulnerable girl or a sexual predator.[76] Sir Toby can be played as a gentleman, a minor Falstaff, a pathetic old man, a sadistic brute, or some combination of these characters, while actresses may portray Viola as a melancholy romantic or a 'cheeky and mischievous' tomboy.[77] Maria has been depicted as a social-climbing gentlewoman, a kitchen soubrette and an elderly spinster, while Feste can be anything from a 'cockney' to a 'humanistic sage' to something like Bob Dylan, although, like Malvolio, he has tended, over time, to become older and less funny.[78]

'Will my revenge find notable cause to work' (2.3.152–3)

That the plot against Malvolio is a justifiable comic revenge is as clear as anything in Shakespeare. Malvolio, we are carefully shown and told, has offended everyone with whom he comes into contact. However, because modern directors and actors are often anxious to make *Twelfth Night*'s subplot 'The Tragedy of Malvolio', and because the politics of a great household's servants is so foreign to most modern audiences, the comic-revenge aspects of the play are often de-emphasized in the theatre. Malvolio is portrayed in various ways, but not generally as a bully who is genuinely dangerous to the livelihoods of those he threatens; although by the end of the play he rarely seems a real danger, it is no accident that his final, famous line is another threat. Yet if we do not perceive Malvolio as a dangerous bully – and perhaps most modern audiences, with their knowledge of the misuse of accusations of insanity and consequent imprisonment, are unable to perceive Malvolio's punishment as anything but torture – his treatment can only appear as cruelty and his adversaries as sadists. Although some productions are satisfied with such a depiction, it drains much of the comedy from the play. Consequently, theatrical companies have three main options: they can perform a hard-nosed (arguably hard-hearted) version in which Malvolio is an overweening servant who gets his comeuppance from a cabal of gentlefolk and lower servants, all of whom he has attempted to intimidate from his position of authority; they can present a sympathetic Malvolio, unjustly tormented by other characters simply for trying to do his job competently; or they can minimize the issues of class and service by setting the play in a place and time that de-emphasizes hierarchy and instead focus on romantic comedy.

'that would alter services' (2.5.157)

Modern audiences' unfamiliarity or discomfort with the play's emphasis on class and with the traditions of service has, arguably, had equally significant effects on the ways productions have represented the main romantic plot. The melancholy main plot, with its themes of unrequited love and mourning for dead – or presumably dead – brothers is often underplayed, since there is little to balance this in productions where so much comedy is leached out of the subplot (Malvolio made more sympathetic, Toby and Maria made less sympathetic, and Feste often just made pathetic). In such circumstances, directors have frequently felt it necessary to add more comedy to the main plot, which has often meant making Orsino and Olivia more comic than the Elizabethans would have expected aristocratic lovers to be.

Trevor Nunn's film is in many ways an excellent example of recent fashions in *Twelfth Night* productions: Malvolio is more tragic victim than comic butt, Feste is more misanthrope than professional entertainer, and much is made of Viola's difficulties in transforming herself into a plausible young man who can handle both a sword and her relationship with the master she secretly loves. A *Twelfth Night* produced by the National Theatre of Craiova, Romania, presented at the tenth annual Shakespeare festival in Gdansk, Poland, in August 2006, also represented some typical trends of twenty-first-century productions of the play: an 'overweight, melancholic' Orsino 'was soon on physically intimate terms' with Cesario despite the duke's condition of 'lovelorn vacuity. Olivia recalled *Sunset Boulevard*'s Norma Desmond in her heavy mourning dress, dark glasses, and black headscarf, but her vivid red lipstick was a hint at other possibilities'; while listening, mainly unseen, to Cesario's suit, she stripped 'to a black bustier, garter belt, and stockings [...] Cesario responded eagerly to her advances, establishing quickly the production's enjoyment of polymorphous perversity.' In the final scene, Olivia 'gleefully embraced *both* Cesarios when confronted with the brother and sister ('Most wonderful!' [5.1.225]).'[79]

Orsino, Olivia and Viola, all servants of those they love, are often depicted on stage and screen as melancholy figures. Orsino, the self-defined romantic servant of a woman who wants nothing to do with him, has been described by Stephen Booth as 'one of the two or three most difficult parts in all of Shakespeare and surely the most unrewarding for an actor who challenges it';[80] the count's worship of a woman he cannot have and failure to recognize Viola's loving service often makes it difficult of audiences to see what Viola sees in him. Directors often try to compensate for this defect in Orsino's character by casting a very attractive actor in the role, although (as in the Romanian production mentioned above) the opposite reaction – reflecting Orsino's unlovely personality in an unlovely body – is another possibility. Olivia, who rejects Orsino's 'service' only to immediately fall in love with her 'servant's servant' (3.1.102), is much more likely in modern productions to be mocked for loving another woman rather than a servant. This is certainly the case in Nunn's production, in which

Viola is wearing what seems to be a military uniform rather than
servant's livery; on the other hand, given her fake moustache and
the scenes in which we see her removing her disguise, we are
unlikely to forget that she's a woman. The Olivia in Branagh's
filmed version is particularly dominating, and when she reacts
strongly against her apparent husband's apparent betrayal, Viola's
'Who does beguile you? Who does do you wrong?' (5.1.138) lands
particularly hard on a woman who has beguiled herself. Viola, an
actual servant to the man she loves (as she thinks, hopelessly), is
easily most rational and attractive of these characters, in or out of
her 'wicked' disguise, and usually the one the audience is most
inclined to identify with. Ironically, however, the varied melancholy of the members of this triangle frequently makes them
laughable: Orsino primarily because of his self-delusion, Olivia
largely because of her confusion, and Viola principally because of
her situation.

The interesting result of our ignorance of service and class in
Shakespeare's world and our distaste for *Twelfth Night*'s focus on
these concerns is that we have turned the play's 'balance' upside
down: for us, the comedy largely inheres in the foolish Orsino and
the confused Olivia, and the drama – not to say tragedy – in the
abused Malvolio and his tormentors. Billington refers to *Twelfth
Night* as 'an extremely elusive play', but if directors can no longer
find the original humour in Shakespeare's play perhaps it is
because they aren't looking for laughs as much as for something
else. Though 'autumnal' is the adjective most commonly applied
to contemporary productions of *Twelfth Night*, one suspects that
'Chekhovian' is the ultimate accolade, and that many of today's
directors are intent on giving the tough-minded Elizabethan social
comedy a tone somewhere between melancholy and despair.[81] The
play continues to interest and delight us, but perhaps only at the
cost of meaning something quite different from what it meant
to its original audience. Perhaps *Twelfth Night* can only survive
because we take literally its subtitle: *What You Will.*

CHAPTER THREE

The State of the Art

WILLIAM C. CARROLL

Major critical statements about Shakespeare's comedies that reshape the field, as C. L. Barber's *Shakespeare's Festive Comedy* did, are rare indeed.[1] Such statements about individual plays occasionally come through a radical production, as with Peter Brook's staging of *A Midsummer Night's Dream*, but can also come through a major edition; it may be – the whirligig of time will tell – that Keir Elam's Arden edition is such an event.[2] Some studies of the play since 2000 have chartered new directions of critical approach, yet most have continued in reaction to the major critical flashpoints of previous decades. Elam's edition, however, is not only master of all it surveys, but casts many elements of the play in newly revealing light. His edition cannot do everything, though, and the more specialized essays examined below illuminate key facets of *Twelfth Night*. I will consider Elam's edition first, and then, by rough-drawn categories of theme or approach (in which there is considerable overlap), some of the most compelling other work on the play published since 2000.

Twelfth Night, ed. Keir Elam

Elam brings to the play a willingness to look and listen anew, in the most acute detail. The Introduction and annotations fully bring out the baffling richness and complexity of Shakespeare's language. One of Elam's most innovative arguments relates to what has usually been seen as a textual crux: Viola's design to present herself 'as an eunuch' (1.2.53). Previous scholars, noting that this plan is not developed, have explained the reference as

a moment when Shakespeare nodded, forgetting what he had
written in moving on to another, more likely plot line; many
productions (ironically) cut the line altogether. Yet Elam makes
a provocative case that the play does carry the theme further;
building on his own 1996 essay relating the concept to the
play's Italian and Roman sources,[3] Elam links Viola as Cesario
to the figure of the castrato singer as well as to literary texts of
Castiglione, Gonzaga, Riche and Terence.

Twelfth Night has often been placed as the climax of a line
of development of Shakespeare's romantic comedies, from *The
Comedy of Errors* on. Among the problems in this teleological
scheme is the circular 'later-is-better' implication that devalues
early work as inferior because it is early, while *Twelfth Night* is
often said to be a 'culmination' of earlier comic themes and tropes.
Elam acknowledges these earlier models, but also points the play
forward, noting the ways in which it is first, not last; innovating,
not just culminating: the play 'is probably Shakespeare's first
seventeenth-century comedy, and is in many ways a beginning-
of-century play, inaugurating a new poetics';[4] it is 'unique among
Shakespeare's plays in having received a contemporary review'
by John Manningham;[5] it is 'in many ways the most material of
Shakespeare's plays, uniquely concerned with cloth and clothing,
dress and dressing, precious and common objects, architecture,
furniture, receptacles, tools, and all the practical and physical
aspects [...] of everyday life';[6] it is 'perhaps Shakespeare's most
class-conscious play' and is 'the only Shakespeare play in which
servants [...] are leading characters, not on behalf of their betters
[...] but in their own right.'[7] Other critics have noted some of
these features, but Elam returns focus to the play's uniqueness
again and again.

Elam produces, to over-simplify, a Feste-centric reading of
the play's strategies: Feste is 'the best guide we have to the play's
underlying themes' and is 'the most astute commentator on
the play of which he is part.'[8] At the centre of the play's many
visual and verbal riddles, Feste embodies Elam's distinctive
argument: that 'perhaps the strongest [desire aroused by the play]

is cognitive desire, the yearning to know and to understand', that '*Twelfth Night* repeatedly professes its own secrecy [...] It is a play "about" interpretation'.⁹ While Elam notes the 'mimetic syndrome' by which many commentators begin to resemble Malvolio, zealously hunting the secrets of the text, he is not immune to the disease himself, offering suggestive readings of the play's many cruxes.¹⁰ Noting the seasonal aspects of its title, Elam suggests that 'it is a play that promises an epiphany – a secret or coded transcendental signified waiting to be revealed – but strategically withholds it.'¹¹ This vision of *Twelfth Night* is at the heart of Elam's edition.

In a related approach that moves towards Elam's argument, Arthur Kinney surveys the long history of Shakespearean criticism that sought 'unity' – in terms of structure, theme, character – in the play, as well as more recent work that stresses its multiplicity and indeterminancy, and attempts a reconciliation of these viewpoints, showing how the complexities set up in Act 1, for example, move toward 'a final resolution, or unity, we long for' at the end 'but are cheated out of.'¹² Still, he says, the search for unity 'lends a sense of unification to what we do have but makes that unification the play's chief object' – the play 'keeps unifying what at first appears to be oppositional.'¹³

Gender/Sexuality Studies

Following Stephen Greenblatt's famous essay 'Fiction and Friction',¹⁴ *Twelfth Night* became a central text in debates over the so-called 'one-sex' model of human anatomy elaborated on by Thomas Laqueur,¹⁵ including refutations of its applicability to early modern England.¹⁶ The critical discourse around Greenblatt's essay represented a quantum leap in complexity from earlier thematic readings and led to many strong accounts of the play's place in early modern debates about the nature of the stage's eroticism and in modern analyses through feminist theory and queer theory. *Twelfth Night* continues to be a central paradigm case for discussions of gender, sexuality, transvestism, the boy actor and anti-theatricalism (all are inextricably interrelated). Much recent scholarship has continued to re-work these issues.

Recent considerations of the play in terms of gender generally conclude that the play, as Robert Maslen says, 'makes it possible to believe that there is no such thing as a stable normality where gender is concerned, either in Elizabethan times or in our own.'[17] Influenced by the work of Judith Butler, Maslen and others have come to see gender as primarily constructed through performance. The instability of gender could even contaminate the early modern audience, according to the anti-theatrical writers, as Stephen Orgel demonstrated in a work that continues to be highly influential.[18] The stage, in such readings, becomes a place where dangerous forms of same-sex desire as well as normative heterosexual desire are played out. While this brief summary represents a scholarly consensus on the subject, Robin Headlam Wells, in a distinctly minority view, dismisses both the cultural anxiety and biological indeterminism arguments in an essay whose title conveys its argument: '*Twelfth Night*, Puritanism, and the Myth of Gender Anxiety.'[19] Agreeing that many elements of the play seem consciously 'inflammatory to Puritan sensibilities', Wells nevertheless argues that Shakespeare 'doesn't seem to regard this sexual ambivalence as a scandal, merely as a charmingly foolish affectation that must sooner or later come to an end.'[20]

Laurie Shannon notes how Renaissance texts

> frequently present gender as a concentrate that is diluted and changed by mixing, whether we consider the symbolic convergence of chastity with power in the female case or the now-established critical viewpoint that effeminacy marks men who become womanly by too strong an interest in women. Renaissance anxieties about such mixing offer heavy weather to an emergent ideology urging a heterosexual marriage that can only preside over just such a mixing. [21]

Shannon further observes that

> In affective terms, affiliation, affinity, and attraction normally
> proceed on a basis of likeness, a principle of resemblance
> strong enough to normalize relations between members
> of one sex above relations that cross sexual difference. In a
> sense, as countless comedies lean on friendship, twinning,
> and disguise (all species of likeness and resembling) to
> bootstrap their way to a leveraged marriage ending, expiring
> as often as not before its threshold, they seem to take
> marriage itself as the thing that warrants explanation and
> accounting, rather than same-sex affects or connection. The
> ideological work of much comedy, then, is less to celebrate
> or to critique marriage and its approach than to find a means
> to make it plausible or even thinkable in parity terms.[22]

She continues the discussion by suggesting that the main reason
Orsino selects Viola/Cesario

> as a proxy to the reluctant Olivia is her nonmasculinity.
> And this is not in order to prevent what eventually occurs
> (Olivia's falling for the messenger) but, on the contrary,
> to make use of a homonormative principle of affect and
> attraction that he supposes will make Olivia more receptive
> than all the previously spurned messengers from the Duke.[23]

Moreover, Shakespeare constructs 'a second order of likeness
in the play: the relatedness of siblings or twins. This species of
likeness, too, is gathered as a way to approach or to approximate
marriage.[24]

Although Valerie Traub only briefly mentions *Twelfth Night*,
her book thoroughly analyzes female same-sex desire in the
Renaissance, and (like Shannon's) shows how *Twelfth Night*
challenges heteronormativity. Traub notes that in contemporary
criticism Cesario's self-indictment (her disguise is 'a wickedness'
and she is now a 'poor monster', 2.2.27, 34) serves

as a summation of early modern attitudes toward female homoeroticism: any woman desirous of another woman could only be viewed as monstrous. Yet, this orthodox position is precisely what much of the action of the play contests. The meaning of femininity has been called into question not only by Cesario's masculine costume [...] but by her obvious delight in playing the erotic part of the man.[25]

Traub concludes that 'It is as object of another woman's desire that Cesario finds her own erotic voice.'[26] Covering much of the same ground as Traub and also only briefly mentioning *Twelfth Night*, Denise A. Walen believes the double wedding at the end signifies Olivia's 'marriage to Viola as much as it does to Sebastian. The play thus closes on a homoerotically constructed passion'.[27]

Tracing female same-sex relations in the play, Jami Ake notes that while the scholarly work of Traub and others acknowledges 'that a discrete "lesbian" identity did not yet exist in the period, [it] has nevertheless worked to recover emergent and recognizable languages of female homoeroticism.'[28] For Ake:

Viola's performance of Orsino's poetic suit to Olivia creates a curious dramatic space in which female characters negotiate and revise the scripts and conventions of the elite, if increasingly clichéd, Petrarchan poetry of Elizabethan courtiers. In the interview scene, the inadequacy of Orsino's ostensibly heteroerotic Petrarchan discourse, surprisingly enough, gives rise to a pastoral poetics of female desire in Viola's conversation with Olivia [...] Viola's successful wooing of Olivia in the interview scene affords us a glimpse of a tentative 'lesbian' poetics as one female character imagines and articulates the words that will seduce another.[29]

Olivia also 'resists the tendency of Orsino's Petrarchan poetics to transform women from pretexts for verse into poetic texts under masculine control.'[30]

Chad Allen Thomas approaches the play through queer theory, but finds that the text's

> playful expression of erotic plurality only goes so far, and within this variety of opportunities, Shakespeare reifies heterosexual endings by prescribing three matrimonial couplings: Sebastian and Olivia, Orsino and Viola, and Toby and Maria. Thus although playgoers experience a variety of erotic encounters [...] in the end, the three unmarried female characters are securely attached to male mates, presumably negating the need for future transgression (transvestite or otherwise).[31]

Nevertheless, Thomas shows how the play can effectively be 'queered' through performance choices. Taking up 'fancy' as a faculty (a power, ability, opportunity) in the play, Bruce R. Smith also reads the play through queer theory. In his account, 'nature' in *Twelfth Night* 'becomes a norm for separating hetero-normativity from homo-deviancy.'[32]

Goran V. Stanivukovic by contrast argues that masculinity in *Twelfth Night* is not represented as heroic and reproductive: 'Rather, this version of normative masculinity is constantly challenged'.[33] He analyzes how early modern prose romances, instead of medical theories, imagine masculinity, starting with how *Twelfth Night* 'comments on the romantic plot of *Parismus* [by Emanuel Forde, 1598] in ways that re-write the representation of masculinity in that romance.'[34] Shakespeare's plot 'registers, through Forde, the cultural shift from chivalric to romantic masculinity', criticizing 'chivalric violence and mock[ing] civic masculinity parading as chivalric', particularly through Sir Andrew: 'Shakespeare's play appeared at the time when romantic masculinity invested in courtship and household management took over as a representational (and cultural) model from the heroic masculinity of the earlier heroic times'.[35]

Laurie E. Osborne analyzes the play in terms of male friendship's conflict with heterosexual marriage, focusing on Cesario as an independent agent: 'Cesario's achievement of open passion and reciprocal devotion with Orsino argues that women "are as true of heart as" men [...] and that sexual passion can co-exist with amity'.[36] Osborne's essay follows recent work on the discourse of male friendship by Paul Hammond, Alan Bray and Shannon. David Schalkwyk follows a different approach, however, 'deliberately ignoring friendship between women and same-sex male relationships to focus on the possibilities of friendship between men and women in Shakespeare [and] Montaigne.'[37] Montaigne denied the possibility of friendship between men and women, asserting that friendship and desire could not coexist; male–male friendship was celebrated 'precisely because it involves none of the costs that constitute the perverse economy of desire.'[38] Schalkwyk shows how 'both Montaigne's exclusion of women from the possibilities of friendship and Orsino's parallel denigration of their capacity for erotic devotion are contradicted by the embodiment, in the *same* actor, of desiring woman and loyal male servant.'[39] Viola as Cesario represents a paradoxical challenge to Montaigne's conception:

> In her male persona, Viola can affirm at least one-half of the bond of loving friendship that Montaigne simultaneously celebrates and mourns, overlaying the erotic intensity of her desire as a woman [...] with the 'constant and settled heat' of her friendship as the duke's favourite courtier.[40]

The play's 'doubled embodiment' creates 'the imaginary space for a woman *performatively* to live up to the demands of friendship'; hence *Twelfth Night* 'reconceptualizes the received family of inherited concepts clustered around the emotional states of love and desire as forms of action.'[41] Tom MacFaul also analyzes male friendship, but while other critics have noted three intertwined courtship plots, MacFaul describes as well 'three distinct plots of friendship, involving Sir Toby and Sir Andrew, Sebastian and Antonio, and Orsino and Cesario', all of which prove to be illusory in some way.[42] Friendship in the play 'is constructed as a danger and a humiliation.'[43] Lesel Dawson focuses on Orsino's male lovesickness in the context of medical discourse.[44]

Two essays consider Olivia's veil in terms of gender roles. Amy L. Smith and Elizabeth Hodgson show how the veil, usually marking the woman as a passive object of desire, is transformed: the play makes

> Olivia a nun, a widow, and a maiden in ways which authorize her to veil and unveil her desires for economic and erotic independence. When Olivia veils herself, her character invokes the power of conventional seclusion for women of the period [...] When her grief converts to amorous desire, but without the usual reprisals or subjection to masculine authority, Shakespeare remakes the lusty-widow narrative. And when she stage-manages her own marriage-choices [...] Olivia remodels the economic exchange of maidenhood.[45]

Indeed, 'in moving Olivia among these roles without comment or narrative punishment, in replacing one veil with an unveiling and then with another veiling and unveiling, Shakespeare makes Olivia into a figure unexpectedly' autonomous.[46] The authors emphasize 'the control Shakespeare allows this character over her relationship with the rather obvious pressures of the outside world and the protection and autonomy he grants her within it',[47] especially in contrast to *Measure for Measure*'s veiled Mariana. Brinda Charry, by contrast, argues that the presence of the veil marks the play's engagement with the process by which Europe defined its relation to forms of racial and cultural difference represented by the Muslim world.[48] The veil complicates the nature of female agency *Twelfth Night* and both evokes and erases the Islamic east.

Loreen Giese examines the '*yellow stockings*' that Malvolio is duped into wearing.[49] Elam glossed 'yellow' as indicating 'that they were hopelessly *out* of fashion', and Giese adds that such stockings would 'signal illicit sexuality and marital betrayal',[50] satirizing and subverting 'Malvolio's desire for sexual domination' by suggesting instead his 'subservience and embarrassment',[51] thus giving class as a dimension to the jealousy usually associated with the colour yellow.

Geography

Many scholars have argued that 'Illyria', although referring to an actual place, was invoked vaguely enough in the play to discourage 'the audience from linking the setting with any contemporary geographical or geopolitical reality.'[52] Ann Blake describes Illyria as 'not only exceptionally remote, as seen from the perspective of a London audience, but also exceptionally unlocalized', thus allowing 'greater emphasis to fall on fantasies and illusions' such as Viola's 'willow cabin' speech.[53] François Laroque describes Illyria as 'a country of the mind, or a nowhere place.'[54] Several scholars with historicist interests, however, have placed 'Illyria' as more central in period discourse. Sara Hanna, Patricia Parker, Elizabeth Pentland and Stanivukovic in effect argue that Illyria 'might be more unfamiliar and foreign to us than to the England of the period we study.'[55] 'We should not forget', Pentland notes, 'that Illyria was also famous to Elizabethans as a commercial and cultural cross-roads where Italian, Turkish, and Greek practices mingled with local custom, and as an ancient kingdom with a long and fascinating history of piracy, resistance to Rome, and female rule'.[56] Parker finds that 'the increasingly fragmented Illyrian territories [were] at the forefront of the conflict between East and West, both before and after the rise of the Ottoman Turk.'[57] While agreeing that Illyria was generally thought of as an unpleasant and possibly dangerous place, Stanivukovic cautions that the 'modern appropriation of Illyria' as 'a specific geographical and topographic location' may be a form of scholarly 'yearning' to 'claim a part of Shakespeare's canon for another culture'; he suggests instead that 'the idea of Illyria in Renaissance England is similar to that of Italy', as 'a space for the inscription of transgressive desire', concluding that the 'geographical and historical Illyria is just like the imagined Illyria of Shakespeare's romance and comedy: a liminal place, partially known, mysterious, and always already provincial.'[58] Catherine Lisak argues for Illyria as a kind of screen, 'an outlandish representation of Renaissance "core middle England" (or central London) that offers scenarios of the foreigner's reception and integration.'[59] The play 'portrays strangers in a remarkably original light, by conjuring dramatic stereotypes while blurring national distinctions', deploying 'a double framework that swiftly absorbs a newcomer's strangeness while enabling the natives' idiosyncratic eccentricities to break through.'[60] Peter Milward, however, claims that Illyria stands

> for two countries, neither of them the real Illyria [...] There is, on the one hand, the Catholic country of Italy, the home of Duke Orsino [...] There is, on the other hand, the Protestant country of England, centred on the court of Queen Elizabeth in Westminster, where the play is being acted for the royal and ducal entertainment.[61]

Richard Wilson's essay on Shakespeare's representations of hospitality to strangers discusses how *Twelfth Night* celebrates exploration like that of the East India Company sponsored by Sir Robert Shirley 'fencer to the Sophy' and mocks parochialism.[62]

Timothy Billings analyzes Toby's geographical reference to Olivia – 'My lady's a Cathayan' (2.3.74; F *Catayan*). In tracing the history of editorial glosses, Billings argues that Cathay was not, as many have asserted, understood as a synonym for 'China', but it 'can best be understood rather as an overdetermined signifier for someone whose speech is not to be trusted (that is, someone who makes empty threats or vain promises, exaggerates, misleads, or lies outright).'[63]

Madness, Malvolio and Puritanism

Twelfth Night's representations of madness and exorcism have drawn much commentary. Manningham's account singled out the trick played on Malvolio as especially memorable, 'making him believe they tooke him to be mad.' Building on work by social historians, Carol Thomas Neely initially explores 'lovesickness' and its early modern cures and then considers Malvolio's madness and confinement as a kind of scapegoating: the scenes draw

> condemnation onto Malvolio, and away from the erotic unruliness, gender fluidity, and willful marriages [elsewhere in the play]. They pathologize Malvolio's status-seeking match to elicit tolerance for those driven by erotic desire. [...] Malvolio serves as a scapegoat who is punished for flaws others share.[64]

Neely relates Malvolio's confinement and exorcism, as other scholars have done, to the debate over possession and exorcism being played out in printed works and in the College of Physicians 1599–1603. Neely argues that the exorcism scene represents this debate as 'unresolvable.'[65] Kathleen R. Sands also examines the possession/exorcism debate, tracing a growing public scepticism,[66] and Marion Gibson links such phenomena with separation and disunity in both the family and the state.[67] Mihoko Suzuki likewise finds Malvolio a victim of social 'scapegoating', in that those characters

> with the most insecure claim to membership in the nobility – Toby, Andrew, and Maria, whose actual marriage to Toby mirrors Malvolio's projected marriage to Olivia – take the greatest pleasure in humiliating him and dissociating themselves from him. [...] all three Malvolio-baiters seek to allay their anxieties about the pervasiveness of social mobility, for they themselves exemplify such mobility.[68]

The play translates 'relations between genders into relation between classes',[69] and ultimately brings about marriages 'between those of different classes' [Sebastian/Olivia, Maria/Toby, Viola/Orsino].[70] In so doing, 'The play displaces its disapproval of all the transgressors onto Malvolio'.[71] Among the play's most positive gender elements is that it allows Olivia an 'anomalous position of independence from patriarchal control.'[72]

Ivo Kamps challenges 'scapegoating' accounts such as Neely's ('I am not sure that Malvolio and Orsino, Viola, Olivia, Toby, and Maria share the *same* flaw [...] nor do I think that their irresponsible behavior is entirely and successfully displaced onto Malvolio in the final act').[73] Instead, Kamps argues that Maria and Toby 'create the impression that Malvolio has gone utterly mad [...] Malvolio is hoodwinked into performing lunacy.'[74] Thus 'to Toby and Maria, Malvolio's social ambition is a form of insanity, and what could be more fitting than to have him act out his desire and to be declared insane for it?'.[75] Kamps offers an alternative vision in which class anxiety produces madness:

> And while Orsino, Viola, Olivia, Toby, and Maria are all disciplined into the societal norm when they enter into class and gender appropriate marriages and thus serve, uphold, and reproduce the social status quo, it is Malvolio's drive for upward social mobility that endeavors to make misrule *permanent* in the shape of an interclass marriage.[76]

In short, 'The repressed Malvolio was perfectly sane by Illyrian standards', but the plot makes him perform his 'madness.'[77]

For some readers, Malvolio's social transgressions – both as a 'festive kill-joy' and as a servant desiring to marry upward – and imprisonment/cure for 'madness' are inextricably linked to his identification with Puritanism, signalled by Maria's comment that 'sometimes he is a kind of Puritan' (2.1.136), but indicated as well by numerous other signs. The implications of this religious/political identification have been discussed since the nineteenth century and include other religious allusions traced in the play, notably Twelfth Night as the feast of the Epiphany. As Elam notes, 'The saturnalian reading of title and play gains force from the oppositional presence of a "Puritan" steward. Protestant fundamentalists reserved special bile for Christmas misrule as a mode of spectacle',[78] and the performance witnessed by Manningham took place on Candlemas, the feast of the purification of Mary, at a 'feast' at the Middle Temple, on which occasions a Lord of Misrule was frequently chosen. In such 'saturnalian' readings, the play's comic plot reflects a 'nostalgia for a pre-Reformation world'[79] in which cakes and ale could flow freely without repression by Puritan kill-joys.

Recent scholarship has continued the investigation of religious, particularly Puritan, elements in the play, in a few cases, such as Ann Lecercle's reading of Olivia's supposedly Catholic household, spilling over into thinly supported biographical speculation about Shakespeare's personal religious beliefs. The text becomes for her – ironically, as the letter does for Malvolio – a 'text encrypted' with hidden allusions.[80] In a more convincing approach, Phebe Jensen sees Shakespeare as a kind of festive traditionalist 'who also aligns his own work, on aesthetic though not theological grounds, with festive energies identified with the old religion.'[81] Jensen's reading (too complex to fully elaborate here) argues that Falstaff 'haunts' the play:

> the play's consideration of Puritan satire, Catholic satire, the history of festivity and theater, and alehouse revelry, represents a return to the not-quite-dead Oldcastle controversy, spinning into a new configuration issues raised both in *I Henry IV* and in the Admiral's Men's rewriting of Falstaff in their own Oldcastle play.[82]

She points out that the 'the festive humiliation of Malvolio does not result in increased self-knowledge [or] spiritual enlightenment.'[83]

Noting the synonyms that Maria immediately offers to her 'Puritan' reference – 'a time-pleaser; an affectioned ass that cons state without book and utters it by great swathes; the best persuaded of himself, so crammed, as he thinks, with excellencies that it is his grounds of faith that all that look on him love him' (2.3.143–7) – Bruce R. Smith observes that 'Reform of religion [...] is not the main thing on Maria's mind. [...] Instead, Maria identifies the Puritan in Malvolio as a matter of social ambition

and exaggerated self-worth.'[84] Indeed, Maria casts doubt on the
sincerity of Malvolio's Puritanism herself: 'The devil a Puritan
that he is' (2.3.142). Kamps has, as already discussed, linked
Malvolio's Puritan madness with his drive for upward social
mobility. G. P. Jones seeks to rebut Poole's comment that while
Malvolio 'is certainly "puritanical" (in the current, modern
sense of the word), he is not, properly speaking, a puritan';
Jones assembles contemporary evidence to demonstrate that 'the
manner in which Malvolio is duped and abused is predicated on
his recognizabiltiy as a kind of puritan.'[85] Brett D. Hirsch links the
'night-owl' (2.3.57) reference to stereotypical Puritan traits: such
figures were conventionally 'purblind' or squinting from reading
the small print of the Geneva Bible.[86] Paul Yachnin develops
another side to the 'social' aspect of Malvolio in analyzing the
representation of Puritans on stage in relation to the institutional
positions of particular theater companies:

> the Puritans are scapegoats for the players and playwrights'
> own profitable but problematic situation between the enter-
> tainment market and the system of rank. These Puritans
> are like the players in that they seek recognition and
> advancement from their social superiors, and unlike them,
> because they do it so poorly. Malvolio [...] is an embod-
> iment of the self-interest and instrumentality of the players'
> 'service' to the nobility.[87]

William Kerwin's reappraisal of medical discourse and
Malvolio's madness shows how medical narratives 'always
follow social narratives.'[88] *Twelfth Night* – 'Shakespeare's play
of diagnosis' – is a fully sceptical interrogation of 'humoralism
and spiritual healing.'[89] Kerwin traces 'three specific issues of
historical contention, debates in which Elizabethans argued about
the meaning of identity, health, and illness.'[90] Firstly, he investi-
gates humoural medicine and the culture of embodiment derived
from the Galenic tradition; here, Kerwin attempts to move beyond
Gail Kern Paster's influential work by showing how humoural

discourse derives as much from identifiable social and political pressures as from its own 'scientific' validity. Secondly, Kerwin argues that lovesickness 'provides another episode of medicine and a volatile social order redefining each other [...] From Duke Orsino's opening speech to his debates with Viola about the relative nature of men's and women's loves, love in the play' is 'defined by a medical language.'[91] Moreover, the 'languages Orsino draws on are crippled by his humoralism. His Petrarchanism is inseparable from his use of a medical model'.[92] Kerwin's third category, centred around Feste, is comprised of the discourses of madness and spiritual healing, which the play subjects to a comparable scepticism. Kerwin, too, contextualizes this topic in relation to the debates about possession and exorcism. While these debates are usually cast in terms of faith vs early science, Kerwin sees them as more the product of Anglican–Puritan conflicts in the arena of public power. Feste's self-identification with the Vice is clearly linked to this debate: 'For the antiexorcists, the Vice [invoked in a surprising number of medical texts] is a parallel to outmoded religious rites; he represents the foolish superstitions that govern practitioners of exorcism'.[93] *Twelfth Night* is 'Shakespeare's most dogged interrogation' of early modern medical discourse.[94]

Darryl Chalk takes the play's interests in love and disease, and the Puritan association with anti-theatrical discourse, in the direction of contagion and plague. He shows that 'the recurrent connection between theatre and contagion in antitheatrical discourse, and in plays like *Twelfth Night*, can be explained through an examination of the emerging understanding of both plague's aetiology and other forms of contagion, such as lovesickness.' For Chalk, the play is a deliberate and self-conscious response to antitheatrical sentiment.[95]

In her study of the theatricality of the exorcism scene, Becky Kemper notes that the F stage direction – '*Malvolio within*' – does not imply an entrance, and that he never appears onstage in the scene. The effect, she argues, would be to reduce audience sympathy for the character and to reduce 'any violence or torturous visual images within the scene.'[96] Production choices since the nineteenth century have thus done much to create the modern sympathy for the character.

Feste, Festivity and Fooling

As is evident from the previous section, festivity – embodied in Sir Toby, Feste and the values they represent – stands in opposition to the kill-joy 'Puritanism' of Malvolio. The 'festive' nature of the calendrical Twelfth Night has often led to arguments based on a Carnival–Lent binary that is both highly attractive and too simple to account for the complexities of the play. Indira Ghose makes this kind of argument, while also (following other scholars) linking Feste's identity to the stage roles of Robert Armin, the actor who played him.[97] As part of her larger argument about Shakespeare's relation to festive tradition, Jensen describes Feste's presence as part of a 'lineage of the stage fool',[98] connected in terms of Feste's 'tabor' (3.1.2) and his proximity, in the joke that follows, to the 'church':[99] 'to put Armin on stage with a tabor and pipe in 1600 was visually to invoke [Armin's theatrical prede-cessors] Kemp [… and] Armin's reported mentor Tarlton, whose signature instrument was the tabor.'[100] In linking them together, the play 'seems to be insisting on the continuity between Tarlton, Kemp, and Armin, and between the professional theater and the tradition of raucous festive misrule and improvisation that they continued and transformed.'[101] The play 'insists on conti-nuity, not disjunction, with a festive past that is at once broadly historical and more narrowly institutional.'[102] Sir Toby's carnival excess, 'a drunken, secular Lord of Misrule',[103] complements 'the Lenten, professional foolery of Feste / Armin.'[104] Paul Dean and Maurice Hunt have traced the Catholic resonances evident in Sir Toby:[105] his homonym Sir Topas has a Catholic history in Marian pamphlets defending transubstantiation, just as Maria's name links her to the Annunciation, while Feste's 'Master Parson' role links him to contemporary parodies of Catholic priests.

Even relatively small linguistic elements, as Thomas Rist demonstrates, may relate to religious issues.[106] Noting the

punning on *merry*, *marry* and *Mary*, and Olivia's initial associations with Catholicism ('chantry', 'madonna'), Rist argues that
Shakespeare's use of 'marry' as an oath (from 'by the Virgin
Mary') leads to a kind of structural/thematic punning as well,
in which 'Olivia's comic trajectory is from a position of noted
Marianism to one of *marriage*.'[107] Rist connects this movement
with the character Maria, whom Feste links with 'Eve's flesh'
(1.5.26): 'Maria is a "second Eve" in a sense wittily contrasting
with Olivia: while Olivia reportedly desires a cloistered life, only
arriving at marriage by accident, Maria actively curries the favour
of Sir Toby Belch […] eventually marrying him'.[108]

Suzanne Penuel's account of the play's Reformation context
begins with a consideration of doubling, which 'can also be
chronological repetition: someone from the past is copied into the
present', then analyzes the play's doubling in 'its connections to
the ambivalently longed for figure of the early modern father' as
a 'response to a specifically post-Reformation hunger […] the
double takes its force from changes in mourning rituals that accompanied the decline of English Catholicism. It serves as a testament
to the power of the father–child tie and ultimately as a fantasy of
its replacement.'[109] Viola's crossdressing transformation 'both in
its very act of doubling and in its female- to-male transvestism,
represents the perpetuation of the father's name and lineage.'[110]
Penuel relates the play's 'obsessive doubling and emphasis on the
death of fathers [… to] a context of rigorist neo–Stoic hostility to
grief. More important, they engage Protestant hostility to traditional Catholic forms of mourning';[111] '*Twelfth Night*'s mourning
is also a hearkening back to a denied form of expression deeply
intertwined with family life'.[112] Penuel then shows how the play's
twinning reveals 'the fragility of the heterosexuality that enables
and is enforced by the ideal of blood descent.'[113]

Intertextuality

Many of the scholarly works described above approach *Twelfth
Night* through its intertextual relation to other cultural discourses,

but the play's links to specifically 'literary' works have always been seen as substantial. Janet Clare argues that *Twelfth Night* is a 'conscious reworking [...] of specific comic devices [such as a comic duel] from [Ben Jonson's] *Every Man Out [of His Humour]* for quite different dramatic ends.'[114] Although the duping of Malvolio has often felt particularly Jonsonian, Clare argues that the relationship between the two plays is

> one of intertextual antagonism. In its response to *Every Man Out (of His Humour)*, there is in *Twelfth Night* a pronounced reworking of Jonsonian motifs which reaffirm both a festive and romantic ethos and an assertion of illusion over mimesis and performance over textuality.[115]

James P. Bednarz delivers a definitive treatment of '*Twelfth Night* at the Center of the Poets' War', describing and unravelling the play's thick intertextuality in relation to Jonson's *Every Man Out (of His Humour)* and John Marston's *What You Will*.[116] Bednarz begins with the chronology of the three plays: Jonson, Shakespeare, then Marston. Jonson's play had satirically stereotyped the typical Shakespearean comic plot as involving 'a duke [...] in love with a countess, and that countess [...] in love with the duke's son, and the son to love the lady's waiting maid [...] with a clown to their servingman.'[117] Bednarz argues that this generic stereotype reflects the comedies that Shakespeare had already written, and that Shakespeare wrote *Twelfth Night* partly in response to Jonson's critique: 'its main plot [...] revitalizes the ridiculous formula of cross-wooing-with-clown that Jonson had rejected [...] its subplot, especially the gulling of Malvolio, echoes comical satire's exposure paradigm only to mock the standard of objectivity on which it is based.'[118] Malvolio is often described as Shakespeare's attempt at the kind of 'humours' character – like Jaques (*As You Like It*) and Ajax (*Troilus and Cressida*) – perfected by Jonson. 'How', Bednarz asks, 'is it possible for *Twelfth Night* to be both Jonsonian and anti-Jonsonian?' The answer is that Shakespeare 'followed Jonson's example' so as 'to contradict him':[119] the 'discovery' moment in the Malvolio plot does not, as it does in Jonson, lead to any kind of reform or rueful self-knowledge, but just the opposite, in his vow to 'be revenged.' Marston's further response to both Jonson and Shakespeare is beyond the scope of this review, but suffice it to say that Bednarz demonstrates Marston's indebtedness to *Twelfth Night*, and not the other way around. One result of Bednarz's study, which ranges far beyond the plays mentioned here, is a sense of how deeply imbedded Shakespeare was in the literary and dramatic culture of his time – not standing aloof, paring his fingernails, but part of the game.

Charlotte Coffin finds that Shakespeare uses 'Ovid's fable of Echo and Narcissus [...] both as subtext and instrument of exploration.'[120] While Ovid's fable has long since been identified and explored, Coffin argues that the play contains 'a more shifting set of identifications' than usually thought,[121] with characters not neatly identifiable as reflecting one or the other. Shakespeare, she concludes, creates 'a different version of the myth [...] Instead of substituting an image of otherness for the pattern of the double, he creates an endless pattern of reproduction', managing 'to subvert the myth by imitating it to excess.'[122] Mark Houlahan argues that Orsino's allusion to 'th' Egyptian thief' (5.1.114) is 'so specific as to prove that Shakespeare knew, by some route we cannot now absolutely determine, at least one form of Heliodorus' famous tale',[123] the *Aethiopica* (translated into English in 1569).

Social and Economic

Materialist approaches to *Twelfth Night* have flourished in the past two decades, opening up new ways of thinking about the play in social and economic contexts. Robert Appelbaum reads it through the material contexts of food and dietary health, locating Sir Andrew's 'I am a great eater of beef' (1.3.83) and Sir Toby's 'hiccup' in a dense network of writing about Renaissance foodways.[124] 'Beef' was supposed to dull the brain – perfectly appropriate for Sir Andrew – but Appelbaum argues that in the world of *Twelfth Night* even beef-eating amounts to a kind of political act. It is an act of deliberate if possibly foolish policy, a decision to live one way rather than another, to take care of the self in one way rather than another, and to do so in a way that has implications for one's class and national identity.[125]

Richard Wilson finds the duelling scenes in *Twelfth Night* anything but comic. Placing the play in 'the first of three English duelling crazes',[126] Wilson (over)emphasizes the comic violence of the play: 'Viewed in the context of the Essex revolt, *Twelfth Night* seems a mirror of the epochal battle between gown and sword, and the duelling mania in which an élite [...] vented its violence upon itself'.[127] Critics who see *Twelfth Night* as mocking the duelling cult underestimate or occlude the 'blood' violence of the play, Wilson claims, and misread Shakespeare's own intentions and beliefs:

> *Twelfth Night* looks like the one play where the dramatist dropped his own authorial guard, since if its subtitle implies that *What You Will* was composed to some political order, its glamorization of hot young bloods also points to a deeper commitment to the aristocratic ethos of Catholic resistance.[128]

Wilson provides a bracing contextualization of duelling and the collapse of the honour code, and explores a surprising number of references to hunting and duelling, yet the evidence is too often stretched to be fully convincing.

Nancy Lindheim proposes to rethink sexuality and class by taking up several 'problems' of recent scholarship that are 'said to darken our reception of *Twelfth Night*'s final scene: the arbitrary pairing of the four lovers; Antonio as outsider, abandoned and hurt; the homoeroticism of Viola's remaining in male costume.'[129] For each, she attempts 'to place the disturbing element in a fuller context of Elizabethan perceptions of the issues, or alongside other factors such as the generic imperatives that shape Renaissance poetics.'[130] Lindheim seeks to resituate Malvolio's rejection of comic reconciliation and Maria and Sir Toby's marriage 'within a spectrum of historically relevant social practices' and 'as consonant with the choices of mature comedy.'[131] The result is an old-historicist reading of the play that attempts to damp down critical accounts of 'anxiety' and 'disorder' by explaining them away.

Both Stephanie Chamberlain and Alan Powers offer analyses of the play's use of rings.[132] Chamberlain considers the exchange of rings in the play through gift-exchange theory, noting that when Olivia sends her ring after Viola/Cesario, it signals that she

> has, in principle, at last agreed to participate in the credit
> network by circulating her body and thus her estate within
> Illyria. The problem [...] is that the object of her desire
> lacks the means by which to repay the debt Olivia's arguably
> magnanimous gesture has created.[133]

The various valuables offered by Olivia and Orsino 'are as much about contracting alliances in an unashamedly monetary marriage market as they are about signaling emotional commitment.'[134] In contrast to most contemporary readings of the play, Chamberlain finds that the flow of gifts in the play finally balances into a 'harmonious outcome.'[135] Lisa Marciano, in contrast to Chamberlain, finds – as her subtitle indicates – a 'dark didacticism' in *Twelfth Night*, deriving from 'an urgent sense that life must be lived well because it is short.'[136] The result of this approach is a reading that seems optimistic and, well, didactic:

> For Viola, Feste, and their fellow Illyrians, the outcome is a
> society which is generally wiser, albeit with a few exceptions
> [... the] characters come to realize the inevitability of death
> and make this knowledge the impetus for a life well-lived.[137]

Valerie Forman reads the play in terms of its 'investments', real and figurative, arguing that the play suppresses 'its material contexts and those of its literary sources. In the consequent derealized noneconomic world it imagines, the play disavows the very conflicts that are at its center and thus loses the opportunity to imagine that profits can be made out of the losses the play earlier sustains.'[138] Using the terms 'profits' and 'losses' in both material and metaphorical senses, Forman shows how the main plot develops from such losses as Viola's loss of her brother and her loss of identity through her disguising. Indeed, her very disguise as a eunuch is (following Elam's work) yet another form of loss. But offering these losses will lead to unexpected gains, just as the new

> idea of investment in the early seventeenth century [...] was a concept developed to explain that losses (bullion sent out of the country) were not really losses, but instead should be understood as expenditure that would lead to a greater inflow of bullion (i.e., profit) at a later time.[139]

Forman enumerates the surprising number of allusions and actions related to monetary flow – Viola's purchase of clothing from the Captain, the odd travels of Antonio's purse through the play (his apparent link to piracy) – though ultimately the play's suppression of its merchant roots allows a refocusing of attention on the 'master–servant relation', which provides 'a way to imagine a happy ending.'[140]

Other critics have focused more directly on master–servant relations in the play. Comparing the play to early modern commentaries on servant-maids, Michelle Dowd argues that it

> marks the shift from feudal to wage-based service through a process of formal displacement; the play transfers the financial logic of service from Viola to Feste. In Viola's transformation from page to Orsino's 'fancy's queen', the play offers a romanticized narrative of female service and upward mobility that is structurally contingent upon the

suppression of other narratives – namely, narratives of limited upward mobility, prolonged service and financial hardship.[141]

Maria's parallel plot as serving-woman – leading to her marriage to Sir Toby – 'is founded on a particular fantasy of early modern female service in which wit becomes a dubious place holder for economic value.'[142]

David Schalkwyk casts new light on the master–servant relation in the play, arguing that 'love and service', as his title indicates, are closely related.[143] Approaching service through the concept of love, rather than desire or power, Schalkwyk denies the standard reading of masters–servants in the play as hierarchically unequal:

> Given the common practice of placing the sons of gentlemen and even the nobility in service with other noble families [cf. Curio and Valentine, *'gentlemen attending on Orsino*], Viola's decision to serve the duke of Illyria does not imply any decline in social status.[144]

The key question: 'Why is the erotic fantasy of Orsino's servant celebrated, while that of Olivia's steward is thwarted?'[145] Schalkwyk points out that '[i]t does not matter to Olivia that Cesario is a servant but rather that he is a *gentleman* servant.'[146] Moreover, '[e]ach of three members of the play's gentry develops an erotic interest in a servant without prompting derisive revenge or suspicions of social disparagement. [...] Service facilitates the erotic dimensions of these relationships' as a reciprocal relation.[147] Still, while service is the condition for the possibility of love, 'it is equally its condition of impossibility,'[148] hence the need for the various revelations at the end. In a later essay, Schalkwyk also brings together the play's tropes of music, food and love in an analysis of the play's 'affective landscapes': Orsino, he notes, 'is an expert in the misogynist, early modern, Galenic or materialist conceptions of male and female passion. As such he is all bluster and contradiction'.[149] Schalkwyk also questions, as does Kerwin, approaching the play through the early modern humoural psychology of affect: if it is 'relevant to the play, it is so negatively: as a form of misrecognition.'[150]

Words and Music

Like moths to a destructive flame, many critics of *Twelfth Night* have been drawn to the riddle in the letter Malvolio reads, crushing it in inventive ways. Elam sees this moment as the 'culminating expression' of the play's 'interpretative compulsion, the desire to disclose illuminating secret meanings.'[151] Cynthia Lewis points out that it is a 'fustian' riddle – usually glossed as 'bombastic, inflated', but by Lewis as 'nonsensical' – hence it is a riddle without an answer, and she arrives at the same position as Elam: it is 'a trap for desiring and even imposing erroneous meaning.'[152] Sean Benson denies the usual reading of this scene, in which Malvolio's style of reading is said to be a parody of Puritan reading habits, and seeks to rehabilitate him as a reader: 'his hermeneutic, far from being the mark of Puritan excess, is remarkably astute.'[153] Benson argues that the play establishes 'a striking parallel between Malvolio's reading of the letter and Sebastian's and Viola's "reading" of each other's identity in the play's recognition scene',[154] but this effort to justify Malvolio's reading, and explain how 'we' have 'in fact misread him',[155] remains unpersuasive. Peter J. Smith argues that the letters M.O.A.I. very clearly allude to John Harrington's *The Metamorphosis Of A Iax*, the allusion advertising what the tricksters think of Malvolio.[156] Lin Kelsey suggests that the letters

> simply represent [... Malvolio's] inadvertent admission that 'I AM O' – I am nought, or not, a musical and social cipher. Far from being 'some sir of note' (3.4.73), as he imagines, his 'alphabetical position' is as precarious as his musicianship; he is one letter short, in effect a 'sir of not.' Far from being 'Count Malvolio' (2.5.35), much less a counterpointer, the suggestion is that he doesn't count, can't count, and is certainly no count, or of no account.[157]

Parker considers how previous editors of the play have corrected and normalized the play in certain passages so that most readers believe, for example, that the forged letter Malvolio reads says '*Some are born great*' (2.5.141), when Rowe and the Douai manuscript actually provide the phrasing to make it agree with two later instances of 'born' (3.4.39, 5.1.364), whereas all four Folios read 'Some are become great.'[158] 'Become' may be 'an easy misreading of a posited copy form "borne"',[159] but whether or not one accepts Parker's justification (too complex to quote here) for 'become', she raises fundamental questions about the editing of the play and its implications for interpretation. In her later essay, she suggests that another hitherto uncited gloss of 'eunuch' is that of the so-called 'eunuch flute', 'an instrument without a true voice of its own, but through which the voice of another could make itself heard, an artificial voice, not natural to the speaker',[160] hence appropriate for Viola's role as Cesario.

Elam provides a useful Appendix of all the music in the play, including musical scores; he notes (as have others) that music 'is not a decorative addition' to the play, 'but an essential part of the play's dramatic economy.'[161] Kerwin observes that

> Orsino's idiosyncratic way of medicalizing language is paralleled by his medicalized view of music. He gives music power to change bodies, and changing a body – his own or Olivia's – is a pattern he repeats obsessively … it displaces him from a world of complexity to a world of simplistic order. [...] The duke's musical nostalgia is consistent with his other efforts at claiming constancy.[162]

David Lindley finds that in *Twelfth Night* there is only a single invocation of heavenly music in the play (3.1.108), while all the other music 'is emphatically, exclusively, and distinctively earth-bound.'[163] One reason for its 'unmetaphysical quality' is because Shakespeare 'gives all the songs to the clown, Feste. He is a professional singer, the most developed representation of such a figure in the whole canon'.[164] Lindley emphasizes just 'how exceptional' the play's opening is: 'no other Shakespearean play [...] begins with instrumental music other than the formal sound of a flourish or fanfare [...] To the more privileged amongst the playgoers it might have suggested that Shakespeare was taking a leaf out of the choirboy companies' book',[165] since opening music was likely a standard feature of their plays. Lindley questions the usual reading of Feste's final song: since plays frequently ended with a song or dance

> not connected in any way with the drama which had preceded it, we cannot assume that this song was expected by its original audience to be integrated with the play itself [...] nor that it necessarily followed every performance of the play.[166]

Moreover, the 'traditional' tune to which Feste's lines are set 'first appeared in the late eighteenth century',[167] and is not necessarily what Shakespeare's audience heard:

> The significance and impact of this final song, then, is profoundly contingent on decisions about the music to which it is to be set, the degree to which Feste stays in character as he sings, and the nature of the address to the audience that he adopts.[168]

Thus, the song may not have been as 'melancholy' and 'serious' as virtually all critics have found it over the past two centuries.

Kelsey offers a witty account of the music that unpacks many a pun, musical and verbal. Kelsey begins by placing the play in the midst of an early modern shift from polyphony to 'the new vogue for the solo voice.'[169] The play's characters are then read as being able to 'keep time' in the sense of holding a note, holding things in a state of suspended animation, and so on, which offers another way of seeing the contrast between Orsino ('unable to hold for more than a minute') and Olivia ('determined to hold for seven years').[170] Kelsey observes that 'the idea of playing a part [...] is not simply a dramatic metaphor but – much more vitally for this period – a musical one.'[171] Ultimately he brings out the punning associations of each character with music, particularly their names, as well as the play's subtitle, *what you will*, as a 'verbal version of the "quodlibet," or "what you please," a popular music form of the period.'[172] Kelsey's own verbal wit reaches a crescendo in describing the main characters as a kind of 'viol consort': 'Orsino (Or-C-no)', 'Sebastian (C-bass-tian)', 'Cesario (C's-ario)', 'Maria (M-aria)' and so on: 'At the very least', Kelsey retreats slightly, 'C provides a key to much in the play that seems puzzling'.[173] Penny Gay examines the aural aspect of the play: 'its seductive musicality, its wit, its linguistic games' that seem 'to be part of the *meaning* of the play', particularly the puns, which she describes as 'the aural equivalent of (near-)identical twins.'[174]

For R. S. White, *Twelfth Night* 'problematizes and raises conversational competence itself to a thematic level', though 'some version of meetings of mind, and even marriage, can emerge', while Illyria seems 'a country where Brecht's *verfremdungseffekt* is a way of life. And nowhere are the alien, alienating, strange manifestations of defamiliarity more disconcertingly treacherous than in the apparently ordinary familiarities of conversation.'[175]

That's All One

The variety of work on *Twelfth Night* published just since 2000 is impressive. Introductions or study guides mainly for students – by Paul Edmondson, Emma Fielding, John R. Ford, Rex Gibson, Sonia Massai, Michael Pennington and Smith – build usefully on current scholarship to make the play accessible to new readers.[176] The fact that so much research published on *Twelfth Night* is of the very highest quality is in part a testament to the energy and imagination of the play's readers and to evolutions in literary scholarship, but even more to the astonishing richness and vitality of the play. If ever there were a play that strives to please every day, and does, *Twelfth Night* is the one.

CHAPTER FOUR

New Directions: 'Ready to distrust mine eyes': Optics and Graphics in *Twelfth Night*

KEIR ELAM

When, in the fourth act of *Twelfth Night*, Sebastian's luck suddenly changes and he finds himself the unwitting object of Olivia's unexpected declaration of love, he promptly blames his own eyesight:

> SEBASTIAN   Yet doth this accident and flood of fortune
> So far exceed all instance, all discourse,
> That I am ready to distrust mine eyes
> (4.3.11–13)[1]

Sebastian's attribution of the Countess's amorous verbal effusion to the field of vision creates a comical paradox, akin to Bottom's 'The eye of man hath not heard, the ear of man hath not seen' (*A Midsummer Night's Dream* 4.1.211–12): if anything it is Olivia's eyes that need testing, in taking him for Cesario and Cesario for a man. At most, it is Sebastian's sense of hearing that needs attention. In the case of *Twelfth Night*, however, the 'eye of man hath not heard' paradox is at the heart of the play itself, since in this comedy everything, including 'all discourse', as Sebastian puts it, passes through the eye. This essay is concerned with the domain of the visual in the play, especially in its interactions with the sphere of the verbal. To put it differently, this chapter discusses the relationship between optics (a concern with visual and ocular processes and their objects) and graphics (a preoccupation with graphic images or signs, including the written word) within the cultural context of a new interest in optical and graphic phenomena in early seventeenth-century England, and in particular English theatre and drama.

The English playhouse was in many ways an emblematic site of early modern visual culture, a veritable meeting point for optics and graphics in practice. The art or science of optics was built into the very structure of the public theatre, with its strategic attention to the crucial question of sightlines, guaranteeing the visibility of the players from every point in the architectonic arc describing two thirds of the amphitheatre. The early playhouses were explicitly dedicated to favouring and facilitating spectatorship. Not by chance the first public playhouse boasted the name The Theatre, in its etymological sense of a site for looking (from Greek θέᾱτρον [*theatron*], a 'place for viewing', itself deriving from the verb θεάομαι [*theasthai*] 'to behold').[2]

The graphics of the early modern stage, meanwhile, were manifold and multifarious. Despite the relative lack of scenery that the need for visibility imposed, the actor on stage was part of what we might term a pictorial continuum: his rich and colourful costume interacted in the field of vision with such iconographic presences as the stage's painted *frons scenae* with its carved statuary; the wooden pillars painted to resemble marble Corinthian columns; the canopy or 'heavens' over the stage displaying paintings of celestial bodies; while according to some scholars the central opening in the *frons* was 'concealed behind a hanging or elaborate cloth woven in panels with pictures of scenes from classical myths.'[3] Other pictorial elements included entire scenic paintings such 'the sittee of Rome' (presumably a painted cloth) mentioned in Henslowe's Diary (c. 1591–1609).[4] Far from being an isolated point of visual focus, the actor was part of a complex stage configuration in which different modes of iconic representation converged. The early modern spectator encountered, moreover, other graphic modes in her or his experience of the performance. Written signs were present both outside the theatre (playbills), at the entrance (in the case of the Globe, the inscribed motto above the gate, '*Totus mundus agit histrionem*') and on stage, not only the virtual or invisible writing of the spoken script, but also, for example, in the form of written placards displaying the title of the play or announcing the next scene.[5]

Elizabethan and Jacobean drama fully and consciously exploited these ocular resources, notably *Twelfth Night*, which is probably Shakespeare's most intensely visual play. Both the comedy's plots, the main Viola–Orsino and the secondary Malvolio, are centred on exquisitely ocular events: in the former, first Viola and then her twin brother Sebastian confound the eyes of both Orsino and Olivia, as well as of other onlookers; in the latter, Malvolio is fatefully trapped by the sight and by the graphic signs of the false love letter, while the scene of his humiliation is itself spied on by the eavesdropping plotters. If the main dramatic theme of *Twelfth Night* is the one announced in the titles of its Italian sources *Gl'inganni* and *Gl'ingannati*, namely deceptions and the deceived, there is little doubt that the primary form that deception takes in the play, as in its sources, is that of optical illusion, *trompe l'oeil*, not only because the theatre is itself the domain of the optical, of spectatorship, but more specifically because the central role played in the comedy by disguise involving almost-identical different-sex twins obliges its spectators, internal and external alike, to keep their eyes wide, if sometimes uncomprehendingly, open.

One result of this prevalence of the visual is that *Twelfth Night* is extraordinarily rich not only in optical illusions but also in what we might term optical allusions, namely its countless verbal indications of visual processes. No other Shakespeare play has so many references to the act of looking and to the fact of seeing, from Orsino's ecstatic 'O, when mine eyes did see Olivia first' in the opening scene (1.1.18), to the Captain's promise 'When my tongue blabs then let mine eyes not see' (1.2.60), to Olivia's confession that Cesario's charms begin to 'creep in at mine eyes' (1.5.290), and so on. Such allusions recall similar ocular references in the Italian sources: for example, the recurrent theme of blindness in *Gl'ingannati* (from Lelia's 'Are you pretending not to see me?' in the first act[6] to Flaminio's 'How can I have been so blind not to recognize her?' and Crivello's 'who has been blinder than me?' in the last;[7] or the theme of multiple spying, associated with multiple crossdressing, in Curzio Gonzaga's *Gli inganni* (1592, 'FILIPPA Alas, who could have imagined that this Cesare was a female? When I saw him, as I was spying through a keyhole, all the blood left my veins. Cast your eye, and you will see that Lucretia has become a male'[8]).

No other Shakespeare play, moreover, points out so frequently the specific objects of such acts or facts of vision. The comedy's fullest and most explicit mode of optical allusion is its unique series of references to the 'picture', a term that occurs four times in the text and that attracts a number of synonyms and cognates, from 'image' (which also recurs four times) to 'impressure' to 'perspective' to specific kinds of image, such as 'map.' The picture is also literally present on stage in the play in the form of a handheld prop, namely the 'jewel' or ornamental miniature that Olivia gives Cesario (''tis my picture': see below). These references show forth a veritable 'picture' gallery in the form of optical or graphic objects presented, represented or described on stage, all of which have to do in different ways with the play's central theme of deceiving the eye.

The first of the play's pictorial allusions is actually to a hidden image, in Sir Toby's enigmatic reference to a portrait obscured by its dust cover: 'Wherefore are these things hid? Wherefore have these gifts a curtain before 'em? Are they like to take dust, like Mistress Mall's picture?' (1.3.120–2). The term 'hid' is a key word in the play, which is dominated by what we might term a poetics of secrecy regarding identities, passions, and more in general meaning (most explicitly in Viola's 'as secret as maidenhead' [1.5.210]), alluding to her concealed gender identity and the impossibility of expressing her passion for Orsino. Secrecy and enigma prevail likewise in the visual field, and indeed Sir Toby's 'Mistress Mall' is itself an enigmatic reference to a sitter of uncertain identity. If, as appears likely, Sir Toby is alluding here to Mary Fitton, erstwhile maid of honour to Queen Elizabeth who fell into disgrace in 1601, the picture in question becomes an optical illusion to the extent that it is the visual representation of social self-deception, figuring an elevated rank at court that no longer exists, so much so that the picture is kept hidden from sight and from the accumulating dust of shame and abandon: one of the comedy's warnings, perhaps, concerning excessive social ambition (Malvolio *docet*).

The same trope of the dust cover reappears – although to the opposite effect, not a covering up but an uncovering – in the comedy's second reference to a picture, namely Olivia's depiction of her own face as a portrait in her first encounter with Cesario: 'But we will draw the curtain and show you the picture. [*Unveils.*]' (1.5.226). This episode confirms the play's visual and verbal dialectic between concealment and revelation. Olivia shows her face, but at the same time offers a playfully deceptive description of her own body: the deception here lies in the fact that Olivia – pretending to be a two-dimensional representation of herself – becomes, as it were, a *trompe l'oeil* in reverse.

A variation on the same conceit of the stage configuration presented as a painted scene occurs in the most enigmatic of all the optical allusions, namely Feste's 'We three' joke in Act 2 Scene 3, in which the clown explicitly calls on us to reframe what we are watching as a two-dimensional image involving a particular mode of optical trickery, namely two figures (Sir Toby and Andrew) supposedly multiplied to three (asses), with the resulting herme-neutic puzzle concerning the identity of the third ass:

> *Enter* FESTE.
> SIR ANDREW Here comes the fool, i'faith.
> FESTE How now, my hearts? Did you never see the picture of 'we three'?
> SIR TOBY Welcome, ass. (2.3.13–16)

Unlike Olivia, Feste cunningly excludes himself from the unflat-tering 'painted' representation he comments upon: if two of the three asses are present on stage (Sir Toby and Sir Andrew), the third is the perceiver of the picture: not Feste but, presumably, the spectator, whose supposed foolishness lies in his or her very endeavour to solve the riddle. Feste's agency in the game is external: he is neither sitter nor viewer of the portrait but, if anything, its painter.

Olivia revisits the relationship between portrait and sitter in her second dialogue with Cesario, reversing it by giving him her 'real' picture of herself in the form of a 'jewel' or ornamental miniature:

> OLIVIA   Here, wear this jewel for me: 'tis my picture.
>   Refuse it not, it hath no tongue to vex you;
>   (3.4.203–4)

Here Olivia plays on the illusionistic ability of the miniature portrait to figure forth a silent and apparently three-dimensional version of her face, just as in the earlier scene she played the part, as it were, of a speaking picture. Olivia offers the miniature as a ludic and erotic substitute for herself that Cesario is to 'wear' about his person, and thus in direct physical contact with his body. The portrait becomes Cesario's 'property', both in the sense of stage prop and in that of personal belonging. As Frances Teague observes, the theatrical property belongs etymologically to a particular individual, it is 'an object on a stage that often has a strong association with a performer, [and] can become a metonymic token of that performer's identity in the role, and even function as a substitute for the actor.'[9] This is even more the case when the property concerned is an actual representation of the character him or herself or of his or her beloved, making its metonymic or substitutive role essential and explicit (compare Emilia's 'Lie there, Arcite', addressed to the latter's miniature portrait in *The Two Noble Kinsmen* [4.2.43]). Since it is to be worn, moreover, the ornate miniature it entertains an intimate relationship with another powerfully visual aspect of stage performance, namely costume (in this case the male clothing that transforms Viola into Cesario).

The illusionistic ability of miniatures to bestow lifelike three-dimensional realism on the subject within a greatly reduced two-dimensional space (the 'portrait in little', as Hamlet calls it

[2.2.305]) is one of the achievements of which Nicholas Hilliard, miniaturist to the Queen, justly boasts in his *Treatise Concerning the Arte of Limning* (c. 1598):

> howe then the curious drawer wach, and as it [were] catch thosse lovely graces wittye smilings, and those stolne glances which sudainely like light[n]ing passe and another Countenance taketh place.[10]

Hilliard reserves special praise for the kind of 'jewel' donated by Olivia, in which the gold and precious stones of the frame or case were made to continue within the portrait itself, thanks to the rich materials, including gold, employed by the miniaturist (Hilliard trained as a goldsmith):

> [Limning] excelleth all other *Painting* what so ever, in sundry points, in giving the true lustur to pearle and precious stone, and worketh the merals *Gold* or *Silver* with themselfes which so enricheth and innobleth the worke that it seemeth to be the tinge it se[l]fe even the worke of god and not of man, being fittest [...] to put in ewells of gould.[11]

This continuity between outer and inner jewels is underlined by Henry Constable's punning compliment in his sonnet 'To Mr Hilliard, upon occasion of a picture he made of my Lady Rich':

> To diamonds, rubies, pearls, the worth of which
> Doth make the jewel which you paint seem rich.[12]

Such material riches are justified by another kind of 'jewel' in play, namely the beauty of the subject, Lady Rich, made to 'seem rich', just as the Countess Olivia's costly gift reflects, and is made even more precious by, the qualities of the sitter.

Olivia's 'jewel', materially displayed on stage, extends the dialectic between secrecy and revelation in the visual field. In offering Cesario her portrait, Olivia appears to perform an act of self-revelation and self-donation analogous to her 'unveiling' ceremony in 1.5. At the same time, however, as John Buxton notes, the ornamental portrait was meant for the gaze of the recipient alone, and was instead strategically hidden to other eyes: 'The jewelled case [...] was intended to conceal from public gaze a private message between two lovers.'[13] This translates in theatrical terms, in the episode in question, into the teasing exclusion of the audience, who witness the exchange of a shining handheld property but are denied visual access to the portrait itself, too small for them to perceive in any detail.

Olivia is, both wittingly and unwittingly, at the centre of the play's optical discourse. A third image associated with her person takes the form of her personal seal abusively pressed on to the false lover letter to Malvolio ('the impressure her Lucrece', 2.5.92), lending – together with her forged handwriting – authority and 'authenticity' to Maria's practical joke. The wax image further excites Malvolio's already steaming erotic and social imagination, not least because Olivia's choice of seal is curiously ambiguous: it is presumably designed to represent chastity (Lucrece's stoic resistance of the assault of Tarquin and her later suicide), but has more immediate and unfortunate associations with rape, and seems in a sense to authorize the steward's amorous reverie. It turns out, however, to be another visual and social deception, the Countess's actual seal adopted without the owner's authorization.

In *Twelfth Night* one 'picture' gives birth to another: the effects of the epistolary joke on its victim are reported by Maria herself in an elaborate simile involving a further image, this time not pictorial but cartographic:

> MARIA   He does smile his face into more lines than is
>   in the new map with the augmentation of the
>   Indies. (3.2.74–6)

Maria's comparison alludes to a specific and well-known image recently published in England, namely Edward Wright's 1600 map of the East Indies, 'augmented' because of its inclusion for the first time of the island of Nova Zembla off the Arctic, a novelty made possible, ironically, by the disastrous 1596–7 expedition of the Dutch explorer Willem Barentsz, which came to a premature end in the icefields off the island. Wright's map, implicitly representing Barentsz's disastrous expedition, is offered as a parable for Malvolio's own dangerous ambitions of vertical social travel, as Fabian's later and more direct allusion to the event suggests: 'you are now sailed into the north of my lady's opinion, where you will hang like an icicle on a Dutchman's beard' (3.2.24–6). Barentsz was led astray by graphic navigational rhumb lines that should have guided him (and to which Malvolio's face is compared), while the steward is in turn disoriented by epistolary lines and betrayed by his own smile lines; both men are fatally misdirected by excessive ambition or hubris. Malvolio's map-face, moreover, is an icon of self-deception, of a delusional state of happiness destined to have a very brief life.

The play's veritable catalogue of visual images involves a wide range of arts and crafts, from the high courtly portraits of Olivia and Mistress Mall to the low popular iconography of Feste's 'we three' to the crafts of cartography and of the wax seal 'impressure.' The evoked images, moreover, bring into play not only optics but also graphics, in the sense that several of the pictures are accompanied by forms of writing. Feste's picture is accompanied by the puzzling caption 'we three.' Likewise, Olivia's 'self-portrait' game involves an interpretative verbal tag, 'such a one I was this present', which is to say, this is what I looked like at the time the portrait was painted (that is, in this very instant). Olivia is rather cryptically evoking the inscription frequently found in Renaissance portraits, including Hilliard's miniatures, *ætatis suæ* (of her or his age), accompanied by the effective age of the sitter and the date of composition. She is thereby playing – again, unlike Feste – on her double presence as painter and subject of her self-portrait, since the composing and viewing of the picture coincide in the real time of performance. A similar inscription is presumably to be found on the 'real' miniature portrait or 'jewel' that she donates to Cesario. In the letter scene, her forged handwriting appears beneath her seal, confirming its authenticity. Maria's augmented map of the Indies is marked by toponyms, including the newly added name of Nova Zembla, together with cartographic rhumb lines and other graphic forms.

The pictures and other images accompanied by writing are all instances of what has been termed an 'image-text'[14] or 'iconotext',[15] namely a mixed-media artefact that depends on the strict interaction between iconographic and verbal components. *Twelfth Night* is not only replete with references to iconotexts, but in a certain sense is itself a large-scale image-text, a play that strategically places the verbal and the visual, the graphic and the optical, in an often difficult and dangerous intercourse. As W. J. T. Mitchell observes, the relationship between the two spheres (visual and verbal) is not necessarily that of harmonious collaboration: 'The image–text relation in [...] theatre is not a merely technical question, but a site of conflict, a nexus where political, institutional, and social antagonisms play themselves out in the materiality of representation'.[16]

Such antagonisms between the two spheres in the early modern theatre are evident, for example, in the dispute between Ben Jonson and Inigo Jones over which element (the visual or the verbal) should prevail in the Jacobean court masque.[17] They are likewise evident in the theoretical discourse of Shakespeare's fellow dramatist Thomas Heywood, whose *An Apology for Actors* (1612) compares the competing expressive claims precisely of verbal discourse and visual images, finding both inadequate. Discourse, in the form of verbal description, fails to register in the crucial domain of spectacle:

> Oratory is a kind of a speaking picture, therefore may some say, is it not sufficient to discourse to the eares of princes the fame of these conquerors [...] A Description is only a shadow receiued by the eare but not perceiued by the eye.[18]

At the same time, pictures are unable to represent the dynamism of the living body and its actions:

> Painting likewise, is a dumbe oratory, […] liuely portrature
> is meerely a forme seene by the eye, but can neither shew
> action, passion, motion, or any other gesture, to mooue the
> spirits of the beholder to admiration.[19]

For Heywood the only complete and, in its etymological sense,
lively mode of representation is theatrical performance, which
brings the rival modes of speaking pictures and dumb oratory
together in living and moving bodies, those of the players:

> but to see a souldier shap'd like a souldier, walke, speake,
> act like a souldier: to see a Hector all besmered in blood,
> trampling vpon the bulkes of Kinges. […] Oh these were
> sights to make an Alexander.[20]

The combination of the visual and the verbal, of optics and
graphics is central to the comedy's dramatic economy, bringing
together as it does the respective emphases of the two plots:
the Viola plot being dominated by optics, the Malvolio plot by
graphics. Thanks largely to Olivia's steward, *Twelfth Night* is an
unusually graphological, or indeed graphomaniacal, play. Not
only does it contain three letters read out loud on stage (not a
solitary record, since *Hamlet* also has three), it also, uniquely,
draws the audience's attention to letters both in the epistolary
sense and, more particularly, in the graphic or calligraphic sense,
beginning with Maria's imitation of Olivia's handwriting ('I
can write very like my lady' [2.3.154]). On discovering Maria's
billet doux, Malvolio is fooled into an amorous relationship with
graphic signs which, supposedly deriving directly from Olivia's
hand – in the double sense of handwriting and of organ – evoke
prohibited fantasies of her more secret body parts and functions:
'By my life, this is my lady's hand. These be her very c's, her u's
and her t's, and thus makes she her great P's. It is in contempt of
question her hand' (2.5.85–8).

Twelfth Night is the only Shakespearian play in which written
alphabetic forms determine a significant part of the action. Its

abiding interest in written characters and other graphic signs and
'lines' also feeds into its intense self-consciousness as a scripted
dramatic performance, most explicitly in Viola's feigned deter-
mination to recite her praise of Olivia, since she has leaned her
written lines by heart: 'I would be loath to cast away my speech,
for besides that it is excellently well penned, I have taken great
pains to con it' (1.5.167–9). In a sense, the graphic sign, and
especially writing, is the privileged semiotic mode in the comedy,
since it is what allows language to register on the ocular plane,
and thus in the sphere of spectacle. The graphic, in this sense,
becomes the model of signification itself; in the words of Jacques
Derrida,

> Even before it is linked to incision, engraving, drawing, or
> the letter, to a signifier referring in general to a signifier
> signified by it, the concept of the graphic [unit of a
> possible graphic system] implies the framework of the insti-
> tuted trace, as the possibility common to all systems of
> signification.[21]

Graphics and optics come triumphantly together in the play's
finale, the climax of the comedy's intensely visual discourse, with
its spectacular onstage reunion of the twins. The presence of
graphics in the scene is again guaranteed by the onstage reading of
two letters, first the irate denunciation, of which Malvolio is, this
time, author rather than victim, followed by the close inspection
by Olivia herself of the forged *billet doux*, drawing fresh attention
to its deceptive calligraphic marks: 'Alas, Malvolio, this is not
my writing – / Though I confess much like the character –'
(5.1.339–40). The graphic sign contributes significantly to the
play's denouement, as it had to the earlier action.

Optics, meanwhile, dominate the finale in the guise of what is
perceived by the internal spectators as a prodigious event within
the field of vision. The simultaneous presence of the visually
identical twins is the object of contrasting perceptions by the
onstage onlookers. Olivia ecstatically perceives two Cesarios,

and thus, perhaps, two prospective husbands: 'Most wonderful!' (5.1.221). The bewildered Orsino, instead, detects some form of optical distortion:

> ORSINO   One face, one voice, one habit and two persons:
> A natural perspective, that is and is not. (5.2.212–13)

Orsino's astonishment at the sight of the doubled Cesario inspires him in turn to a double paradox: not only his riddling gloss 'that is and is not', but also the oxymoronic 'a natural perspective', since perspective, in its early modern sense, was by definition unnatural, the result of some mode of *trompe l'oeil*. Precisely what form of deception the Duke is alluding to has been the subject of considerable critical and editorial debate, in which competing interpretations depend partly on how we read the grammar of the phrase. 'Perspective' is usually taken as a modifier with a missing noun, implying the abbreviation of the term 'perspective glass.' If this is the case, what Orsino claims to see is the 'natural' equivalent of an illusory picture produced by one of several kinds of optical device equipped with lenses designed to project a multiplied image from a single object, or, on the contrary, containing a faceted lens making multiple objects converge into a single image.

The most immediate point of cultural reference for such multiplicational optical trickery is probably Reginald Scot's denunciation of the pseudo-magical effects of glasses or lenses in *The Discovery of Witchcraft* (1584). Scot's marginal note, 'Strange things to be doone by perspective glasses', reads:

> But the woonderous devises, and miraculous sights and conceipts made and conteined in glasse, doo farre exceed all other; whereto the art perspective is verie necessarie. For it sheweth the illusions of them, whose experiments be seene in diverse sorts of glasses.[22]

The doubled image of Cesario becomes, according to this 'magical' reading of Orsino's phrase, the spontaneous counterpart to the special effects of optics put to the service of pseudo-magical chicanery. Perspective glasses were not, however, the monopoly or indeed the invention of the English magus or trickster. They were primarily the domain of Italian artists, architects and theorists, beginning, at least according to iconographic lore, at the end of the fifteenth century with Brunelleschi's perspective lenses that supposedly enabled the Florentine architect to project and superimpose images for artistic and architectonic purposes.[23] What Orsino and the play's spectators supposedly see, therefore, may not be so much 'natural' witchcraft as equally 'natural' visual artistry. The decisive difference is the cultural context: early modern English or Renaissance Italian respectively.

The ambiguous grammar of Shakespeare's oxymoron, however, leaves open other interpretative options. 'Perspective' can be read not as a modifier implying an abbreviation but as a self-sufficient substantive, a grammatical role that the word fulfils in its other appearances in Shakespearian drama. In *All's Well that Ends Well*, Act 5 Scene 3, Bertram employs it metaphorically in order to represent the distorting psychological effects of his own ill-judged disdain, which led him to produce or project a perceptual monster, namely the unjustly deformed image of the virtuous Helena:

> BERTRAM   Contempt his scornful perspective did lend me,
>   Which warp'd the line of every other favour,
>   (5.3.48–9)

In this case the optical reference unequivocally involves the distortion rather than multiplication or superimposition of images, and there is little doubt that the term 'perspective' here alludes to the somewhat extreme early modern artistic device known as perspective or oblique anamorphosis, which presents a warped image requiring an unconventional angle of vision in order to 'straighten' its definition.[24] Bertram's vision is distorted by contempt and needs to be straightened by love. The same metaphorical allusion to a distorted image occurs in

Richard II Act 2 Scene 2, where the term 'perspective', again a self-contained noun, appears at the centre of an elaborate simile in Bushy's philosophical discourse designed to console the melancholy Queen, grief-stricken at her husband's departure for Ireland:

> BUSHY   Each substance of a grief hath twenty shadows,
> Which shows like grief itself, but is not so;
> [...]
> Like perspectives, which rightly gazed upon,
> Show nothing but confusion; eyed awry,
> Distinguish form. (2.2.14–20)

The Queen's grief warps her perception of all that she sees, and must be straightened by philosophy and patience.

Again the iconographic context of these tropes may be primarily Italian, since Leonardo da Vinci is often credited with the first known example of perspective anamorphosis in his experimental 1485 drawing of an eye, although what were probably more directly known to Shakespeare and at least part of his audience, instead, were indigenous anamorphoses such as Hans Holbein's celebrated *The Ambassadors* with its anamorphic skull, painted at the court of Henry VIII in 1533, or the portrait of Edward VI by Holbein's successor as Henry's court painter, the Dutchman William Scrots, painted in London in 1546. In the light of this familiar iconographic and specifically Shakespearian tradition, Orsino may perceive the twins as a 'naturally' distorted anamorphic-perspective picture rather than as a mechanically doubled image.

There is, however, a final possible cultural and hermeneutic context, again primarily Italian, for Orsino's phrase, no longer magical or pictorial but more specifically – and perhaps more appropriately – theatrical. This context is probably evoked in another Shakespearian use of the term 'perspective', this time unequivocally adverbial, namely in the finale of *Henry V*:

KING HENRY V   It is so: and you may some of you
               thank love for my blindness, who
               cannot see many a fair French city for
               one fair French maid that stands in
               my way.
FRENCH KING   Yes, my lord, you see them perspec-
               tively, the cities turned into a maid;
               for they are all girdled with maiden
               walls that war hath never entered.
               (5.2.313–18)

Henry, conqueror of France, magnanimously compliments
both French cities and the French Princess or 'maid', his
bride Katherine, prompting the defeated French King's polite
and erudite visual metaphor. The Cambridge Shakespeare
editor Andrew Gurr glosses the adverb 'perspectively' as 'in
a "prospective glass", or a distanced and distorted view',
thereby evoking at once both the alternative traditions
discussed so far, the optical–mechanical and the pictorial.[25]
The Arden 3 editor, T. W. Craik, instead, glosses it more
generically (perhaps with a view to *Twelfth Night*) as an
'unnatural' image: 'i.e. in another form than their natural one.
The sense here is "symbolically"' (Craik does not specify
what kind of symbolism is at work).[26] On closer inspection,
the French King's 'symbolic' metaphor seems less optical—
mechanical or pictorial than exquisitely theatrical, and more
particularly scenographic: Henry fails to perceive clearly the
French cities because they are in the background of the scene,
whose foreground is entirely occupied by the female protagonist of the historical moment, and of the play itself, the fair
French maid Katherine. In other words, what seems to be
called 'symbolically' into play here is the 'perspective' scenery
that had been employed for decades on the continental, and
especially Italian, Renaissance stage, in which an apparently
three-dimensional – but in reality painted – city serves as the
setting for the foregrounded human figure.

According to the *Oxford English Dictionary*, the term
'perspective' was introduced into the English language by the
artist John Shute in his introduction to *The First and Chief
Groundes of Architecture* (1563) and specifically in the context of
his discussion of the perspective scenery designs of Sebastiano
Serlio, which had powerfully influenced the development of stage
sets in Italy:

> Opticke sheweth us how and by what meanes the lightes
> should be set into the House, And howe they should be
> brought from place to place, as to serue the hole house, and
> euery place therin, [...] whiche Optica, is properly called
> perspectiue, and is a furder speculacion then therin can
> or nedeth to be exprest: which of Sebastian Serlius, in his
> second booke first second and thirde Chapiter is partely
> declared.[27]

It is curious that the earliest use of the term should have been
theatrical, suggesting a precocious interest in the scenographic
implications of perspective art or science, even if the latter would
receive its actual stage application in England only half a century
later. The kinds of 'Optica' or 'perspective' that Shute has in mind
are probably Serlio's recommended representations of tragic,
comical and pastoral scenes in his *Second Book of Architecture*
(1545): Serlio prescribes a forest for pastoral, a formal street of
classical palaces and monuments for the tragic scene, while the
comical set (see Illustration 2) should show forth a city street
comprising more private buildings, not all of them respectable:

> The first [scene] shall be Comicall, whereas the houses must
> be slight for Citizens, but specially there must not want a
> brawthell or bawdy house, and a great Inne, and a Church;
> such things are of necessitie to be therein.[28]

There may be unsuspected Shakespearian implications in Serlio's
scenographic prescriptions and in Shute's 'Optica.' It is possibly

2 Sebastiano Serlio, from Tutte l'opere d'architettura di Sebastiano Serlio bolognese, *Book II (Venice, 1584).*

just such a comical (French) urban landscape that the King of France has in mind in the politically 'happy' finale to *Henry V* ('you see them perspectively, the cities'). It was almost certainly in such 'comical' Serlian perspective sets, moreover, that the earliest stage versions of the *Twelfth Night* story were performed. In the original Sienese staging of *Gl'Ingannati*, as the comedy's most recent editor, Marzia Pieri, has observed,

> it is probable that on the wooden stage erected in the Great Council Hall [of the Municipal Palace in Siena], which had been turned into a theatre, [...] a perspective set of

city scenes had be created, comprising a painted canvas and movable booths, akin to the *mansiones* of medieval religious drama. [...] The characters enter and exit from their respective houses, they meet, they hide from each other's sight, they monologue without being heard, they spy each other in a relatively restricted space, which alludes to a street of the city of Modena where the action is set.[29]

The presence of a perspective set lends a particular optical angle to the revelation scene of in Act 5 Scene 3 – equivalent to *Twelfth Night* Act 5 Scene 2 – in which the discovery of the true gender of the female protagonist Lelia (disguised as Fabio) takes the form of the unveiling of a picture within the overall stage picture, directing the audience's (like Henry V's) gaze towards the female protagonist in the foreground:

CLEMENZIA   This, Master Flamminio, is your Fabio. Look at him carefully: do you recognize him? Are you amazed? [...]

FLAMMINIO   I don't believe there has ever been in the whole world a finer deception than this. How can I have been so blind not to recognize her?[30]

Likewise, the first edition of Curzio Gonzaga's *Gli inganni* (published in Venice in 1592, but probably written and performed in Rome around 1570) includes illustrations of characters on stage defined within a Serlian cityscape representing contemporary Rome, as in the episode in Act 4 in which the protagonist Ginevra (disguised as Cesare) encounters the spying governess Filippa and the ingenious servant Guindolo (Illustration 3), and risks the premature unmasking of her gender identity under Filippa's penetrating gaze ('CESARE: I am undone: she has discovered that I am female!'):[31]

Here again the somewhat baroque disguises and deceptions of the plot (in which both different-sex twins crossdress) are

3 Scene from Curzio Gonzaga's Gli inganni *(Venice, 1592).*

intimately linked to the deceiving of the spectator's eye through scenographic perspective trickery.

At the time of the composition of *Twelfth Night* (c. 1601), the century-long use of perspective sets on the Italian and European stage was becoming known in England, especially after the first Italian sojourn (c. 1598) of Inigo Jones, who in the opening years of the seventeenth century began to introduce perspective scenery into English court and private theatres. The theory and practice of perspective painting, including scenery painting, had also become better known in England though publications such as Richard Haydock's 1598 translation of Giovanni Paolo Lomazzo's *A Tracte Containing the Artes of Curious Paintinge Carvinge and Buildinge*. In the fifth book of his tract, entitled 'Of Perspective', Lomazzo praises the 'virtue' or efficacy of perspective in terms of its powers of deception (*inganno*):

Such is the virtue of Perspectiue, that whiles it imitateth the *life*, it causeth a man to oversee and bee deceaued, by shewing a small quantity in steed of a great; the onely reason wherof is, because the eye is never offended with seeing a naturall body in anie place, whether aboue, belowe or else where, because it is daily acquainted wherewith.[32]

The virtue of perspective lies in its ability to create, in Orsino's words, that 'that is and is not', something out of nothing: depth out of flatness, 'life' out of paper, optical effects ('decietful sightes')[33] out of graphic forms ('a science of visible lines'[34] all of them strictly and strategically unnatural ('never [...] a naturall bodie').

When applied to the stage, Lomazzo's science of visible lines achieved its most spectacular deceitful sights, namely apparent three-dimensional space out of a flat painted surface, thereby creating the illusion of depth and distance to frame and expand the visual field of the stage action. This science was put to good use especially in the indoor rooms or halls in which Italian comedies such as *Gl'ingannati* were performed. At the same time, however, the early Serlian picture sets imposed severe limits on the movements of the actors themselves:

> The perspective illusion allowed for little interaction between actor and scenery. [...] Until [the introduction of multipoint perspective in 1703] all perspective scenery had a single vanishing point – for a spectator seated in an ideal position, the scenery seemed to disappear at a single point in the distance.[35]

The fixed-focus vanishing point of early perspective scenery meant that the actor playing, say, Lelia or Ginevra could not move along the perspective axis, up and down the depth of the stage, without destroying the optical illusion by revealing the true size and the two-dimensional character of the scenery itself, especially its lack of real depth. The final scene of *Gl'ingannati*, with its simple foreground unmasking of the heroine, or likewise the somewhat static finale of *Gli ingannti*, with its intricate narrative disclosures, posed little threat to the pictorial stage illusion of which they were part.

The final scene of *Twelfth Night*, on the contrary, with its crowded stage and the hectic movement of actors across the width and along the depth of the platform, allowing each of them to witness the reunion of the twins from a different visual and psychological perspective, could hardly have been achieved in an Italian picture box set, where, instead of creating the 'natural perspective' of the twins' identical appearance, the entire episode would have risked destroying the unnatural perspective of the illusionistic stage picture, even in an indoor space such as the Middle Temple Hall, where the first known performance of the comedy was staged. In any case, such internal spaces were unequipped with scenographic equipment until Inigo Jones adapted the Whitehall banqueting house (1619–22). In the outdoor 'public' theatre, such as the Globe, the Italianate perspective picture set was still less achievable, even if Shakespeare's company had wished to do so, since instead of the more or less fixed frontal focus and distance on which the illusion of depth depended on the scenographic stage, the Elizabethan amphitheatre was characterized by multiple points of view along a 270° axis, with no orchestra dividing audience from stage. The visible lines of the pictorial set, moreover, would have been all too visible on the Elizabethan stage, obstructing the sight lines for most of the audience. Unlike the 1532 performance of *Gl'ingannati* in the great hall of the Sienese Municipal Palace, therefore, the 1602 performance of *Twelfth Night* in the great hall of the Middle Temple very probably offered no perspective illusion, no painted canvas and no movable booths, just actor–characters who entered and exited from the play's two houses (Orsino's and Olivia's) by means of the stage doors, thereby allowing the decidedly non-urban space of Illyria to be rapidly and fluidly transformed from one domestic interior to the other, and from interior scene to open air scene ('This is the air, that is the glorious sun', affirms

Sebastian at the beginning of Act 4 Scene 3, leading us outdoors after the domestic interior of Act 4 Scene 2, set in Olivia's house).

This brings us back to Orsino's natural perspective, seen, as it were, from a theatrical viewpoint. The finale of *Twelfth Night* is the only episode in Shakespeare in which the term 'perspective' is used not metaphorically or symbolically to refer to an imaginary or offstage event or object (such as the cities of France or the absent Helena) or to an abstract concept (the Queen's grief), but literally, and indeed with reference to the onstage spectacle simultaneously perceived by the theatre audience. Orsino's underlining of the 'naturalness' of this scene and its participants – in direct contrast to Lomazzo's proud exclusion of the 'naturall body' – can be read as a vindication of the characteristics and of the mimetic 'virtue' of the non-perspective English stage. The optical process at work is the exact opposite to the perspectivism of the Italianate stage: what looks like a painted perspective trick turns out instead to be three dimensional, made up not of visible graphic lines but of real bodies with little or no scenographic support, costumes apart. We might term this phenomenon optical *dis*illusion, a mode of visual and dramatic dénouement that we also find elsewhere in Shakespeare, for example in the finale of *The Winter's Tale*, in which the supposed statue of Hermione turns out to be a living character or actor.

The *inganno* achieved in Shakespeare's finale, therefore, is not so much pictorial as proudly actorial, whereby two male actors, one playing a young man and the other playing a young woman disguised as a young man, succeed in appearing identical to the discriminating gaze of the Globe or Middle Temple audience. Evidently the Lord Chamberlain's Men were confident of being able to pull off such a demanding illusionary effect – difficult to achieve on the modern stage, but more feasible with the use of two boy actors – despite Ben Jonson's complaint 'that he could never find two so like others that he could persuade the spectators they were one.'[36] Here is a *trompe l'oeil* brought about not by two-dimensional Italian graphics or optics but by three-dimensional English theatrics: not, as Thomas Heywood affirms in his apology for actors and for the contemporary English stage, by a speaking picture, but by living, moving and speaking players: 'Those eyes with which you all the world suruay', affirms Heywood, paraphrasing Ovid, 'See in your Theaters our Actors play.'[37]

The vindication of the 'natural' body of the actor lends added meaning to Olivia's reference to herself as a portrait in Act 1 Scene 5. Paradoxically, the literally speaking picture of Olivia's three-dimensional face portrays itself as a mute and static two-dimensional icon, through words that issue from it in the dynamic flow of theatrical performance. Indeed, by pretending to be a painted image, Olivia underlines precisely the fluidity of Elizabethan dramatic art, which, try as she may, she cannot suspend: she can never become an Italianate stage picture, only a moving and breathing English body. Her 'draw the curtain' thus takes on specifically theatrical connotations, evoking the tiring house door of the Elizabethan stage, a fact underlined by Cesario's sarcastic 'Excellently done, if God did all' (1.5.229), hinting at the fact that Olivia is played by a made-up (and thus not altogether 'natural') male actor. When Olivia unknowingly changes the object of her amorous eloquence in Act 4 Scene 3, Sebastian is right, after all, to distrust his eyes.

CHAPTER FIVE

New Directions: Shipwreck and the Hermeneutics of Transience in *Twelfth Night*

RANDALL MARTIN

Trevor Nunn's 1996 film of *Twelfth Night* draws in movie-goers with a dramatic back-story of shipwreck. In a smoky dining room on board a turn-of-the-(last-)century passenger ship, Viola and Sebastian perform in after-dinner theatricals *en travestie*. A sudden storm batters the ship and hurls the twins into the sea, struggling to cling to each other before being separated. The film cuts to a rugged sunlit shoreline beneath towering cliffs (present-day Cornwall). From above, Feste observes the survivors washing up on the beach and hiding from Orsino's approaching cavalry. When all are gone, Feste descends to recover a gold necklace Viola has left behind that he will later enigmatically return to her during her reunion with Sebastian. In that closing moment, if not before, there is a sense that Feste has recognized something of himself in Viola's responses to shipwreck and survival.

Nunn's prologue usefully distinguishes the critical transience of shipwreck from the predictable passing of end-of-season festivity registered by the play's holiday title and subplots. Shipwreck and foreign survival traumatize Viola and Sebastian and permanently dispossess them of their former lives. *Twelfth Night*'s romantic comedy gradually eases their shock and re-orients them towards conventional happiness through its wooing-and-marriage intrigues, but it can never fully recover what is lost. If carnival's internal time-clock always promises a cyclical return to orderly behaviour and social discipline, the unfinished business of Malvolio and the Captain, and other often-noticed contingencies and deferrals in the final scene, suggest that shipwreck's aftershocks have penetrated the romantic comedy, destabilizing its generic aspirations towards inclusive harmony.[1] I'd like to begin this essay by outlining how the temporal and existential implications of shipwreck differ from carnival rhythms of release and restraint.

Mirabile dictu

Compared to classic studies of Elizabethan pastimes and holiday patterns in *Twelfth Night* by C. L. Barber, Northrop Frye and others, Viola and Sebastian's shipwreck experience has received relatively little attention as an event that redefines normative orders of knowledge and being.[2] Most obviously, the terrors of near-drowning and bare survival in an unknown country sever physical and personal connections. Such negations seem to confirm classical and biblical traditions of sea-travel as both fatally risky and metaphysically transgressive. Shipwreck produces a remnant of eye-witnesses to watery near-death whose stories of virtually miraculous preservation on dry land prompt a re-evaluation of what it means to live and be human.

In his suggestive survey of shipwreck from ancient to modern times as a literary metaphor for *Lebenswelt*, or living-in-the-world, Hans Blumenberg observes that Stoic philosophers and early modern sceptics such as Montaigne reversed the ancient baleful associations of sea-voyaging by reading the survivor's experience as a positive test of endurance and a welcome jolt into existential self-awareness and philosophical speculation. For those who live though its extreme physical and mental dangers, shipwreck creates an opportunity for 'self-possession achievable through the process of self-discovery.' Tossed up on a foreign shore but discovering signs of human presence and civilization, the survivor undergoes what Blumenberg calls a 'conversion' to new horizons of knowledge.[3] Josiah Blackmore's fascinating study of shipwreck's dislocation of early modern Portuguese narratives of imperial discovery and conquest similarly observes that survival produces a feeling of 'salvation',[4] or revelatory re-positioning of inner beliefs and convictions.[5] In *Twelfth Night* Shakespeare represents Viola and Sebastian's life-altering experience of shipwreck as a comparable rupture and reshaping of subjective identity. It inaugurates the changing perspectives, perceptions and knowledge that characterize the play, as discussed in Keir Elam's essay in this volume.

As an event, shipwreck also represents a *peripeteia*, or reversal of fortune, in the play's romance narrative. In *The Sense of an Ending* (1967) Frank Kermode relates classical and later ideas of *peripeteia* to the early Jewish–Christian condition of eschatology represented in Paul's letters, the earliest New Testament texts. This historically limited but culturally far-reaching episteme was shaped by expectations during the period in-between the messianic revelation of Christ and the traditionally prophesied *eschaton*, or end of the world.[6] Giorgio Agamben has recently argued that Paul's letters are 'the fundamental messianic [or eschatological] text for the Western tradition.'[7] Agamben is more concerned with recovering the Jewish messianic Paul than with the construction of his universalizing authority by nascent Christianity. But his work brilliantly demonstrates that both worldviews are present in the contradictory representations of temporality and social practice found in Paul's letters.[8] On the one hand, as Agamben and modern theologians observe, at many points Paul's original texts authorize radical equality, the hollowing out of hegemonic laws and power-structures in the face of an imminent end-of-times, and the adoption of new unbounded identities.[9] On the other hand, the prospect of final judgement dissolving all earthly orders shaped much of Paul's conservative advice to eastern-Mediterranean Jewish and gentile communities about hierarchical social relations and deferential personal conduct (for instance, by women and slaves in Corinth and Ephesus). Yet significant numbers of people in cities such as Corinth, living in the new existential freedom of messianic time and loyal to local leaders and syncretic religious traditions, evidently rejected Paul's censures. Their resistance is legible in the deliberative rhetoric, or persuasive speech, of his letters (as we shall see later). The dynamism of these competing views began to be shut down after the first century as the emerging Christian church institutionalized St Paul's disciplinary voice and patriarchal preferences. Christian universalism thus instantiated Carnival's cyclical rhythms by licensing limited seasons of simulated 'eschatological' freedom that always reverted to 'Lenten' structures of canonically formulated authority.

Twelfth Night's action of correcting festive suspensions and inversions by attempting to reinstate social hierarchies and gender conventions symbolically dramatizes the earlier historical process of subordinating the messianic state of nullified generic categories that began in Paul's writings and ultimately became routinized in Western culture. The world-dissolving shocks of shipwreck, on the other hand, reintroduce the ethos of exceptional contingency and end-of-times detachment into Illyria. Personalized encounters of these opposing conditions in the play re-stage the original clash between existential experiment and social conformity found in Paul's debates with his antagonists in Corinth and elsewhere. *Twelfth Night*'s multilayered representations of an eschatologically figured shipwreck can thus become analytical tools for historicizing carnival transience, undoing its reflexive valorization of social and gender distinctions, and questioning the basis for these divisions in Paul's textual authority.

In this discussion I will argue that contrasting ideas of eschatological and diachronic time and knowledge, and their related hermeneutic tendencies – one rupturing and dispersive, and other stabilizing and logocentric – illuminate respective shipwreck and holiday epistemologies in *Twelfth Night* and clarify its incomplete dramatic closure as a positive affirmation of open subjective potential. Viola and Sebastian's traumatic experience of losses and negations leads them to embrace a survivor's mode of improvised self-invention, expressed in the full-body theatrics of cross-dressing and role-playing. These reactions connect them to Feste, who seems to have been figuratively shipwrecked by previous personal loss, and who expresses his conversion to itinerantly constituted knowledge through wry parodies of Pauline and other cultural narratives. Returning to Olivia's household, he bridges the imaginative worlds of extreme transience and holiday licence by acting as a survivor–spectator of *Twelfth Night*'s carnivalesque intrigues. His passing references to Pauline texts and Reformation controversies have led previous critics to connect his outlook to the Pauline–Erasmian tradition of wise folly. But Feste's ludic adaptations of such discourses introduce shipwrecking ruptures, suspensions and alterity into the play's presumed deferential relationship to scriptural authority. Moreover, Feste's performative dialogues and impersonations imitate Paul's classically derived rhetoric of self-invention and persuasive argument, whose aim was to secure agreement to possibilities rather than absolute certainties. These structural and interpretative aspects of Paul's original letters were being rediscovered by Humanist-educated readers and spectators in Shakespeare's time. Such people attended to the ways Paul's meanings were pluralized by the rhetorical textures and historically differentiated contexts of his writings, rather than being understood as once-for-all-time dogma. The intertextual effect of *Twelfth Night*'s shipwreck and rhetorizing horizons redirects audiences' critical imaginations back to Paul's texts. There, readers could recognize him in the process of simultaneously constructing the time-space, or chronotope,[10] of eschatological liberation, and restricting it with the traditional Jewish–Hellenic ethos of hierarchical discipline and civic organization that eventually modulated into Christian and Elizabethan polities. Most radically, *Twelfth Night* makes audiences aware of how shipwreck-and-survival's personal conversions into subjective and rhetorical self-invention could conceptually challenge Pauline determined roles and identities with an alternative epistemology of oceanic human potential. I propose that we think about the play subtitled *What You Will* as Shakespeare's subversive Letter to the Illyrians.

'as boundless as the sea'

In *Twelfth Night* and his other sea romances, Shakespeare stages
shipwreck as much as a (mis)fortune to be embraced as a catas-
trophe to be lamented. Despite its strong ethos of mourning,
shipwreck's erasures clear new imaginative spaces for personal
and cultural rediscovery. Their dismantling of subjective convictions corresponds historically with the epistemic shift recorded in
Paul's first-century letters. As Agamben explains, the messianic
end-of-times internally refigured the Jewish–Christian subject,
nullifying its categories of religious and social difference while
leaving their outward forms unchanged. Prevailing laws and
markers of cultural identity were internally cancelled but did not
cease their everyday forms and operation. They remained 'as not',
or 'as if' they still had value – virtual rather than real. Eschatological
time was therefore not dialectic in character. Its stance was not to
set up valorized categories of difference – for example, of post-
Pauline tropes of materiality versus transcendence, or flesh versus
spirit, which Shakespeare stages in plays such as *The Merchant
of Venice* and *Measure for Measure*. Instead it was a worldview in
which diachronic or historical time was terminally suspended in
the 'the time of now' – the subtracted period in which the world
would come to an end.

Viola and Sebastian's experience of shipwreck and survival
represents an oceanic figure of this archetypal rupture. As she
struggles to comprehend the new wonder of dry land, Viola's
inward gaze traces a cosmic arc between the physically real but
alien Illyria of the seashore and her brother's afterlife journey:

VIOLA	What country, friends, is this?
CAPTAIN	This is Illyria, Lady.
VIOLA	And what should I do in Illyria?
	My brother he is in Elysium.
	Perchance he is not drowned. What think you sailors?
CAPTAIN	It is perchance that you yourself were saved.

VIOLA   O my poor brother! And so perchance may he be.
CAPTAIN   True madam, and to comfort you with chance
            ... (1.2.1–7)[11]

The tangled semantics of 'perchance' in this exchange suspend
Viola between past memories and vestigial hopes. Outwardly
bare life continues. But inwardly her world has utterly changed.
Like the ship she travelled on, Viola's sense of herself as a
forward-moving subject with a destined future has been violently
interrupted.[12] When she later tries to make sense of this cancelled
state, she expresses her feelings in the fictional history of a dead
sister, whose life-journey ends in a 'blank' (2.4.110).

In this subjectively adrift condition, Viola tries to re-orient
herself. Her first move is to attenuate the feeling of blankness. The
Captain's description of the grief-stricken Olivia seems to mirror
her own trauma, so she resolves to join Olivia in seclusion until
the shock of vertiginous death has ebbed into quotidian life ('not
to be delivered to the world / Till I had made mine own occasion
mellow / What my estate is' [1.2.39–41]). But this plan is cut off
by the Captain's report of Olivia's briny vigils for her dead father
and brother, which seem to domesticate the elemental negations
of the sea. Viola thus improvises a new identity to try to forget the
unforgettable. Hearing of Orsino, she decides to serve the duke as
'not Viola', disguised as a eunuch, a role she defines (for obvious
reasons) not as sexual lack but positively as the multilateral connec-
tivity of courtly performance: 'for I can sing, / And speak to him
in many sorts of music' (1.2.54–5).[13] Shakespeare dramatizes
Viola's response to shipwrecked identity and existential transience
in the mode he knew best: the performing body. Embracing a
theaticalized alterity will allow her to express her grief through
'as if' words and gestures of emotional release – possibilities that
increase after she shifts into the more mobile role of page. This
move also keeps alive hopes for her brother's survival that she
associates with the utter arbitrariness of her own 'escape', which
'unfoldeth to my hope', substantiated by the Captain's account of
Sebastian binding himself to the ship's mast (1.2.10–16).

Viola's errands between Orsino's and Olivia's households allow her to translate her transfixing encounter with the abyss into ex-stasis performances. As Cesario she juggles the inherent instabilities of her crossdressed role by taking increasingly greater risks. Frustrated by the impasse of Orsino's wooing assignment and put out by Olivia's mockery of its stale Petrarchanisms, she shifts into a veiled performance of her own passion for Orsino ('Make me a willow cabin at your gate' [1.5.257ff.]). She explores and tests living in the moment, drawing on emotional turmoil within to try performing new convictions and identities without. Her instinctive knowledge of female body language and non-verbal patterns of communication also breaks down Olivia's inner barriers and encourages her to extemporize her own passions. 'You might do much', Olivia responds, on the edge of a thrilling journey into uncharted waters, before she pulls back into the harbour of social propriety ('What is your parentage?' [266–67]). The transparent ruse of sending her ring grooms her breakthrough performance during their next meeting (3.1). Olivia apologizes for her trickery in the hope that a new level of honesty combined with their now shared intimacy might draw out Cesario's feelings. When none are forthcoming, she again edges towards brinkmanship by seizing on the fortuitous cue of a striking clock ('There lies your way, due west' [132]). The bridging exchange of mutual 'as not' identities puzzles Cesario into a show of anger but prompts Olivia, like Juliet before her, to bid farewell to 'compliment', suspend ordered time and leap into fearless desire: 'Stay […] I love thee so' (3.1.135, 149).

Sebastian responds to the de-essentialized world of shipwreck by also adopting a transitional identity. The Captain's account of his possible survival strikes a prophetic note owing to his double perspective as both survivor and spectator. But rather than the apocalyptic overtones of Viola's first reaction on shore, the Captain figures Sebastian merging mythically with the sea at a vanishing point on the horizon:

[…] I saw your brother

Most provident in peril, bind himself –
Courage and hope both teaching him the practice –
To a strong mast that lived upon the sea,
Where like Arion on the dolphin's back,
I saw him hold acquaintance with the waves,
So long as I could see. (1.2.1–16)

Sebastian's mast, bucking against the waves, ramps up a human will to live which seems momentarily to harness the sea's power into a preternaturally co-operative rather than tragically hostile force. It's the epic (and gendered) counterpart of Viola's first more passive impulse to retreat into self-possessing isolation. And as a signature image reminiscent of Antipholus's drop-of-water-in-the-ocean trope in the earlier *Comedy of Errors*, the Captain's report anticipates a new protean subjectivity emerging from the sea's rescaling of human consciousness. But for the moment the Captain's report leaves Sebastian's destiny hanging until we learn that he has been rescued from 'the breach of the sea' by Antonio (2.1). Unlike Viola, Sebastian is certain his twin sibling has been drowned. He struggles with a grief so intense that the misfortune feels malignant (4). But he has also experienced a miracle in the form of Antonio's unconditional courage and love. Sebastian tries to create some clarifying distance from the unreality of this star-crossed survival by adopting the 'as-not' persona of Roderigo. The trust which Antonio tactfully establishes over three months finally encourages Sebastian to go much further than Viola's veiled confession to Olivia ('I am not that I play' [1.5.176]). Yet still whirled in the emotional storm of physical shipwreck and its losses, Sebastian is unable to settle his identity as Antonio's object of devotion. Letting his still-watery body run its course leaves him open to more outlandish roles: 'My determinate voyage is mere extravagancy' (2.1.9–10). Ultimately, he follows Olivia's leap into a tangibly real yet wondrously virtual 'flood of fortune' (4.3.11).

Feste shares Viola's and Sebastian's habits of performative self-invention as a reaction to personal upheaval. Although his backstory is not as clear as the twins', it seems that he too has suffered some inward form of shipwreck, to which he has responded by travelling abroad. When he returns to Olivia's household (1.5) he sidesteps Maria's questions about where he's been and tries to regain his former favour by turning his absence into a verbal souvenir of wry adages, syllogisms and catechisms on the theme of transience: 'As there is no true cuckold but calamity, so beauty's a flower' (1.5.46–7). Later we learn Feste's reason for going away was the death of Olivia's father and the loss of their close personal relationship. His situation mirrors that of Lavatch in *All's Well That Ends Well*, another philosophical clown sad for the death of his master (4.5.65–6). Lavatch's conventional remedy for human mortality is sex-in-marriage, the generic goal of romantic comedy. Feste's strategy is to existentialize transience as a mode of living 'calamitously', which he acts out as a whirligig of 'as if' discourses (e.g. sage, cleric, with distinct Pauline overtones, as we shall see). These personae, which resemble Viola's role as singer who tailors her words and music to different audiences, mediate the pain of human shipwreck that Feste shares with the twins and perhaps intuits in Cesario. They also become part of his professional routine, which Malvolio belittles as more studied than inventive. But Olivia's sharp correction and Maria's later disclosures reveal that Malvolio is projecting his envious anxieties, since it is he who takes pains to 'con state' to acquire the politic language he thinks will help him move into the circles of his social betters. Malvolio's jibe also reminds audiences of Cesario having to mimic Orsino's ridiculous speeches. Both Viola and Feste are conscious of living precariously in-between their stripped-down selves and tempest-tossed performances in a way that Malvolio learns only after suffering a shipwreck of his own.

'[H]e's a rogue, a passy-measures pavan'
[*pagan?* F1 paynin] (5.1.199)

There is no New Testament epistle to the Illyrians, but in the mind of Shakespeare and his audiences the reputation of other eastern Mediterranean cities such as Corinth and Ephesus could easily stand in for it. Goran Stanovukovic observes that the Roman province of Illyricum on the eastern shore of the Adriatic was converted to Christianity by Paul and Titus. According to legend, the Apostle preached in its main city, Epidamnum, setting of Plautus's *Menaechmi*, which Shakespeare shifted to the more notorious Ephesus in *The Comedy of Errors*.[14] Paul's single mention of Illyria situates it on the frontier of a regional sphere of revelation that recalls Viola's shipwrecked telegraphing of Illyria and Elysium:

> For I dare not speake of anie thing, which Christ hathe not
> wrought by me ... With the power of signes and wonders ...
> so that from Ierusalem, and rounde about vnto Illyricum, I
> haue caused to ab[o]unde the Gospel of Christ. (Romans
> 15:18–19, Geneva Bible translation)

Illyria shared with Corinth and Ephesus a reputation for vice and lawlessness, especially on the seas. In *2 Henry VI* the haughty Suffolk tries to dismiss the Captain's perceptive indictment of his abuses by comparing him to Bardulus (or Bargalus) 'the strong Illyrian pirate' (4.1.108).[15] Shakespeare also associates Illyria with Corinth and Ephesus as quintessential spaces of saturnalian inversion. The Eastcheap drawers in *1 Henry IV* credit Hal for being 'no proud Jack, like Falstaff, but a Corinthian, a lad of mettle, a good boy' (2.4.11–12). In *Part Two*, the Page refers to Falstaff and his Eastcheap companions as 'Ephesians [...] of the old church' (2.2.142). The Fool in *Timon of Athens* invokes Corinth's reputation for prostitutes, echoing both the ill fame of the classical city and Paul's anti-female directives towards it (2.2.71–3). In Paul's accounts, the hybridized religious customs

and relaxed attitudes towards sex in these eschatologically insou-
ciant communities served to spur his emergent master-narrative
of patriarchal hierarchy that eventually displaced the messianic
ethos of social and gender equality.

Shakespeare's Falstaff had riffed brilliantly off these scriptural
contentions and paradoxes, and Sir Toby and the Illyria of cakes
and ale continue his legacy, albeit in a more sodden vein. This
includes the Falstavian trick of twisting Reformation readings
of Pauline texts into mock-pious soundbites (e.g. Toby's 'Give
me faith, say I' [1.5.122–3]) in order to deflect criticism of the
fleshly vices which Paul and his early modern puritan followers
denounced (e.g. as 'pagan', the possible word behind F1's 'paynin'
in Toby's ironic complaint cited in this section's headtitle). Their
discursive interplay indicates that Illyria, Ephesus and Corinth
function interchangeably as metonyms for subversive personal
autonomy and horizontalized social relations. *Twelfth Night*'s juxta-
position of shipwreck end-of-times and temporary carnival licence
clarifies Paul's attempts to regulate public behaviour and local
forms of spirituality in the latter two communities as proto-Lenten
discourses that imposed a cultural paradigm of asymmetrically
empowered temporalities. Except that in the original contested
context of Paul's letters his 'Lenten' model had not yet won out.
Rather, it clashed with the vigorous dissent of the same communities, whose hybridized traditions of knowledge and messianic
freedoms Paul's letters seemed at certain points to authorize (e.g.
Philippians 1.15–18; Galatians 3.28; 1 Corinthians 1–6 below).

My reading of *Twelfth Night*'s relationship to Pauline discourse
differs from that of earlier critics who have understood Feste's
prominent references to Pauline–Erasmian paradoxes of wise folly
as 'hermeneutic keys' to the play, by which is meant the trans-
cendent Paul of Western, and especially Reformation, Christian
theology.[16] I would argue, however, that Feste's adaptation of
Pauline and other biblical discourses, like Falstaff's, does not
represent a code for resolving the play's varied actions into a
single humanist interpretation or implicit social programme.
Feste's scriptural allusions are never simple or straightforward,

but continually interwoven into ambiguous parodies and ironic dialogues. These transpositions overlie epistemological and discursive differences that proliferate semantic contradictions and speculative possibilities in concert with the diverse reception by on- and off-stage Elizabethan spectators.[17]

Linda Hutcheon's discussion of parody and irony clarifies the mediated effects of Feste's Pauline references. Allegorical and traditional humanist readings posit deferential and unifying correspondence with a source-text or tradition to extend the latter's ideological worldview into the derivative work. This is the way Shakespeare's scriptural allusions have conventionally been understood to operate, and one reason they have been largely ignored by modern criticism. Parodic adaptation on the other hand creates an ironic doubling of meaning that draws attention to contrasts between, and contradictions within, the original and adapted texts and their plural interpretation by readers or spectators. Whereas the force of traditional hermeneutics is centripetal, the dynamic of parody is para-relational. The creation of free-standing but irreducibly connected differences, Hutcheon concludes, gives parody and irony their critical charge.[18] Mirroring *Twelfth Night*'s actual and symbolic ruptures of shipwreck, Feste's comic 'as not' re-inventions not only intermingle Paul's sacred words with moments of 'present mirth' and 'laughter' in the secular space of the Globe Theatre, but also redirect audiences back to original texts with the experience of Shakespeare's play as a salty hermeneutic. These contemporizing and defamiliarizing perspectives jointly dismantle the closed interpretative framework of divine paradoxes and typological binaries which, like the Carnival and Lent dyad, became formalized only after the radical absolutism of the early Jewish messianic was assimilated by Christian hermeneutics and institutionalized as civil Christian politics.[19] Feste's virtual Pauline discourses draw attention to the open-ended potential for experimental identities in eschatologically framed shipwreck-and-survival, as well as the naturalizing construction of carnival's cyclical reversion to ordered patriarchy.

'You must allow *vox*' (5.1.288)

Feste also raises awareness of the play's comically 'shipwrecked' discourses by mimicking Paul's protean and persuasive rhetoric. Appropriately, it is Viola who identifies this Pauline aspect of Feste:

> This fellow is wise enough to play the fool,
> And to do that well craves a kind of wit.
> He must observe their mood on whom he jests,
> The quality of persons, and the time,
> And like the haggard, check at every feather
> That comes before his eye. This is a practice
> As full of labour as a wise man's art,
> For folly that he wisely shows is fit,
> But wise men, folly-fall'n, quite taint their wit. (3.1.59–67)

Commentators usually focus on the final two lines of this speech, connecting the idea of 'wise men, folly-fall'n' to Malvolio's pratfalls and, more symbolically, to the Pauline paradox of militant Christian faith, a strong inner conviction that appears simple-minded by rational standards (for example, 1 Corinthians 3:18–20). But Viola pays more attention to the way Feste fits his witty jesting to the variable disposition of his hearers. This practice imitates Paul's ambiguous 'language of accommodation'; that is, his public strategy of performing as different kinds of people to local audiences, and of varying his arguments to match his local listeners' expectations or to undercut their dissent (1 Corinthians 9.19–22). Humanists such as John Colet and Desiderius Erasmus admired Paul's rhetorical versatility because they believed it served the higher goal of spreading Christian truth.[20] Others observed its potentially duplicitous nature. Christopher Marlowe, for example, called Paul a 'juggler' who practised a sly form of pragmatic 'wit.'[21] Feste expresses Marlowe's early modern scepticism about the doubleness of rhetorical manipulation when he observes: 'To see this age! A sentence is but a chev'rel glove to a good wit, how quickly may the wrong side be turned outward' (3.1.11–13). The age's solution, Feste explains, has been to turn orality into textuality, to convert verbal to written words, and to move from informal to legal contracts, all in an attempt to fix a one-way relationship between words and referents and restore the integrity of public language ('words are very rascals since bonds disgraced them' [3.1.19–20]).

But this shifts the medium rather than remedying the inherent instability of all forms of representation. Olivia's wobbly performance of her shipwrecked emotions makes her aware of this problem. Just before her breakthrough dialogue with Cesario she deplores the artificiality of socially bounded language that gets in the way of expressing true feelings: "Twas never merry world/ Since lowly feigning was called compliment' (3.1.96–7). Her observation glances back to the artfully constructed personae Viola and Feste recognize in each other (but which turn into a bewildering present-absence when Feste mistakes Sebastian for his sister: 'Nothing that is so, is so' [4.1.8]). More theoretically, Olivia's complaint raises questions about gaps between rhetoric and truth, and the sincerity of persuasive speech, which originally troubled Paul's communications with the citizens of Corinth. But like Paul, Feste is too worldly and too personally invested in the elasticity of rhetoric as a tool of interpersonal relations to forego it. Paradoxically foolish wit and ludic mimicry are his and the wider play's leading mode of accommodationist speech. They are calculated practices despite the naturalizing pretence that arises in Shakespeare from the semantic slippage between 'fool' and 'natural' (i.e. born idiot). During their crisscrossing service in Orsino's and Olivia's households, Feste compliments Viola's own version of accommodating practice: 'I would be sorry, sir, but the fool should be as oft with your master as with my mistress. I think I saw your wisdom there'. This seems to comment on both their personae: 'I've seen you operating in both places', and 'I noticed the (ambi-)dexterity with which you play to your audiences' [3.1.38–40]). Feste's insights into Viola's performative masks create an unspoken understanding between them that modern productions have signaled in various ways.[22] Nunn's film, for example, captures the sense that Feste has always known how Viola's post-shipwreck story will play out in his retrieval and wordless return of Viola's necklace.

The ambiguities of accommodating speech become most obvious during Feste's interlude as Sir Topaz. His clerical impersonation mimics the official *Book of Common Prayer*, parodies the rhetoric of authoritative citation and ventriloquizes the moralizing cant associated with puritan, and hence strongly Pauline-oriented, preachers ('Talkest thou nothing but of ladies?' [4.2.27]).[23] Toby's admission midway through the scene that Feste's 'knavery' is risking Olivia's greater displeasure also recognizes at a more basic level the unpredictable consequences of 'juggling' with people, an insight Viola gained after her first meeting with Olivia as Cesario (2.2.18–30). Toby's and Maria's hesitations undercut Feste's swaggering gloss on Paul's boast about being able to create different personae for every kind of audience: 'I am for all waters' (4.2.63). But Feste doesn't immediately take the hint and can't resist indulging himself a bit longer at Malvolio's expense (4.2.94–102). His prolonging of the latter's mental torment may leave modern audiences feeling uneasy, and justify sympathy for Malvolio's charges of abuse and vows of revenge in the final scene.[24]

The physical characteristics of Feste's adopted name develop the associations of 'waters' further to suggest an intertextual trope for re-examining Paul's writings. The topaz's 'water' may refer to its lustre, as editors note, as well as its colour, which changes according to local settings and light. Thomas Nicols's *A Lapidary, or, The History of Pretious Stones* (1653) observes that the topaz interacts visually with surrounding foils and continually changes hue with the day's light (Q2v-3r). These qualities suggest that Feste's 'I am for all waters' includes the colours of rhetorical invention and persuasion as the juggling Sir Topaz. Such associations recall another watery gemstone mentioned by Feste, the opal, whose dynamic reflection of ambient light he slyly compares to Orsino's 'changeable taffeta' mind (2.4.73).[25] Feste's topazine adaptations of Pauline and other authoritative discourses suggest a refracting perspective through which Paul's original texts might reveal their variable rhetorical colours.[26]

To see how this might work, let's briefly turn an opalizing light on a couple of Paul's most controversial arguments. The First Letter to the Corinthians opens with a disclaimer reminiscent of many Shakespearian wits: Paul denies using 'the wisdom of words', or the arts of rhetoric, to influence his hearers. He claims simply to speak the truth – in this case the apparently far-fetched news of the Christ-event (1:17). Yet as I noted earlier, Paul later boasts about inventing different personae for particular communities in order to 'gain them' for 'gospel's sake' (9.19–23). In 2 Corinthians he re-states this strategy while also implicitly acknowledging its ethical slipperiness:

> And I will most gladly bestow, and will be bestowed for your souls, though the more I love you, the less I am loved. But be it that I charged you not; yet for as much as I was crafty, I took you with guile. (12.16–17, Geneva Bible translation)

Paul remains proud of the fact that, like a good stage actor, he could vary his public manner to manipulate his hearers' hearts and minds. Erasmus praised this contentious practice in his widely read *Paraphrases upon the New Testament*.[27] Yet seen from the perspective of *Twelfth Night*'s ironic and sometimes cautionary contexts of crossdressing and play-acting, Paul's protean performances raise typically Shakespearian questions about the relationship of his private and public identities: 'Who was the real Paul?' 'Do his rhetorical means justify his ends?'

Such questions evidently destablized Paul's interventions into various gender, marital and sexual controversies in messianically indifferent Corinth. One of the most notorious of these appears in 1 Corinthians 14, which concerns female public speech. Paul initially presents himself as both reasonable to his potentially hostile audience and sensitive to Corinthian traditions of female participation by arguing that women as well as men should be allowed to prophesy and speak in tongues (verses 1–6).[28] Here, as both early modern and modern commentators observe, Paul's letter is following classical conventions of deliberative rhetoric. Its aim was to persuade an audience to accept probable or possible assertions, and it allowed for rational opposition. From the audience's viewpoint its interpretive hermeneutic was open and dialogic. Deliberative rhetoric was taught to Shakespeare and his contemporaries in grammar school, and this knowledge made Paul's letters susceptible to literary, rather than exclusively doctrinal, interpretation.[29] These readers would have noticed that Paul's rhetoric changes towards the end of this chapter. Erasing his initially accommodating gesture of equality and now arguing dogmatically from personal authority, he orders Corinthian women to be silent in church and to ask questions of their husbands only at home (14.34–8). Despite the contradiction with Paul's earlier arguments, this command, like other scriptural restrictions, became a universal imperative. Lear, for example, recalls admiringly of Cordelia, 'Her voice was ever soft, / Gentle, and low, an excellent thing in woman' (sc. 24.268–9), referring to both the aural pitch and obedient chastity of her public voice. But early modern women readers and writers, seeking to create space for their own voices, wrestled with and resisted these scriptural fiats, partly by re-interpreting the rhetorical texture of Paul's letter to qualify or dissent from its established meanings.[30] Scripturally literate audiences recognizing the pluralizing herme- neutic generated by *Twelfth Night*'s eschatological-shipwreck and end-of-carnival paradigms would also have paid fresh attention to the rhetorical shifts and ideological faultlines (first-century and early modern) of 1 Corinthians 14, re-reinvigorating it with the disputatious energy of messianic Corinth to open up potentially challenging re-interpretations.

The respective provisional and determining temporalities of shipwreck and carnival also reframe the play's climax as a crossroads of existential options. When Sebastian rushes in to be recognized as the identical twin of Cesario, Orsino tries to make sense of the 'One face, one voice, one habit, and two persons' he sees by describing it as 'A natural perspective, that is and is not' (5.1.209–10). Commentators relate 'perspective' to early modern optical glasses that created illusions or distortions, while focusing on 'natural' as the correcting revelation of what Sebastian later calls nature's 'bias' (5.1.254).[31] In this reading a 'natural perspective' reverses the aberrations of women dressing like men, men loving men and women loving women, and the blurrings of same-sex and heterosexual desire. It announces a proper return to normative social identities and patriarchal authority in keeping with the inevitable termination of holiday exemptions, emblematized by the final heterosexual couplings and expected re-appearance of Viola in her 'woman's weeds' (5.1.267). The play's staging of shipwreck-and-survival's 'as not' conversions, however, focuses attention on the second part of Orsino's description: 'is and is not.' This recalls the virtualized identities and suspended value-conventions of messianic time. A 'natural perspective, that is and is not' suggests the experimental subjectivities associated with post-shipwreck 'conversion.' Moreover, early modern perspective glasses came in many forms and performed a variety of enhancing functions. 'A natural perspective' indicates that *Twelfth Night, or What You Will* sustains the possibilities of expanding and re-inventing the boundaries of gender and desire, 'represent[ing them] in diuerse colours, & them most gorgeous.'[32] The energies of this 'natural bias' have branched out along daring pathways that remain imaginatively open amid the generic closures of romantic comedy.

Twelfth Night's presentation of 'is and is not' structures of human experience not only reflects the contested rhetorical and epistemological time-spaces of Paul's controversial texts. They also positively revalue the many deferrals and ambiguities in the play's formal ending as potential routes of continuing self-discovery and vocation, rather than human shortcomings endemic to idealized comic transcendence. In the epilogue of Nunn's film, for instance, we see a smartly suited Malvolio, no longer a servant, leaving the grounds of Olivia's house with just an umbrella and a suitcase, apparently not bent on revenge but remaking his unburdened life. We also see Antonio turning up his collar to the wind and the rain as he strides away from the main gate. Openness to emotional and subjective risks does not prevent turns down blind alleys, where Antonio has apparently journeyed with Sebastian. Yet Antonio is moving on.

In owning up to his role in the sportful malice against Malvolio, Feste accepts living in the accidented condition of calamitous living. Implicitly he discards any notion that conventional wisdom, foolish or straight, will detach him from, let alone resolve, the existential knot of life's mingled yarn. He puts his faith in the tougher knowledge of nature's indifference to human exceptionalism revealed in the 'blind waves and surges' of physical transience (5.1.223). And he acts out this heightened consciousness of human liminality in parodic accommodations of Pauline and other master-discourses. His performances do not serve any lofty goals. They do not aspire to incite virtue. They decline to correct his fellow travellers' waywardness from any self-conferred position of militant benevolence. Instead his jesting dialogues – with Orsino, for example – seem mainly to reflect his own life-choices: 'I would have men of such constancy put to sea, that their business might be everything, and their intent everywhere, for that's it that always makes a good voyage of nothing' (2.4.74–7). Like a character in Beckett, Feste's multilateral performativity simply keeps him going. It supports living from hand to mouth – *viz.* Feste's regular gambits for money – and eases acceptance of the finality of death in nature which Viola and Sebastian's initial experience of shipwreck reveals with terrifying intensity.

From the perspective of comedy's journey towards quotidian social realities leavened with dreams of escaping or improving those conditions, the twins' integration into the play's romantic narratives counterpoints Feste's pragmatic materialism with the promise of 'golden time' to come. Malvolio's clamour for revenge and his suit against the Captain – supposing he pursues these options – are motivated by a related ideal of ultimate justice along a more hazardous route. Feste's final song dilates these divided hopes and outcomes, although theatre productions often try to resolve them into some kind of comforting vision. Trevor Nunn's film continues the popular tradition, setting Ben Kingsley's words to upbeat music which leads into final shots of Viola and Olivia in splendid gowns dancing with their husbands in marriage celebrations. But at least since John Barton's revisionist RSC production (1969–71), modern stagings have often gone the other way, using watery soundscapes not only to give the wind and the rain greater affective pull, but also to recall the tragic energies of the play's opening *peripeteia*. These seem to reverberate through Feste's ballad of a shipwrecked life. Its final stanza, 'A great while ago', hints at some kind of closing wisdom emerging from the tosspot's itinerary of drunken beds. But 'that's all one our play is done' ruptures this expectation, suspends judgement and finally synchronizes the waters of oceanic transience with the unknown approval of the theatre audience.[33]

CHAPTER SIX

New Directions: 'Let them use their talents': *Twelfth Night* and the Professional Comedian

Andrew McConnell Stott

It was C. L. Barber's contention that *Twelfth Night* was 'Shakespeare's last free-and-easy festive comedy', a play that had the power to delight audiences by 'making distinctions between false care and true freedom', and recommitting them to those 'powers in human nature and society which make good the risks of courtesy and liberty.'[1] This sounds inviting, but even if we were to focus our attentions solely on Malvolio's comeuppance, the festive spice of crossdressing and the incorrigibly gluttonous Sir Toby Belch, 'free-and-easy' remains a gassily optimistic assessment of a play that ends in summary imprisonment, promises of revenge and a song that takes as its subject the world's stubborn refusal to improve. Even more problematically, if there is one character we can point to who best characterizes this failure of simple comic resolution, it is Feste the clown, whose convoluted speech and ironic detachment actively tip the scales against 'release and clarification', the phrase Barber uses to describe the loosing of social restrictions and subsequent strengthening of social bonds that he believes define Shakespearean comedy.

Barber's study of festive comedy may be more than half a century old, but its central concepts have proved impressively resilient, especially with regards to their urge to associate Feste – as his name emphatically begs – with the traditions of festivity and misrule.[2] For Marjorie Garber, Feste is a master of revels, 'less like a person than like a sprite or a spirit of music [...] much akin to Puck.'[3] François Laroque has likewise emphasized his role as an 'allowed fool', the embodiment of permissive holidays whose music and joking encapsulate the solstitial cheer of 'cakes and ale', to remind us that in a period of misrule 'the world is nothing but a hall of mirrors.'[4] At the heart of this view is, of course, Olivia's reaction to: the quibbling 'catechism' in which Feste aims to 'prove' the lady 'a fool' (1.5.53),[5] an exchange which subsequently prompts Malvolio to object that those who stand for such impertinence are no better than fools themselves. While Olivia's response – 'There is no slander in an allowed fool' (1.5.88–9) – has been read as the definitive assertion of the 'licence' clowns are granted to speak truth to those in power, and therefore the broader suspension of repressive social expectation during the holiday period, to read Feste as a social corrective ignores the fact that he himself repeatedly rejects the role. Leaving aside the question of whether the licence of early modern clowns might not have been systematically overstated by literary critics, Feste tells Olivia that 'I wear not motley in my brain' (1.5.51–2), as if to assert that he is not the incarnation of a Puckish spirit, but rather a man with a job. Furthermore, to see Feste guiding the community to greater awareness and so knitting it together in happiness seems to disregard his fundamental elusiveness, not to mention detachment from and clear indifference to, his fellow Illyrians – a detachment so extreme that at one point he drops out of the play entirely. Such indifference is often accounted for by presenting him as a floating, choric abstraction in the mold of *As You Like It*'s Touchstone, or *All's Well that Ends Well*'s Lavatch, and, of course, *King Lear*'s fool, an apocalyptic figure limning the world as a Möbius strip of paradox in his enigmatic and religiously-inflected language. Leading people through the labyrinth of language to find the way to larger meaning, however, seems not to concern Feste as much as the speed with which words can deteriorate from sense to incomprehensibility: 'A sentence is / but a cheveril glove to a good wit', he tells Viola, drawing her attention to the continuity of meaning and nonsense, 'how quickly the / wrong side may be turned outward!' (3.1.11–13). It is fitting, then, that when Viola asks if Feste's is Olivia's fool, he says no: 'I am indeed not her fool, but her corrupter of words' (3.1.34–5).

As with his relationship to festivity, Feste's addiction to 'misprison in the highest degree' (1.5.50) has been used to draw analogies between the characteristics of his clowning and the early modern concept of Folly as it is personified in Desiderius Erasmus's *Praise of Folly* (1511, 1515).[6] Erasmus's Folly possesses a powerfully ironic identity that she uses to disperse self-delusion throughout the world in order to make it work. All human interactions, Folly claims, are made possible because of her, the font of all the vanity and ambition and the willful blindness in the world that makes it and its inhabitants endurable to one another. Folly smoothes relations between people, makes lovers bearable, and commerce and community possible. 'No association or alliance can be happy or stable without me', she declares,

> People can't tolerate a ruler, nor can a master his servant, a maid her mistress ... unless they sometimes have illusions about each other, make use of flattery, and have the sense to turn a blind eye and sweeten life for themselves with the honey of folly.[7]

Such blindness is certainly observable in Illyria, where people consistently fail to see what lies directly before them. And Folly is also an 'allowed fool', licensed to address the powerful without fear of retribution. 'The fact is', she says,

> kings do dislike the truth, but the outcome of this is extraordinary for my fools. They can speak truth and even open insults and be heard with positive pleasure; indeed, the words which would cost a wise man his life are surprisingly enjoyable when uttered by a clown. For truth has a genuine power to please if it manages not to give offence, but this is something the gods have granted only to fools.[8]

Ultimately, however, the concept of Folly proves to be a vehicle for spiritual meditation, which, in its purest form, graduates from the concept of mere permissive foolishness to become a kind of divine madness, the 'folly' of religious insight that descends when one has been granted a vision of eternity beyond the quotidian veil. True folly is true knowledge, and while perhaps something similar is implied in Feste's assertion that 'the rain it raineth every day', *Twelfth Night*, in spite of a rather complicated relationship to religion, shows little sign of promoting madness as a route to religious insight.[9]

What unites these readings of Feste, then – as Folly or Festival – is a tendency to see the comedian as a dual citizen of both sub- and superlunary realms, a mercurial trickster at once in the world, but able to stand at an ironic remove from its dealings. Yet what gets lost here is the possibility that this might all be an act. As Karin Coddon has persuasively argued, there is a clear suggestion that the ideas of folly and festivity are already faded and anachronistic in the world of *Twelfth Night*: Sir Toby and Sir Andrew are irredeemably *stuck* in their observance of 'uncivil rule' (2.3.115), for example, whereas Orsino's melancholy appears to feed on nostalgia as much as love.[10] Where Feste is called upon to give voice to the spirit of festivity, therefore, it is in the open knowledge that such things already belong to past, as when Orsino, reflecting on the power of Feste's 'old and antic song' (2.4.3), describes it to Cesario as 'old and plain' and belonging entirely to an earlier age:

> The spinsters and the knitters in the sun,
> And the free maids that weave their thread with bones,
> Do use to chant it. It is silly sooth,
> And dallies with the innocence of love,
> Like the old age. (2.4.43–7)

Orsino's admixture of innocence and old age draws our attention to the song's anachronistic discontinuity, and suggests that Feste's relationship to festivity belongs more to his ability to evoke sentimental longing for it rather than being its inherent, fully embodied representative. This would certainly be in keeping with the historical fact that is a rise in the amount of fool and folly literature that appears at the end of the sixteenth century at the same time as there is a commensurate decline in the retention of jesters at court and in private houses, a fact that suggests that simply to write about fooling was already to look backward with nostalgic intent.[11] The fact that Feste is such a talented purveyor of nostalgia, however, does help to bring into focus what the court jesters had become – professional performers who know their audiences well enough to provide them with the specialist entertainments they want: old songs, and a repertoire that includes ventriloquism, mock-Latin disquisitions and dexterous riddles.

Instead of embodying a concept, therefore, Feste might be more productively read as a professional comedian, even if, as a long-term dependant of Olivia's household, he may not obviously belong to a world of modern 'careers', but to an older, organic network of extended kinship groups and feudal hospitality. There is more flexibility in this arrangement than at first meets the eye, however. Country households were not necessarily synonymous with fixed and unwavering servitude, but, as Barbara Palmer has shown, for professional performers at least, they represented profitable sites of accelerated social mobility. Clowns and fools especially were in a position to become influential messengers and well-remunerated mediators by virtue of the unprecedented access to men of influence they were granted through their roles and the logistics of their touring schedule. The fooling of clowns in country houses, then, writes Palmer, was 'shaped by creative mobility rather than rooted in provincial isolation.'[12]

Similarly, Feste's harsh, admonitory attitude towards Olivia and ultimately vengeful persona clearly does not participate in what we might call the comedy of social appeasement, where, in the words of Michael Bristol, 'self-abjection and self-ridicule are significant elements in an elaborate system of deferential gesture and compliment.'[13] Furthermore, as a pure 'sprite or spirit of music', we would expect him to be less economically conscious than he constantly proves himself to be. Feste is only character who explicitly takes money during in the play (with the sole exception of Sebastian, who agrees to be Antonio's 'purse bearer

[...] for an hour' (3.3.47–48), and his presence onstage inevitably results in some payment of some kind. Indeed, the question of payment is so prominent with Feste that Shakespeare seems to make it a condition of the clown's appearance, either showing or describing him being paid multiple times in multiple locations – twice at Olivia's house, twice at Orsino's court, and twice by Viola and once by Sebastian somewhere in-between. Performers are vendors and they need to be paid, the play seems to be saying, an idea Feste himself acknowledges when he tells Maria 'God give them wisdom that have it; and those / that are fools, let them use their talents' (1.5.13–14).

If there is a tendency to conceive of clowns as manifestations of cultural ideas, it is because the role itself places a premium on eliding the artifice of its craft. Richard Tarlton (d. 1588), for example, the popular clown of the Queen's Men, presented himself as a rustic man of the people, concealing his professional identity and tradecraft beneath the carefully constructed persona of a shrewd but uncultured rural immigrant. In fact, Tarlton was on a very comfortable financial footing, the landlord of two taverns, a Groom of the Chamber and a Master of Fence, who frequently performed before Elizabeth I.[14] In Feste's case, such elision manifests itself in the constant deflection and refusal of interpellation inherent in his punning rejoinders. Not only does such a move work unceasingly against definition, but also highlights the extent to which the question of identity itself appears to be folded into the professional description of what it means to be a clown. The aim of this chapter, then, will be to ask what it might mean to consider Feste first and foremost as a professional comedian, and what might a broader understanding of a professional context for comedy bring to a reading of *Twelfth Night*.

The Vocational Clown

The term 'professional' requires some gloss, although any rigorous definition was something the period was itself unable to provide as a result of the many transformations taking place around the early modern world of work. The word 'profession', with its long and relatively stable history in relation to those employments traditionally marked by gentility – Medicine, the Church, and the Law – which have been defined by the historian of professionalization, Wilfred Prest, as 'non-manual, non-commercial occupations sharing some measure of institutional self-regulation and reliance upon bookish skills and training', held a more capacious meaning at the time of *Twelfth Night*, and one that could be understood as any activity conducted with a sense of vocation.[15] The traditional Aristotelian distinction between the 'liberal' and 'mechanical' arts, those employments that relied on literacy as opposed to those that drew on practical skills, had become muddied as an increasing number of trades took on an enlarged sense of their own dignity in an expanding economy, especially among occupations where regulation and literacy were becoming increasingly important, such as apothecaries, surgeons, the military and various merchants.[16] This is also period in which, according to the *Oxford English Dictionary*, the word 'professional' is first coined, recording the first usage in relation to 'professional clengers', a Scots word for 'cleaners.' Certainly Shakespeare was comfortable using the word to refer to both genteel and more common pursuits, referring at once to the 'high profession spiritual' of priests (*Henry VIII*, 2.4.115) but also to a wide variety of gardeners, tinkers, fortune-tellers, brothel-keepers, knaves and Gadshill thieves. By 1600, the most important factor when determining a profession, then, was not the nature of the work so much as the extent to which it is tied up in notions of industriousness, social credit and personal worth.[17]

From this perspective, not only do stage clowns fit the definition of a profession well, but some, such as Robert Armin, the performer most likely to have first created the character of Feste, specifically refer to themselves in such terms: 'it is my profession', wrote Armin in 1600, 'To jest at a jester, in his transgression'.[18] As is well documented, the status of actors in the early modern period was a confusion of overlapping and oftentimes contradictory practices, responsibilities and affiliations.

Players were technically servants of their aristocratic patron, but might also be members of guilds and trade associations, as well as stockholders in their companies, taking part, in Jean Howard's words, 'in a theatrical industry at once proto-capitalist in its joint-stock arrangements and yet tied to older structures of service and patronage.'[19] Yet this mixed terrain is exactly the result of a move towards increased professionalization that, as Tom Rutter has argued, players had been making from the fifteenth century onwards. Professional acting companies, he reminds us, did not spring in to existence fully conceptualized with the passage of the 1572 Act for the Punishment of Vagabonds (14 Eliz. I c.5), but had been evolving continually as the result of a 'gradual reorientation in relation to the idea of work brought about by wider social, economic and religious trends.'[20] Such trends include the decline of amateur civic drama (most notably mystery plays) in the wake of the Reformation, and the increasing uniformity of labour practices throughout the sixteenth century, especially in the rapidly growing metropolis of London where labour was becoming, in Rutter's words, 'repetitive, geographically-fixed, [and] carried out on weekdays.'[21]

One effect of this realignment of urban labour was the space it created for more clearly defined leisure time, and, as such, the more specialized and commodified leisure market that grew to fill it. In turn, this prompted theatre companies themselves to fashion better regulated means of instruction by which they might replenish their ranks and ease entry into the profession. While actors had no guild or livery company to represent them either by law or custom, the London livery companies still played an important, if indirect, role in the training of players by providing them with a clear blueprint for apprenticeship that helped to place them on a secure professional footing.[22] This was especially true in the case of the twelve 'great' livery companies of London – the Mercers, Grocers, Drapers, Fishmongers, Goldsmiths, Merchant Taylors, Skinners, Haberdashers, Salters, Ironmongers, Vintners and Clothworkers – that enjoyed an enormous influence on civic and economic life. Almost all of London's early modern theatre companies contained at least one member or shareholder who had completed an apprenticeship with a livery company at some stage of his youth, going on to become a full member of the association and thus a 'freeman' and citizen of London.[23] Once elevated to this rank, freemen were able to take on apprentices of their own, although the peculiarities of the system meant that they could train them in whatever trade they wished rather than the one in which they were themselves trained. Thus, those freemen who had gone on to pursue theatrical careers were at perfect liberty to bind apprentices to them who studied nothing but playing.

At the age of twelve, for example, Shakespeare's collaborator and co-editor of the 1623 First Folio, John Heminges, was apprenticed for nine years to the Worshipful Company of Grocers, from which he emerged a freeman of the city. He in turn bound ten apprentices to the Grocers' Company, all of whom studied to become players.[24] Playing and grocering were mutually beneficial activities, as membership of the Grocers' Company greased the wheels as Heminges dispatched his managerial duties for the King's Men. Richard Tarlton was made a freeman of the Company of Vintners in 1584, binding his first apprentice ten days later, by which time he had already been a popular member of the Earl of Sussex's company for over five years.[25] Similarly, Robert Armin served an eleven-year apprenticeship under John Lonyson, a London goldsmith and master worker of the Queen's mint at the Tower of London. When Lonyson died, Armin completed his training under a man named John Kettlewood, before becoming a freeman via his membership of the Goldsmiths' Company in 1604, by which time he had already been a member of Shakespeare's company for five years.[26] A possibly apocryphal story has it that Tarlton hand-picked Armin to be his successor as London's premier clown, having been impressed by the witty verses the young man left behind after calling on some non-theatrical business that concerned Tarlton and his master. Regardless of its veracity, the story works to demystify somewhat the ritual origin of the clown by suggesting a process of 'talent spotting' and promotion that serves to remind us of the overlapping spheres of commercial life, professional advancement and the adoption of stage personas inherent to being a 'career' comedian.[27]

Armin's entry into the Lord Chamberlain's Men has been commonly seen as a turning point in Shakespeare's conception of clowning, providing the playwright with a new texture and range in the construction of his comic voices than was previously possible in the clowning of Armin's predecessor in the company, Will Kemp. Though extremely popular and influential in his own right, Kemp's clown was firmly in the tradition of Tarlton, who epitomized the rustic booby, and was beloved for his bawdy improvisations and athletic jigs. Such overtly visceral activity, however, was exactly what Armin's clown avoided. Where Kemp was physical, explosive and unruly, Armin was ruminative, satirical, witty and lyrical, his humour originating in the plasticity of language.

The most prominent exponent of the argument for Armin as an iteration of clown reform is without doubt Richard Helgerson, for whom the switch from Kemp to Armin is indicative of a new level of conscientiousness among theatre practitioners concerning the quality and consistency of their product. Armin entered the company at a time when the landscape of London theatre was expanding to meet increased demand. Shakespeare and Burbage's Globe had opened in 1599, followed a year later by Henslowe's Fortune in 1600, and a third adult company, Worcester's, who came to fill the newly vacant Rose. To this can be added two private companies who had started offering performances: Paul's Boys and the company at Blackfriars. The increased competition in London, Helgerson contends, resulted in an assertion of managerial discipline that produced tension between what he calls the old 'players' theater' – performances that made room to showcase the skills of particular performers and had scripts loose enough to allow for improvisation – and an emerging 'authors' theater' best represented by Hamlet's advice to the players:

> Let those that play your clowns speak no more than is set
> down for them, for there be of them that will themselves

> laugh to set on some quantity of barren spectators to laugh
> too, though in the mean time some necessary question
> of the play be then to be considered. That's villainous,
> and shows a most pitiful ambition in the fool that uses it.
> (*Hamlet*, 3.2.37–44)[28]

While it is possible to read Hamlet's injunction against comic
improvisation that pits the 'pitiful ambition' of getting a few laughs
against the importance of preserving the aesthetic integrity of the
text, as a rationale for replacing Kemp with the more ensemble-
minded Armin, it is worth noting that from the 1590s onwards there
had been a more general move away from the history plays and rural
comedies that suited Kemp-style clowns towards satires, romances
and city comedies (not to mention that Helgerson may be guilty
of simply mistaking Hamlet for Shakespeare.)[29] As Nora Johnson
has argued, the idea that Shakespeare was determined to tame his
unruly clowns depends on enforcing a strict separation between
the performances of Kemp and Armin, where in fact there is reason
to see many continuities, not least of which is the fact that both
were 'authors' of their own performances and collaborators within
the larger play, a fact that Shakespeare appears to acknowledge by
granting Feste such autonomy within the Illyrian world.[30]

However, the fact that the role of the clown was becoming
more institutionalized in other ways as Kemp gave way to Armin
is undeniable. Evidence from printed plays suggests that the early
seventeenth century saw a noticeable move to assimilate the clown
more fully into the overall fabric of the play-text. While stage
directions sometimes referred to Kemp directly by name ('Enter
Will Kemp' is one such instruction in *Romeo and Juliet*), by the
time of *Twelfth Night* the names of individual performers had
been elided in favour of the roles they performed. In the case of
clowns, this can be taken as evidence that the role was no longer
identified with the unique qualities of any single individual, but
had become a fully formed construct in its own right, referring
both to a particular kind of part, and also to the specialist actor
tasked with performing the role within the company.[31]

Clearly, Armin was working at a moment in the history of comic performance when the nature of comedy was undergoing important revisions, even if those revisions do not care to organize themselves in such conveniently binary terms. For example, almost all accounts of early modern clowning remind us of the difference between 'natural' and 'artificial' fools, a distinction which Enid Welsford claimed in 1935 was 'often made in the Elizabethan times' and which could be traced back as far back as the twelfth century.[32] 'Natural' fools were innocents, men whose deviant, eccentric or otherwise risible behaviour was explained by a mental defect or physical deformity beyond their control; 'artificial' fools consciously performed their antics for profit or acclaim. Armin, as an actor, has been placed squarely in the latter camp, one which became increasingly dominant towards the end of the sixteenth century as professional drama began to question the propriety of using 'natural' fools as comic butts and began to explore alternative means for making audiences laugh (indeed, the braided plots of *A Midsummer Night's Dream* might be read instructively as a meditation on what properly belongs to comedy, and how an audience might best respond).[33] The change can be partly accounted for by changing manners and standards of civility that rejected the laughter of ridicule and saw derision as an unbecoming and ungentlemanly trait. However, a look at Armin's own writings on comedy shows that Armin himself saw the distinction between natural and artificial fools to be much more ambiguous than the critical literature would have it. In particular, his *Foole Upon Foole, or Six Sortes of Sottes* (1600) illustrates amply the how blurred those lines might be. This text is comprised of biographical sketches of six historically verifiable individuals: Jack Oates, Jemy Camber, Lean Leanard, Jack Miller, Will Somers and John of the Hospital. Somers was the celebrated court fool of Henry VIII, Camber was fool to the Scottish court, and Oates a fool in the household of Sir William Holles, Lord Mayor of London in 1539. Jack Miller and John of the Hospital were both known to Armin himself, who had met Miller in Worcestershire while touring with Lord Chandos' Men, and had seen John of the Hospital in the streets of London, where he had become notorious enough for Armin to write him into a play entitled *The History of the Two Maids of More-Clack*.

That Armin takes such care to let the reader know which fools he has known personally, and which he has merely heard of, is just one feature of a text that is notable not only for the scholarly attention and taxonomic detail it brings to the history of clowns, but to the scant regard it has for the critical distinctions between natural and artificial fools. It is true that all of the men in *Foole Upon Foole* suffer from some kind of disability, whether it be stuttering, dwarfism or deformity, yet their mental capacities vary wildly. Leanard, a servant to a gentleman in the vicinity of Sherwood Forest, for example, seems not so much merry as horribly troubled, his 'jests' demonstrating behaviour that is uniformly violent and unsettling and more compatible with psychological disturbance than mirth. Jack Oates, meanwhile, while being referred to as an 'Idiot', shows great mental sharpness as he plots against his enemy, the cook; similarly Will Somers' only disability appears to be a hunchback which in no way impedes upon his verbal acuity or inventive comic intelligence.[34] Clearly, Armin would not lump together the amateur and the professional, the cunning and the unhappily afflicted if strong distinctions between natural and artificial were being enforced. Instead, the portraits of *Foole Upon Foole* suggest that fooling cannot be so simplistically organized, but rather that clowning constitutes a spectrum of activity from which it is possible for a professional comedian like Armin to construct a repertoire. One explanation for compiling a text such as *Foole Upon Foole*, therefore, might be that Armin sought to simultaneously highlight the tradition within which he was working even as he unmoored it from any firm ontological categories. If this is accurate, then the main difference between Armin's clown and those of Kemp and Tarlton is not that he falls rigidly in line with the author's tyrannical vision, but in the fact that he does not elide the comedian's labour, but rather actively historicizes his profession and thereby places himself within a lineage of other 'workers.' Such an idea is reinforced in Armin's

Quips Upon Questions (also 1600) in a verse that makes the case for fooling as an instrumentalized activity, a tool in the hands of a well-trained expert just like a carpenter's chisel:

> True it is, he playes the Foole indeed;
> But in the Play he playes it as he must:
> Yet when the Play is ended, then his speed
> Is better then the pleasure of thy trust:
>> For he shall have what thou that time hast spent,
>> Playing the foole, thy folly to content.
>
> He playes the Wise man then, and not the Foole,
> That wisely for his lyving so can do:
> So doth the Carpenter with his sharpe toole,
> Cut his own finger oft, yet lives by't to.
>> He is a foole to cut his limbe say I,
>> But not so, with his toole to live thereby.[35]

The pride Armin appears to take in his sphere of labour is further referenced in the frontispieces his printed works, where he refers to himself once as 'Clonnico de Curtaino' ('Clown of the Curtain', the home of Shakespeare's company prior to its occupancy of the Globe), and subsequently as 'Clonnico del Mondo' ('Clown of the Globe'), descriptions that delineate both his professional identity and his place within the Chamberlain's and King's Men.[36] It should be noted that Will Kemp also made a number of explicit references to the 'labour' of his clowning, particularly when drawing attention to his bodily exertions and the many injuries sustained in the service of entertainment, especially in the course of his remarkable 'Nine Daies wonder', a dance from London to Norwich. But while Kemp's allusions to his work evoke the register of manual labour, Armin was anxious to associate himself with more vocational occupations.[37] *A Nest of Ninnies* (1608), for example, bears a dedication to 'the youthfull and rightly compleat in all good gifts and graces, the generous Gentlemen of Oxenford, Cambridge, and the Innes of Court', itself suggesting the pride

Armin appears to take in the fact that he keeps the company of more conventionally 'professional' men.[38]

Illyrian Professions

It is possible that Armin first made his acquaintance with the gentlemen of the Inns of Court while appearing in *Twelfth Night*, which had its debut performance as a private entertainment at Middle Temple Hall, a professional setting that lends itself nicely to the play's unlikely preoccupation with work. It is not for nothing that Keir Elam has dubbed *Twelfth Night* 'Shakespeare's most class-conscious play', as while on the surface it appears to be an indolent territory of boozing, lovesickness and mourning, Illyria is rife with competitive tensions that arise as a result of its various inhabitants' efforts to trade up their social status, from Andrew Aguecheek hoping to bag a fortune to Malvolio imagining himself as Olivia's lord.[39] Worrying about issues of social status and social mobility was, of course, one of the recurring themes of early modern comedy, and which perhaps explains Olivia's question to Cesario – 'Are you a comedian?' (1.5.174) – that so clearly aligns *arrivistes* and social cuckoos with comedy. According to Keith Thomas's classic essay on the early modern uses of humour, comedy most frequently found its subject-matter around issues of deviance and inequity, what Thomas labelled 'areas of structural ambiguity in society itself.'[40] The means of addressing these issues could be profoundly conservative, as in the phenomenon of the *charivari*, a brash community performance deployed to shame those who had fallen out of line back into orthodoxy. Similarly, as Chris Holcomb's study of early modern jest books has shown, the social tensions at the heart of jesting revolved particularly around questions of civility and deportment. Jest books, Holcomb contends, divide society according to those deserving of scorn and those who provide reproofs, offering examples of 'liminal moments when two social types communicate across the boundary that normally separates them' for the purpose of drawing distinctions between, say, uncultured rustics in the thrall of their unchecked impulses, and courtiers who use laughter as a means of shaming them into reform.[41]

Twelfth Night, however, seems less interested in the process or social reform than the mechanics of social friction, friction that provides the play with a dark core that is never far from tipping into cruelty or violence. Feste, the professional fool, has to find a place in a cut-throat world characterized by frequent allusions to blood and blood-sports, especially hunting and bear-baiting, forms of violent competition that appear to offer a template for much of its action, from Orsino's imagining of himself as Actaeon devoured by Olivia's hounds to the tethering of Malvolio in a dark room.[42] Malvolio's torturous humiliation is of course the play's darkest turn, but literal violence also manifests itself in the more knockabout interlude in which Antonio gives Sir Andrew his bloody coxcomb, the report on Sebastian's arrest for piracy that reveals he was responsible for Orsino's nephew losing a leg (5.1.57) and Orsino's angry threat to 'sacrifice the lamb' Viola to avenge himself against Olivia (5.1.127).

Given the competitive environment of Illyria, then, Feste's frequent requests for financial reward are not only not out of place, but they positively reinforce the contradictions of self-interest and service that seem to encapsulate the status of early modern performers. Within three short days of her shipwreck, for example, Viola already finds herself 'much advanced' (1.4.2) in the service of Duke Orsino (an advancement Valentine reflects upon with something like an incredulous eyebrow), whereas Malvolio muses on the example set by the eponymous 'yeoman of the wardrobe', who married the 'Lady of the Strachey' (2.5.36, 35). Indeed, the potential for sudden social mobility is the central conceit of the play, which revolves around parallel and bifurcated considerations of the consequences of marrying servants, whether it be through the prism of Malvolio's deluded imaginings, or the fact that both Viola and Maria end up at the altar, providing a sense of fluidity that is further redoubled by the fact that these women are performed by boys dressed as girls to suggest that nothing is more opportunistic nor more profitably traded – on stage as in Illyria – than sexual identity.[43] Both Viola and Maria are, of course, gentlewomen, so hardly required to traverse yawning class divisions. Rather, the characters in the play negotiate what David Schalkwyk has called the 'subtle but decisive class distinctions within the household', a series of small, incremental differences that inflame the most passionate rivalries.[44] The enmity between Malvolio and Sir Toby, for example, derives not simply from antipathy towards the Steward's nominal Puritanism, nor disgust at his having taken on unconscionable airs, but also from the friction that stems from both men having arrived at positions of approximate authority and influence within Olivia's court in spite of quite different social origins. The same consideration motivates Malvolio's prickly reception of Cesario, which arises from the fact that for all the difference in their roles, ages and backgrounds, no single element is definitive enough to clearly anchor their status in relation to one another, a status that appears, from Malvolio's point of view at least, to be chafingly close.

As for the importance of work, we see this reflected clearly in Viola, who quickly identifies its necessity, and throws herself into it immediately, animating the play with her busy energy. In this, she puts herself in the position of competing with Feste for a job – 'for I can sing / And speak to him in many sorts of music / That will allow me very worth his service'(1.2.53–5) – responding to Orsino's prompt to 'prosper well in this' (1.4.38), by diligently undertaking her commission as a go-between, writing and delivering speeches, and rarely, if ever, standing idle, in stark comparison to her employer who embodies the static world of the brooding, cloistered aristocracy.

Comedy and Identity

Viola and Feste share something of an affinity. The young woman's freedom and entrepreneurial drive are matched by the clown's itinerancy in which he deploys his services wherever there is need, hiring himself out freely to Orsino while remaining notionally attached to Olivia's court and living separately from both. Both characters have blank spaces in their immediate pasts – Viola is birthed from the sea, whereas Feste's introduction to the play comes on the back of an unexplained absence and a refusal to appear overly concerned about the prospect of losing Olivia's favour, or even being hanged. Such disinterest is typical of the importance he places on his freedom, not only flatly denying that he is 'Lady Olivia's fool', but simultaneously emphasizing his itinerancy: 'I would be sorry', he tells Viola, 'but the fool should be as oft with your master as with my mistress' (3.1.38–9). Such resistance to enforced identity brings into relief the extent to which both characters address the central question that permeates *Twelfth Night*, namely the consequences of perpetually misrecognizing people, symbols and desires. But whereas it is Viola's ultimate fate to reconcile appearance and reality, Feste's role is geared towards bringing the contingency of identity more dramatically into relief. The shared scene between Feste and Viola underlines both the differences and similarities of these two central characters, as both look to conceal important truths from one another while sharing a kind of mutual insight. For Viola, exposure to Feste's relentless doubletalk serves to draw her into sharper focus as a woman both through Feste's clear penetration of her disguise, and her own admission of her love for Orsino:

> VIOLA   Nay, an thou pass upon me, I'll no more with thee.
> Hold, (*giving money*) there's expenses for thee.
> FESTE   Now Jove in his next commodity of hair send thee a beard.
> VIOLA   By my troth I'll tell thee, I am almost sick for one, though I would not have it grow on *my* chin.
> (3.1.41–7)

It should be remembered that both characters are in disguise here. Feste appears in this scene carrying a drum and tabor, instruments associated with an older clowning tradition, specifically those of the rustics Tarlton and Kemp. This is a curious outfit, as

Feste is quite clearly not that kind of fool, and the joke is further compounded when Viola asks 'Art thou a churchman?' (3.1.4). This layering of personae uses sumptuary signals to gesture towards a professional lineage (both within Illyria and the space of the theatre), and the religious associations of holiday that again recall the anachronistic echoes of festivity in the play as if Feste himself were trying to recall a performance. That this is typical of Feste's relentless shift of identities relative to his interlocutor is not lost on the perceptive Viola, for as even as she admits that he has her verbally well-beaten, she is still able to clearly perceive the labour elided in both Feste's insistent glibness, and the degree of skill required by his endless manoeuvres around meaning:

> This fellow is wise enough to play the fool,
> And to that well craves a kind of wit.
> He must observe their mood on whom he jests,
> The quality of the persons, and the time,
> And like the haggard, check at every feather
> That comes before his eye. This is a practice
> As full of labour as a wise man's art,
> For folly that he wisely shows is fit. (3.1.59–66)

It is fitting that this encounter should also involve a financial transaction in which Feste manages to extract a double payment, as the scene itself is doubled soon after when the clown encounters Sebastian in what we might safely assume is the exact same spot. Here, it is Feste's turn to be exasperated by the answers he hears, as insight is replaced by unintelligibility, understanding by rancour, and the only constant is payment.

FESTE   Will you make me believe that I am not
             sent for you?
SEBASTIAN   Go to, go to, thou art a foolish fellow,
             Let me be clear of thee.
FESTE   Well held out, i'faith! No, I do not know
             you nor I am not sent to you by my lady

>   to bid you come speak with her, nor your
>   name is not Master Cesario, nor this is not
>   my nose neither. Nothing that is so, is so.
> SEBASTIAN   I prithee vent thy folly somewhere else,
>   Thou know'st not me.
> FESTE   Vent my folly! He has heard that word of
>   some great man, and now applies it to a
>   fool. Vent my folly! I am afraid this great
>   lubber the world will prove a cockney. I
>   prithee now ungird thy strangeness, and
>   tell me what I shall 'vent' to my lady. Shall
>   I 'vent' to her that thou art coming?
> SEBASTIAN   I prithee, foolish Greek, depart from me.
>   There's money for thee: if you tarry longer
>   I shall give worse payment. (4.1.1–19)

Despite his own habitual resistance to accepting an externally imposed identity, questions of identity are at the root of all the performing services Feste offers, each of which appears to be specifically geared towards enhancing or transcending the personhood of those he serves, and which are able to take the form of either sickness or cure. For Olivia, 'addicted to a melancholy' (2.5.192), Feste provides palliative care in accordance with the early modern belief in the benefit of laughter as a means to restore the body's humoural balance.[45] This ability, however, is clearly secondary to the clown's 'excellent breast' (2.3.18), a superb singing voice he uses to fashion delicate aesthetic experiences that complement the dispositions of his listeners, as Tiffany Stern's essay in this volume discusses. Feste sings four songs in the play, each one perfectly tailored to its audience, and which, taken together, reveal an uncanny ability to anticipate and give external shape to their inner feelings, leading them to a place where they are able to experience a purer, more abstract version of the impulses they believe compel them. 'Would you have a love-song, or a song of good life?' (2.3.34), he asks Sir Toby and Sir Andrew during their drunken carousal, before transporting both on what

Sir Toby dubs his 'contagious breath' (2.3.52), a phrase that
invokes the peril of the plague in its ability to enter into them 'by
the nose' (2.3.54) and hasten them away. As with Orsino who finds
that 'Come away, come away death' 'did relieve my passion much'
(2.4.5), thereby reconfirming him as a lover that needs soothing,
Feste scripts hypostasized identities for his listeners where they
might be re-affirmed in their fictional idea of themselves.[46]

Feste's facility in this area is most keenly displayed, of course,
in his harrowing of Malvolio, a stillborn exorcism which makes
the most overt statement about the uses and logic of comedy
in *Twelfth Night*, as it distills perfectly the way in which Feste's
comedy creates a comic plane beyond the body that opens up
into fantasy and the loss of subjectivity. Questioning Malvolio
imprisoned in his dark room, we witness a sustained encounter
between two false realities, whose focus is the voice. As a set comic
piece, the exchange requires quoting in its entirety:

FESTE	Fie, thou dishonest Satan – I call thee by the most modest terms, for I am one of those gentle ones that will use the devil himself with courtesy. Sayst thou that house is dark?
MALVOLIO	As hell, Sir Topaz.
FESTE	Why, it hath bay windows transparent as barrica-does, and the clerstories toward the south-north are as lustrous as ebony, and yet complainest thou of obstruction?
MALVOLIO	I am not mad, Sir Topaz, I say to you, this house is dark.
FESTE	Madman, thou errest. I say, there is no darkness but Ignorance, in which thou art more puzzled than the Egyptians in their fog.
MALVOLIO	I say, this house is as dark as ignorance, though ignorance were as dark as hell; and I say, there was never man thus abused. I

	am no more mad than you are. Make the trial of it in any constant question.
FESTE	What is the opinion of Pythagoras concerning wild fowl?
MALVOLIO	That the soul of our grandam might haply inhabit a bird.
FESTE	What think'st thou of his opinion?
MALVOLIO	I think nobly of the soul, and no way approve his opinion.
FESTE	Fare thee well. Remain thou still in darkness. Thou shalt hold th'opinion of Pythagoras ere I will allow of thy wits, and fear to kill a woodcock lest thou dispossess the soul of thy grandam. Fare thee well. (4.2.31–60)

The flat-out denial of the evidence of the senses and the barrage of questions in which Malvolio's only option is to be wrong create a space of dissociative disembodiment that leaves Malvolio fighting to retain a grip on his identity. The reference to Pythagoras contains a further clue as to Feste's comic practice, as the concept of metempsychosis – the posthumous transmigration of the soul to another body – serves as a fairly useful description of the way Feste conceives of joking. For him, it is not that there are inherently comic subjects or modes – a 'festive' comedy, say – but rather, like the cheverel glove, anything has the potential to be inhabited by the comic should it choose to alight there in the fluid and heterodox movement of context. Rather than focusing our attention back on conventionally 'festive' themes such as the body, the rhythm of the seasons, and the therapeutic importance of pleasure, therefore, the professional comedian in *Twelfth Night* repeatedly places obstacles in the way of such a turn.

CHAPTER SEVEN

New Directions: Inverted Commas around the 'Fun': Music in *Twelfth Night*

TIFFANY STERN

As its title heralds, Shakespeare's *Twelfth Night* is a festival play: the Twelfth Night of Christmas, the eve of Epiphany, was a time for feasting, holiday, the exchange of gifts and the playing of music. But it was also the end of Christmas. The topsy-turvy period of misrule that begun on All Hallows' Eve, when a King or Lord of Misrule was appointed to oversee the Christmas festivities, was, on Epiphany, celebrated one last time and concluded; holiday yielded to the cares of daily life once more.

At court, Christmas ended on Twelfth Night with feasts accompanied by a series of farewell revels. Masques – entertainments consisting of music, singing, dancing and acting, embellished with elaborate costumes and stage designs – were typically mounted on Twelfth Night, perhaps because their music added poignancy to the occasion, perhaps because they were events in which the whole court could participate. In the time of Henry IV, 'on Twelfth night according to his custome, was a stately Maske of Knights and Ladies, with solemne Daunsing and a most Magnificent Banquet';[1] in the time of Richard III, however, 'the Dukes of *Amerle*, of *Surrey*, and of *Exeter*, [...] made great provision for a Maske to be presented before the King upon Twelfth night'; it was called off when news reached the king that 'the foresaid Lords & gentlemen had made a solemne conjuration to kill [the king] in the said Mask.'[2] How often Twelfth Night masques continued to be mounted in the time of Queen Elizabeth and King James is not clear; suggestions are, though, that the tradition continued unabated. A good scattering of printed masques witness performance on Twelfth Night. Thomas Campion publishes 'The discription of a maske, presented before the Kinges Majestie at White-Hall, on Twelfth Night' in 1607;[3] *The Maske of Flowers* was '*Presented by the gentlemen of Graies-Inne, at the court of White-hall, in the Banquetting House, upon Twelfe night, 1613*';[4] Ben Jonson's *Time Vindicated to Himselfe* was shown 'at Court on Twelfth Night. 1622';[5] Jonson's *Neptune's Triumph* was 'celebrated in a Masque at the Court on the Twelfth night 1623.'[6] Twelfth Night, then, was an occasion that mingled celebration and misrule with regret at the end of the holidays, often displayed through scenery, poetry and music, the combined arts of the masque.

What does this say of Shakespeare's *Twelfth Night*? The piece is obviously a play, not a masque; it does, however, flirt with masque elements – music in particular – and is often thought to have been, when first performed, a Twelfth Night masque-substitute. Critics, in the wake of Leslie Hotson, generally assume it is the entertainment, not recorded by name, that the Lord Chamberlain's Men, Shakespeare's company, mounted for Queen Elizabeth on Twelfth Night in 1601, when the royal guest of the evening had the telling name of Don Virginio Orsino.[7] A 1601 Twelfth Night performance would explain the play's title; the name of its hero Orsino; and the reason behind its musical homage to the masque form.

Yet if the title, *Twelfth Night*, is day-specific, why was it also used for Middle Temple performance on 2 February 1602 ('At our feast we had a play called Twelve Night', writes John Manningham), particularly when the play had a more generally applicable subtitle, *What You Will*?[8] The answer cannot be connected to the play's content, for the drama's story takes place over at least three months ('Three months', says Orsino about Viola, 'this youth hath tended upon me', 5.1.94); none of these months even obviously occur during the winter season.[9] That means that the words 'Twelfth Night' must say something specific about the play that is not linked to content – something, then, about its 'feel.'

Looked at in terms of atmosphere, 'Twelfth Night' qualities do seem to imbue the play irrespective of day of performance. The theme of reversal and 'misrule' is a consistent *Twelfth Night* topic, from the girl who dresses as a boy to the Puritan who dresses as a fun-loving dandy. The feasting that typified Twelfth Night celebrations, too, is present in the drama, both through the drunken revelling of Sir Toby Belch and his cronies, and through poetic analogies that conflate music with food. Most crucial, however, is the fact that, from the opening of the play onwards, music, often in the form of sophisticated and plaintive songs with telling lyrics ('art songs'), is employed repeatedly. *Twelfth Night*, originating, perhaps, in Twelfth Night celebrations, continues to negotiate with Twelfth Night qualities whenever it is performed; its themes relate to the 'farewell to Christmas' masques that combined revelry with regret.

This discussion will look at the role of music in *Twelfth Night*, exploring the dose of melancholy it often adds to the play's festivity. It will investigate the three different forms in which music is employed in the play: as song, which combines melody and poetry – a tension that has its own additional resonance; as wordless instrumental performance, where music contributes to the play's sound; and as verbal description, where music is part of the play's text. Considering traces of an earlier version of *Twelfth Night*, perhaps closer to the play's probable Twelfth Night performance, it will ask what *Twelfth Night* gained and lost as it moved away from its point of origin.

Song Lyrics

Much has been made of the importance of songs in *Twelfth Night*, but only the snatches sung by Sir Toby and his crowd are integrated into the dialogue of the play – and for those characters, words, rather than tune, are of primary importance: 'My lady's a Cathayan, we are politicians, Malvolio's a Peg-o'-Ramsey, and "Three merry men be we"' sings, or says, Sir Toby to Sir Andrew and Feste. 'Am not I consanguinious? Am I not of her blood?

Tilly-vally, lady! "There dwelt a man in Babylon, lady, lady'"
(2.3.71–4). This passage mingles 'Peg-o'-Ramsey' from a popular
ballad, 'Three merrie men' from George Peele's play *Old Wives'
Tale* and 'There dwelt a man' from a religious-themed ballad.
These snippets, however, function to construct an argument
showing that Olivia ('my lady') and Malvolio ('Peg-o-Ramsey')
are unlike the three revellers present ('three merry men'), though
Sir Andrew would make an ideal husband for Olivia ('There dwelt
a man' is a ballad about the husband of the biblical Susanna).[10]
Melody for this interchange may or may not be present; if it is,
then single musical phrases gesture towards songs that will not be
completed.

Later, when Sir Andrew repeatedly insists that the others join
him in a 'catch' – a 'round' in which successive characters sing the
same words and tunes at different times, creating harmony – it is
words, again, to which attention is drawn:

SIR ANDREW   Begin, fool. It begins 'Hold thy peace.'
FESTE   I shall never begin if I hold my peace.
SIR ANDREW   Good, i'faith. Come, begin.
          They sing the catch.
          Enter Maria.
                    (2.3.65–7)

A catch that begins 'Hold thy peace' survives in a couple of
forms, one from 1580 and one from 1609, for both of which text
is supplied; the 'Hold thy peace' song sung here, which is almost
certainly one of them, will have consisted either of the words
'Hold thy peace, and I prethee hold thy peace, thou knave' or the
simpler 'Hold thy peace, thou knave.'[11] Either way, given that the
song is a catch, 'thou knave' will resound repeatedly on stage,
each character calling the other characters 'knave' and being
called 'knave' in turn, depicting the three to one another and all
three to the audience. 'Hold thy peace', also repeatedly sung, is
ironically the phrase that wakes up the household, as well as the
joke that precedes the song. Thus the song celebrates the play's

language and the foolishness of its clowns, while securing music's role as disruptive, discomforting and the opposite of 'peace.'

Awakened by 'Hold thy peace', Malvolio, who arrives to castigate the singers, is then twitted, also through the medium of song snippets. Yet once again, it is verbal content that is important. Robert Johnson's popular song 'Farewell, dear heart' is turned by Sir Toby and Feste into part of a dialogue exchange; its words progress from 'Farewell', which is what Malvolio wants to bid Sir Toby, to 'Shall I bid him go', which is what Sir Toby wants to bid Malvolio (2.3.102–3). That the real song is about a forlorn lover is an extra-textual irony that the audience may realize but that seems to pass the singers by. Collectively, then, the revellers' use of song reminds the audience to think about the words of lyrics and to be alert to meanings beyond those heard by the actual characters. As music, however, these snatched passages eternally deny what they seem to promise – the opportunity to listen to or sing along with known popular tunes.

It is, however, the three full songs in the play, sung by Feste, which are regularly written about. Yet unlike Desdemona's 'Willow Song' in *Othello*, which is later echoed by Emilia as she dies, or indeed, unlike the snippets sung by Sir Toby and his friends, the substance of these *Twelfth Night* songs is not acknowledged in the play. Their narratives stand aside from the text they are in, suggesting that they may be in the play through – or because of – circumstance as well as design.

Looking at the sole text that survives for *Twelfth Night*, that in the Folio (1623), it will be visibly clear that Feste's songs stand apart from the dialogue. All his songs are printed in italics, for instance, though the dialogue is in roman type; one of them, 'Come Away', additionally has a heading 'The Song.' Italics and a 'The Song' heading alike supply information about the manuscript behind the surviving printed text. Both were used by playwrights and prompters to signal passages that were to be extracted by a scribe on to a piece of paper that could be brought on stage; the manuscript of *Twelfth Night* behind the Folio might have contained this information. Alternatively, the manuscript behind the Folio was a performance one, consisting of dialogue alone; the songs, with their separate information, may not have been in the actual play-text, but handed over to the printing house as separate stage documents to be (re)integrated into the printed play. Whatever has happened has ramifications for what the songs are. As separate and separable documents, 'resting' in the play but not necessarily integral to it, they might originate in Shakespeare's drama, but need not; they might have been chosen by Shakespeare, or added by others at some later stage; they might be authorial, or by actors, composers, poets or other playwrights.[12]

Eighteenth- and nineteenth-century writers, certainly, assumed the play's songs had no connection to the drama in which they were placed. Of 'O Mistress Mine', William Chappell wrote that 'in accordance with the then prevailing custom [...] an old song, [was] introduced into the play';[13] of 'Come Away', Howard Staunton observed that 'the privilege of the singer' was 'whenever the business of the scene required a song, to introduce one of his own choice';[14] and, of the final song, 'When That I Was and a Little Tiny Boy', George Steevens maintains:

> It is scarce credible, that after [Shakespeare] had cleared his stage, he should exhibit his Clown afresh, and with so poor a recommendation as this song, which is utterly unconnected with the subject of the preceding comedy. I do not therefore hesitate to call the nonsensical ditty before us, some buffoon actor's composition, which was accidentally tacked to the Prompter's copy of *Twelfth-Night*, having been casually subjoined to it for the diversion.[15]

Though current criticism of the songs views them as crucial to the drama, it should be borne in mind that the relevance they have to the text may arise simply from the fact that they are (now) there.

What can be said of the songs collectively is that, however tenuous their connection to the play, they seem likely to relate to one another. Each is sung in the first person; each has a narrative;

each is 'male' and is voiced by Feste. That gives the impression
that the three separate songs may even be about the same fictional
person; perhaps they supply passages of one man's story traced
across the progress of his life as well as the drama. In the first,
'O Mistress Mine', a man begs his mistress not to wander but
to stay and 'kiss me' (2.3.49); in the second 'Come Away', a man
demands a funeral because 'I am slain by a faire cruel maid'
(2.4.53); and in the last, 'When that I was and a little tiny boy',
a man compares his carefree childhood with his subsequent life,
the downturn of which seems to have happened when 'I came,
alas, to wive' (5.1.387). As one single narrative, the songs link a
man's decline in life with his relationship to a woman; as separate
narratives, the songs connect love with frustration and despair.
Creating the play emotionally, the songs, with their bleak outlook,
undercut the drama's comedy.

'O Mistress Mine', performed for Sir Toby and Sir Andrew
during their evening of drunken revelry, is Feste's first song.
Having asked Sir Toby and Sir Andrew whether they would prefer
a 'love song' or 'a song of good life', he is, supposedly, supplying
the first. Yet the words he sings are not about the wonders of love
fulfilled: though in the first verse a maiden is told not to roam but
to stay for her true love, in the second, she is reminded to kiss her
lover now, as 'youth's a stuff will not endure' (2.3.50). This is a
carpe diem ('seize the day') song, warning the listener to relish the
fleeting moments love supplies as decay and death are around the
corner. How, then, can the song be interpreted *in situ*?

Though the song is notionally sung for Sir Toby and Sir
Andrew, neither are its subjects or objects: they are not female,
young and coy; the people they are pursuing are, in Sir Andrew's
case, the strong-minded, lengthily mourning Olivia, and in Sir
Toby's, the knowing trickster Maria. Perhaps, as John Ford
suggests, the song is designed to parody Sir Toby and Sir
Andrew's delusions about the connection between love and the
good life.[16] Or perhaps, as David Lindley argues, the song is
designed to persuade Sir Andrew that he may yet be successful in
his suit for Olivia; if that is the case, Feste, in singing it, chooses to

promote Sir Toby's purpose.[17] Yet as the song concerns a woman's
unreadiness to commit to her true love, it may not be directed
to its fictional listeners at all. To Auden, the song's ironies
overwhelm the play, but are audible to the theatre audience only:

> True love certainly does not plead its cause by telling the
> beloved that love is transitory; and no young man, trying
> to seduce a girl, would mention her age […] These lines
> are the voice of aged lust, with a greed for possession that
> reflects the fear of its own death. Shakespeare forces this
> awareness on our consciousness by making the audience to
> the song Sir Toby and Sir Andrew, a couple of seedy old
> drunks.[18]

It might at least make better sense to see this as a song for the
actual audience who can apply the text to Olivia, a lady who needs
to put aside her grief and confront love again. John Hollander
argues for this notion – though it would be hard to claim that
Olivia is actually the song's subject: she certainly is not (yet)
'roving.'[19] Nevertheless, Olivia fits the subject matter more clearly
than anyone else; the true love that the lady is told to wait for,
who 'can sing both high and low' (2.3.39), may, then, refer either
to a boy with a voice breaking (the player of Viola, perhaps), or
to the combination of Viola–Sebastian, who can sing high in one
persona and low in another. In that sense, too, the song would
engage in *Twelfth Night*'s themes of transitoriness and reversals.
Yet the range of people it might be about or to whom it might
be applied should give us pause. Perhaps it really is a song that
is simply placed in the text, an interlude more important for
musicality than words at all.

'Come Away' is a song whose tune has already been played
during the scene, so its melody will be familiar, allowing, when
it is sung, for concentration on the words. Its story tells of
a melancholy lover who wants a shroud, a black coffin and a
friendless funeral because a cruel woman will not accept his love.
Surprisingly brutal, the song concentrates on the suicidal misery

of the abandoned man and, by extension, the viciousness of the woman who has rejected him. Feste may be using this text to poke fun at Orsino's posturing, but the ditty is bitter against the loving possibilities celebrated in the play. Again, though, the audience for the song is not entirely clear. Orsino, who has asked for the song, may be imagined thinking it depicts him and his unfulfilled love for Olivia; Viola may be imagined seeing it as a reflection about her unfulfilled love for Orsino – or about the love she has for the brother she thinks is dead. Yet when the song is over, Feste makes a telling comment about Orsino's habit of changing. Calling Orsino's mind 'a very opal' and suggesting he choose to wear 'changeable taffeta', Feste accuses Orsino of inconstancy (2.4.73–4). Perhaps he has observed that Orsino is now in love with Viola/Cesario; perhaps he does not believe Orsino is in love with anyone. Whatever he means, the song had portrayed eternal suffering because of fixed and permanent love – but Orsino's love is, as Feste seems to point out, already changing its object. As before, the meaning, then, may be for the theatre audience rather than the fictional characters, for the song's refrain of death recalls the 'dying fall' that Orsino so enjoyed. Auden is, once more, insightful here:

> Outside the pastures of Eden, no true lover talks of being slain by a fair, cruel maid, or weeps over his own grave. In real life, such reflections are the day-dreams of self-love, which is never faithful to others [...] It would be painful enough for [Viola] if the man she loved really loved another, but it is much worse to be made to see that he only loves himself, and it is this insight which at this point Voila has to endure.[20]

The final song sung by Feste, 'When That I Was and a Little Tiny Boy', appears to be some kind of epilogue to the play. It is placed after the story ends and concludes by observing that 'our play is done' and promising to 'strive to please you every day' (5.1.398). But what is the relationship between the song and the rest of the text? There need be none, of course, and indeed the song has sometimes been thought to be a post-play jig,[21] or a non-play-specific nonsense song with a refrain in which the crowd could join.[22] Both these explanations cast the song as merry or meaningless – perhaps even a drinking song (a 'song of good life' [2.3.34]) like – or, in fact, the one – Feste had offered to Sir Toby and Sir Andrew.

But is the song merry? The narrative considers four phases of a humble life: childhood, manhood, marriage and (drunken) sleep. Adult life is described cynically – the narrator marries 'alas' and ends his story sleeping near 'tosspots' (5.1.393). Here again, then, the singer partly shapes what the song is. The spokesman is a clown; the song he sings, though savage, could be seen as lighthearted burlesque or bleak premonition. Maybe this is even Feste's autobiography, in which case the 'foolish thing', which in childhood was 'but a toy', but that comes to have more meaning later on, might be the fool's bauble, or the sexual prowess for which it stands (5.1.381).[23] When, in old age, the subject collapses into his 'beds' without a partner, the drunkenness of later life would, then, be substituting for sex (5.1.391). According to this reading, it is meaningful that the song closes on the line 'that's all one', for that recalls the lines in which Feste dismissed the part he had had in fooling the imprisoned Malvolio: it was 'all one' (5.1.364).

Alternatively, the song is simply a further disconsolate story told through music, setting the seal on the undercutting process that songs have performed throughout. Its regret at marriage certainly gives a dismal cast to the end of a marriage-bound comedy; its burden of 'hey ho', the sound said to be made by a sigh, and 'the rain it raineth every day', which maintains that the only depressing certainty in life is continual rainfall, is resigned at best. The chorus collectively recalls '*Oh the winde, the weather, and the raine*', said in Tourneur's *Laugh and Lie Downe* to be the song that is to be sung in 'purgatorie.'[24] According to this reading, during the progress of the song, the fool, then the acting company, and finally the audience are left to the wind and the rain, and the company's hope to please the audience is pitched against despair. Whatever is the case, the play is not resolved in simple harmony, for the song's narrative is brutish, or melancholy – which seems intentional in a play that is obsessed with the emotional effects of music.

As ever, though, the issue with which this section began needs to be borne in mind. The songs may have ended up in the text after original composition, rather than been placed there. That does not mean that we should not interpret them, of course, for they are where they are, and their nature will naturally affect the play that surrounds them. It should be recalled, however, that their meaning may be contingent rather than elemental.

Tune

Unlike any other Shakespeare drama, *Twelfth Night* both starts and ends with music – it is framed by melody. Indeed, as Orsino's first words tell the musician[s] to 'play on' (1.1.1), the audience must already have been listening to music by the time Orsino begins to speak. That means that a player or players may have been visible on stage performing before the drama started. If this is the case, 'music' has appealed to the audience's senses of listening – and sight – before it has been placed in the drama. Alternatively, as no entrance or exit is given to a musician or musicians, the sound of the tune may have emanated either from 'within' the tiring house or, if there were one, from the music room – generally a curtained space 'above'; heard rather than seen, such music may have enchanted and intrigued the audience without revealing its source. Whatever is the case, spectators have experienced music before they meet Orsino, and they may well be surprised that the tune they thought preceded the play is also in fact part of it. As the play begins and we realize that Orsino has been hearing and responding to the same music as us, we are made to identify with Orsino, our shared experiences conjoining our fact with his fiction.

Yet our pleasure and shared experience is brought to a sudden stop when Orsino turns against the tune that is playing: 'Enough,

no more' (1.1.7). In mid-tune, his – and so our – experience is,
in David Schalkwyk's phrase, 'curtailed, in a crisis akin to coitus
interruptus.'[25] Now we identify with Orsino in a different way: the
sexual frustration experienced by Orsino and expressed through
music is conveyed to and into us through melody denied. Music
is crucial to the start of this play: the play's emotional sensa-
tions of pleasure and frustration began with and through music
well before the words have started. However, what the opening
melody actually is has not been identified, any more than its
instrument or instruments are known. Of the music itself, all we
know comes from Orsino's description of it: that it has a repeated
'strain', a melodic movement heard more than once, and a 'dying
fall', a melodic falling cadence (1.1.4). Some musicologists have
proposed contemporary early modern tunes that have these
features: Orlando Gibbons' 'The Lord of Salisbury his Pavin',
suggests E. W. Naylor;[26] John Dowland's 'Lachrimae Pavan',
suggests Philip Gordon.[27] Orsino may, of course, be listening to a
new tune altogether, though the notion of his being entranced by
a tune familiar to the audience is appealing. As for instrument(s),
the fullest theatrical music of the time tended to be played on a
mixed or 'broken' consort – usually four instruments consisting of
a mixture of woodwind and strings. Bringing a band of musicians
on and offstage during important textual moments, however, is
unlikely: if a mixed consort were used, they are particularly likely
not to have been visibly staged. If a single instrument, a lute,
cithern or viol, were used, however, a musician may have entered
and played on stage, for the sound of a single stringed instrument
travels better if it is not muffled from 'within.' There might, too,
be a theatrical impetus for seeing a lone musician walk offstage in
dejection when his or her music is no longer required.

The second piece of instrumental music is played when, at
the start of 2.4., Orsino demands 'Give me some music'; shortly
afterwards, as the stage direction makes clear, *'Music plays'* (2.4.1;
2.4.13). Again, what instrument or instruments are responsible
for the music is unclear; again, no entrance is provided for an
actual musician. As with the opening piece, too, the music itself

is unknown. It, however, can be more clearly defined: it is music to 'Come away', which Orsino asks the musicians to 'play [...] the while' until Feste can be found to sing the words (2.4.13). The music with which, in the fiction, both Orsino and Viola/Cesario are familiar seems to aid and perhaps provoke the conversation the two then have about love. Perhaps this is the tune that, subliminally, makes Orsino fall in love with Viola, even while describing what is putatively his love for Olivia. Underscoring the conversation between the two, it brings the audience not intellectually but emotionally into Orsino's – and Viola's – sensual world. When its words are later heard, however, the spectators may be shocked or alienated: they and the characters have been emotionally swayed by what turns out to be 'Come away [...] death', a song more about funerals than about love (2.4.50).

The rest of the music in the play is performed as an accompaniment to songs. As ever, the instruments for it are unknown, as are many of the tunes. We know that Feste plays the tabor – a small drum that was often played together with a pipe – for in 3.1 Viola and he have byplay on the subject: 'Save thee, friend, and thy music. Dost thou live by thy tabor?' 'No sir, I live by the church' (3.1.1–3). It is just possible, then, that Feste beats a rhythm to the songs that he sings in the play, which would give them a heartiness not generally imagined, that might itself highlight ironies in the text. Yet as Feste largely sings sophisticated art songs, he is more likely to have accompanied himself on a melodic instrument – there was a strong association between art songs and stringed music, and Robert Armin, the company fool who almost certainly performed Feste, seems to have been proficient at playing the lute and/or cittern.[28] Perhaps Feste's tabor accompanies his songs with Sir Toby, leaving the lute/cittern for Orsino, and visually dividing the singing according to which of the two groups Feste is entertaining.

Music to the song 'O Mistress Mine' is sometimes said to be extant. The composer Thomas Morley published a tune, without words, to which he gave the title 'O Mistress Mine' in 1599. As he and Shakespeare were living near one another in Bishopsgate at the time, Morley is sometimes said to have been asked to compose the play's music. The fact that Morley wrote another melody called 'Mistress Mine', however, should give us pause: the words are highly conventional and the composer need not have had a specific lyric in mind for either tune. Indeed, he may not even have been the composer of 'O Mistress Mine' in the first place. The melody published by that name in Morley's *Consort Lessons* of 1599 is also recorded in the manuscript *Fitzwilliam Virginal Book* (c. 1619), where it is said to have been composed by William Byrd.[29] More problematic still, however, is the fact that a seventeenth-century inventory gives the tune an expanded title, 'O Mistress Mine I Must', thus implying different lost words to which the tune applies.[30] A musical commonplace book gathered by John Gamble gives the tune a different accompanying text altogether, by Thomas Campion, 'Long have mine eyes gazed with delight.'[31] As Shakespeare's words do not easily fit 'Morley's' tune – the first two lines of the stanza have to be repeated to make the words fit, which is not an Elizabethan device – the melody probably has nothing to do with *Twelfth Night*.[32] We are reliant, then, on extracting effect from words while imagining what music might have done to them.

For the play's other music, the snatches of text sung by the revellers, some tunes survive. Robert Johnson's 'Farewell, Dear Heart', used to annoy Malvolio, was published in 1600 and will have been a strikingly up-to-date occurrence in the play. Its tune, which is constructed as a series of musical ascents and 'falls', may even double as the tune at the start of the play. If that is the case, then Orsino is linked to the world of fools by musical analogy. Perhaps, however, the tune simply provides another example of a 'dying fall', emphasizing the play's underlying theme of melancholy through music.

Speech

That leaves us with the little we do actually have: the depiction of music *verbally* in the play, for music in *Twelfth Night* is important not just aurally but as part of the text. It is, for instance, hinted at in the vocabulary of the play itself, which is set in what Bruce Smith calls 'Il-lyre-ia', a land that encloses a lyre or musical harp within its name;[33] it stars 'Viol-a', a heroine who encloses the six-stringed instrument, the viol or 'viola-da-gamba', within her soubriquet – the reference to Sir Andrew playing 'o'th' viol-de-gamboys' (1.3.23–4) may exist to point the parallel. Music as text is elemental to meaning in *Twelfth Night*.

Music is consequently part of characterization. It is not a new observation to say that characters' approach to music is as revealing about themselves as it is about tune. But character in *Twelfth Night* is also complicated through music. Sir Toby Belch desires, and illustrates, the carnivalesque side of music and general revelry. He learns that Sir Andrew can 'cut a caper' in a galliard – a popular dance – and has 'the back-trick simply as strong as any man in Illyria' (1.3.115–16); he exploits this information to make his friend literally dance to his tune – 'let me see thee caper. Ha, higher! Ha, ha, excellent' (1.3.131–2). The only dancing in the play is ludicrous and perhaps has something of the antimasque about it (though the habit of preceding a masque with an antimasque was not formalized until 1609); it shows that Sir Andrew is dupe to Sir Toby, that both men are clowns, and that music for the two men will be a site of comedy.

As in other Shakespearean dramas, hating music is suspect. Malvolio describes the singing of Sir Toby, Sir Andrew and Feste bitterly, asking them why they have chosen, late at night, 'to gabble like tinkers' and 'squeak out […] coziers' catches' (2.3.82–3, 85). He may be being precious about the quality of the revellers' singing or their music, of course, but this is, in its moment, a character statement that later contributes to another of the play's Twelfth Night reversals. Towards the latter half of the play, forced into yellow-stockings and obliged to smile constantly in a misguided attempt to woo Olivia, the music-hater will say or sing a line not just out of a popular song, but out of a song thought to be by the former playhouse clown Tarlton: 'please one, and please all' (3.4.22).[34] Malvolio will unconsciously reveal that he has now taken on the clown's mantle, showing he has truly become the antithesis of his actual self.

Approach to music, in particular, is generally said to delineate Orsino. This is because he and music are introduced together, his poetry accompanying but perhaps also drowning out the music that it is notionally extolling. He is often said to be in love with music, and sometimes to be in love with love, because he asks for 'excess of' music/love – but he is more wayward than that. Opening by drawing a parallel between music, appetite and love, Orsino actually maintains that he wants to be not delighted, but nauseated by music, so that his 'appetite' for it, like his appetite for food, may be glutted:

> If music be the food of love, play on,
> Give me excess of it, that surfeiting,
> The appetite may sicken and so die. (1.1.1–3)

In the beginning, then, Orsino hopes to be repulsed by music and so cured of his love. Alert to the tune's eroticism, its 'dying fall' that 'came', says Orlando pointedly, 'o'er mine ear', he reveals himself to be, against his will, enraptured rather than sickened by what he hears (1.1.4–5). No sooner has that new emotion overtaken him, however, than his delight in it really does cease; he is not nauseated so much as bored by the taste: ''Tis not so sweet now as it was before' (1.1.8).

Joining Orsino in his house, Viola (dressed as Cesario) mimics not just Orsino's interest in music but also his interest in the close connection between music and death. She would, she relates, create funeral songs were she unhappy in love (1.5.259–60). Later, talking to Orsino about 'Come away, come away, death' she describes it as giving an 'echo to the seat / Where love is throned' (2.4.20–1). Through this Viola perhaps reveals that she and Orsino are psychologically compatible, sharing a sickness that the two can cure or indulge together, though she may simply show that she is cravenly prepared to become the person Orsino wants her to be.

It is, however, Feste, the singer, who is most strongly depicted through his connection to music – and yet his attitude is the hardest to determine. Feste's name descends from the Latin for 'feast': he, of all characters, should be the embodiment of Twelfth Night revelry. In a sense he is. Not confined to one social group or one set of people, his audience in the play is everyone: he sings in Olivia's house for the revellers, in Orsino's house for Orsino and Cesario, and at the play's end for us. Yet his songs, conflating love and death, may seem to reflect or even dictate Orsino's attitude. Feste's own death-fascination is pointedly highlighted in his musical conversation with Sir Toby: 'But I will never die', sings Sir Toby, a line from Johnson's 'Farewell Dear Heart', to be answered by the Clown, in lines not in the original song, 'Sir Toby, there you lie' (2.3.99–100). Having imbued *Twelfth Night* with death in melodious form, Feste's final song, 'When That I Was and a Little Tiny Boy', leaves us with that theme too, depicting a man's progress through life, which obviously only has one end.

Yet Feste is, throughout, also darkly playful. His use of song to reveal home truths is particularly obvious when he sings 'Hey Robin' to the falsely imprisoned Malvolio. That song, with words by Thomas Wyatt, asks 'how thy lady does'; it draws vicious attention to the fact that Malvolio had imagined Olivia was in love with him (4.2.73). Using the fool's right to know things that other characters do not, Feste's songs seem repeatedly to goad his listeners. Feste's own interest, however, is presented as being largely linked to payment. For 'O Mistress Mine' he begs sixpence from Sir Toby and a 'testril' (another sixpence), from Sir Andrew; for 'Come Away' he gets payment of an unclear amount from Orsino, first for his 'pains', and then for his 'pleasure', because 'pleasure will be paid, one time or another' (2.4.66–70); for his tabor playing and general foolery, he coaxes 'expenses' from Viola (3.1.42). The suggestion is, then, that he sings not so much what is 'true' but what people will pay to hear. Ultimately, then, the uncomfortable implication is that what the characters, but also what we, the paying audience, most want in the midst of comedy are songs of loss and death. This of all reversals in *Twelfth Night* is most complex, for it puts Orsino's questionable concerns on to all of us and asks us whether what we desired was comedy at all.

Music and the Earlier *Twelfth Night*

Much of what has been said above is reliant on the relationship between the text of *Twelfth Night*, the words of its songs and the songs' singer, Feste. Yet, as has also been argued, the songs and even their singer may be a late entrant into the drama. Though only one version of *Twelfth Night* survives, published in the Folio in 1623, the text itself gives signs of significant revision. It is particularly disturbed around its musical moments in ways that suggest that some songs, which may or may not be these ones, were, in a lost form of the play, sung by Viola. When we first meet Viola washed ashore in Ilyria, she decides to serve Orsino. She instructs the captain to:

> present me as an eunuch to him.
> It may be worth thy pains, for I can sing,
> And speak to him in many sorts of music
> That will allow me very worth his service. (1.2.53–6)

Viola originally suggests, then, that she will go to Orsino's house as his musical eunuch. Yet in the text that survives, she is neither. This may, of course, be an over-reading of the comma after 'sing' – perhaps Viola is merely declaring that she will speak to Orsino in musically elegant rhetoric, though that leaves the 'eunuch' suggestion dangling. Yet throughout the play the suggestively musical timbre of Viola's voice is repeatedly described. Orsino talks, in a series of musical analogies, of Viola's 'pipe', her 'organ' and her 'sound' – 'thy small pipe / Is as the maiden's organ, shrill and sound' (1.4.32–3) – and even Malvolio remarks that Viola 'speaks very shrewishly' (1.5.154), which, though critical, draws attention to her voice's pitch. When Olivia prefers Viola's speech to 'music from the spheres' (3.1.108), and tells Orsino that his suit, after hearing Viola, would be like 'howling after music' (5.1.15), she not only praises Viola's voice but its musical nature. All of these may, of course, simply serve to link Viola to music, the sound that Orsino enjoys, except that Viola goes on to describe herself as a singer, telling Olivia how she would, if rejected by one she adored, burst into 'cantons' (songs) 'of contemned love / And sing them loud even in the dead of night' (1.5.259–60). Viola is a character with intensely musical speech; that speech, however, is described as having an outlet in singing.

That is further suggested by the start of Act 2 Scene 4. At the scene's opening, Orsino asks Viola, dressed as Cesario, a question concerning a song from the night before:

> Now good Cesario, but that piece of song,
> That old and antic song we heard last night.
> Methought it did relieve my passion much, [...]
> Come, but one verse. (2.4.2–7)

Orsino apparently asks Viola to sing one verse from a song they both heard the previous day. That also implies, of course, that Viola knows the song – which raises problems when Orsino later explains it to her as though she does not:

> Mark it Cesario, it is old and plain.
> The spinsters and the knitters in the sun,
> And the free maids that weave their thread with bones,
> Do use to chant it. It is silly sooth,
> And dallies with the innocence of love,
> Like the old age. (2.4.42–7)

Descriptions, like this one, of the song in Act 2 Scene 4, together with Orsino's earlier depiction of the song as 'old and antic' (2.4.3), insist collectively that the song that is to be sung will be plain, old fashioned, unsophisticated and of a kind adopted by spinsters; its description is said by Katharine Garvin to recollect the old French weaving songs known as 'chansons de toile.'[35]

'Come Away', the song then supplied, however, is none of these. It is a sophisticated, metrically elaborate conceit written in a strikingly up-to-date form: 'come away' songs were a popular modern genre, employed by Jonson and Campion as well as Shakespeare himself (or perhaps Middleton) in *Macbeth*; they were prized for their valedictory qualities and often used in plays to supply exits.[36] The song, then, is actually similar to the kind of ditty that Orsino, in the same scene, says that he does not like: 'light airs' full of 'recollected terms / Of these most brisk and giddy-paced times' (2.4.5–6). The scene appears to be set up for one song, but to feature another. Richmond Noble concludes from this that 'Viola's song was different to Feste's', and that what we have here is a description of Viola's lost song, followed by Feste's new one.[37] Given Viola's projected 'cantons' of 'contemned love' (1.5.259–60), of which 'Come Away' seems to be an example, however, it may be that we have Viola's original song in Feste's mouth and have lost Feste's original, humbler contribution to the scene.

Feste's entrance into the scene itself raises some further questions about the singing. After Orsino appears to request a song from Viola ('Come, but one verse', 2.4.7), he is corrected by Curio:

CURIO   He is not here, so please your lordship, that should sing it.
ORSINO   Who was it?
CURIO   Feste the jester, my lord. (2.4.8–11)

The suggestion that Orsino cannot remember whether his favourite boy or an elderly clown had sung to him, itself odd, is made stranger by Curio's explanation that Feste 'is about' in Orsino's house, and can be summoned to sing the song again (2.4.12). Feste is Olivia's fool, and there is no reason for him to be in Orsino's house. As Curio, moreover, speaks his part of this exchange in prose, though that section of the scene is otherwise in verse, his lines appear to be late additions to the drama.

Music-based revision, as this seems to be, was normal in

Shakespearean dramas and its traces often survive around songs to be sung by boys – for boys' voices have a habit of breaking. An obvious example is in *Cymbeline* when the two boys who initially intended to sing to Imogen suddenly decide, instead, to speak the words of the song to her:

> ARVERIGUS   Let us, Polydore, though now our voices
>   Have got the mannish crack, sing him to
>   th' ground [...]
> GUIDERIUS   I cannot sing. I'll weep, and word it with
>   thee [...]
> ARVERIGUS   We'll speak it then. (4.2.236–43)[38]

In this instance, voice-breaking appears to have brought the changes about. Perhaps something of a similar kind has happened to the boy actor of Viola. Both Dover Wilson and W. W. Greg conclude that the *Twelfth Night* text we have is a reworked version of the play, changed to reflect the fact that a singing Viola was no longer available.[39] As *Othello* was written shortly after *Twelfth Night* and assumes a singing Desdemona for the 'Willow Song', and as a second surviving version of *Othello* is revised so that Desdemona no longer sings, it seems reasonable to suggest that the company had a singing boy in around 1601–4 for whom several parts were written, and that plays were changed along song lines when he ceased to be able to sing.

That, of course, has a knock-on effect on the nature and characterization of Feste. Textual oddities in the play certainly suggest revision around what Feste is to do and consequently what his original role was in the play. Maria originally maintains that Feste will be the third eavesdropper on Malvolio ('I will plant you two – and let the fool make a third – where [Malvolio] shall find the letter', 2.3.161–162), though when it comes to it, the third eavesdropper is Fabian, a substitution that allows Feste to open the following scene, Act 3 Scene 1, by playing on his tabor. Perhaps Feste's role was reshaped as songs were taken from Viola and given to him; perhaps the character of Feste was rewritten when the company acquired for Robert Armin, a musical clown.

Were the songs for the original *Twelfth Night* performance, then, originally sung by Viola alone? Or were they once divided between Viola and Feste? Clearly, in a musical play, a musical boy who could directly indulge Orsino's love of melody would have made for a suggestive but different story. But would that version of Viola have sung the same songs that the text now contains, or different ones? If the songs were the same, then 'Cesario' would have voiced male songs about hard-hearted women – from the position of being a broken-hearted woman, a pleasing textual irony that would work well with the play's reversals. As, however, a verse with a chorus of 'hey ho, the wind and the rain', analogous to the final song in *Twelfth Night*, is sung by the Fool in *King Lear*, that ditty at least may be Armin-specific, used to show how variants of the same character can exist across numerous plays, including a tragedy and a comedy. Indeed, 'When That I Was' might even be the autobiography not of the fictional Feste, but its clown singer, Armin; the phrase, 'that's all one', also picks up Armin's guide to fooling, *A Nest of Ninnies* – 'all is one', he declares, 'and one all.' In his *Foole upon Foole*, he writes about weather and the current times in the same dour vain as the song: 'Why, do we not know that sometimes the ayre purgeth with uncomfortable sleete, as profitable raine? Are all Wits ever prosperous? no, times are leaden, dull: Age weakens, and Wits must needes decline'.[40]

Thus although in the *Twelfth Night* that survives all the songs are potentially ironized by their singer, a fool, the ironies supplied in the lost text may have been stronger or simply different. Perhaps Orsino was once lured by what he thought was sound, but was, if he dared notice it, the singer; or perhaps he was moved by the songs' fictional persona without immediately being conscious of the singer at all. On the other hand, the words of the songs may have been so different that the play had another nature altogether, just as *Henry V* with chorus (as it is in the Folio) and without (as it is in Quarto) are vividly different dramas.

Yet all this is, of course, to ignore a different lost quality of the play that this essay has repeatedly hovered around: the music of the songs themselves. Up to a point, whether these songs are male or female, sad or happy, ironic or frank, would have been dictated by their melodies: much about *Twelfth Night* is lost, not only because we lack the play's earlier version, but because of what we still lack in its current version: the tunes and the emotional content that they carried.

Conclusion

Framed by music, *Twelfth Night*, in the form in which we have it, details a musical progress as well as a narrative one. As befits the upside-down world of the title, however, song in the version of *Twelfth Night* that survives contradicts or questions the progress of the story it tells. The play's songs become ever more negative, which is telling in a world in which musical harmony or 'concord' was thought to reflect the divine resonance said to join planet to planet – the music of the spheres of which Olivia speaks of (3.1.108). Lack of harmony, 'discord' – the 'caterwauling' made by Sir Toby, Sir Andrew, and Feste, for instance – could seem to speak disorder not just locally but in the heavens (2.3.68). As a result of these connotations, the music of the play, with its 'dying falls' and its melancholy, has a serious effect. Given that 'hey ho, the wind and the rain' is an uncomfortable and uncomforting burden, the music seems to ensures the continued irresolution of the play's close.

In a play about misrule and upside-down worlds, however, music, whatever it is or was, helps constitute the 'Twelfth Night' nature of the play. It seems to ensure that the feel of Twelfth Night revels – their compulsion but also their regret – is maintained whenever the play is performed, with the result, too, that the play will always have, as Auden puts it, 'inverted commas round the "fun." '[41]

CHAPTER EIGHT

Learning and Teaching Resources

Peter Kirwan

Twelfth Night offers a world in which teaching and learning appear to happen spontaneously and reactively, in which the acquisition of new skills and knowledge occurs with surprising ease. Early in the play, the Captain tells us that he saw Sebastian 'Most provident in peril, bind himself / Courage and hope both teaching him the practice / To a strong mast that lived upon the sea' (1.2.11–13).[1] Much later, Antonio accuses Cesario (mistaken here for Sebastian) of a similarly quick self-education:

> [I] drew to defend him when he was beset,
> Where, being apprehended, his false cunning,
> Not meaning to partake with me in danger,
> Taught him to face me out of his acquaintance (5.1.81–4)

Learning is a natural reaction, based on survival and adaptation to events. The teachers are courage, hope and cunning; the learners are victims of circumstance. Learning is a passive activity, as Cesario later tells Olivia: 'The rudeness that hath appeared in me have I learned from my entertainment' (1.5.208–9). The responsibility for behaviour and action is deferred to the circumstance and environment that has occasioned it, and in this sense the student becomes a product of the abstract teacher. Jane Hwang Degenhardt's recent take on the contemporary geopolitical resonances of Illyria positions the figure of the castrated eunuch at a border point between a Christian West and Islamic East, in which Shakespeare seems to 'refuse the specificity of setting [...] Illyria is less a timeless and placeless setting devoid of meaning (as some critics have suggested) than a place packed with too many meanings.'[2] If the play deliberately stages a conflicted and ambiguous world into which an unweaponed youth is deposited, then it becomes more essential that educators provide tools to help navigate and confront at least some aspects, if not the whole of this world. This chapter offers an overview of a broad sample of the resources available to educators at all levels for shaping the physical, intellectual and social environments in which *Twelfth Night* is encountered, with a particular attention to accessible resources and recent criticism, and the possibilities for classroom discussion that emerge.

Pedagogy

While most educators would agree that knowledge tends to be much harder won than for the twins of *Twelfth Night*, there may yet be something to be said for Socrates' notion of *maieutic*, of 'giving birth' to knowledge that students already possess. As David L. Norton elucidates, *maieutic* 'tells us that the learner, as he [sic] originally presents himself, is not to be regarded as a blank page to be written upon, or a container to be filled, but as a potentiality to be fulfilled.'[3] Viola and Sebastian's protean adaptability emerges when the correct circumstances and environment tease it out of them. A growing trend in secondary and tertiary education prioritizes the creation of appropriate environments for learning, whether in the adoption of new online resources (the 'virtual learning environment') or in the creation of dynamic physical environments, as in the work of the CAPITAL Centre at the University of Warwick which, between 2007 and 2010, increasingly relocated undergraduate English literature teaching of Shakespeare to rehearsal rooms and theatrical studios. As Nicholas Monk, Carol Chillington Rutter, Jonothan Neelands and Jonathan Heron put it, 'Participants learn not only the detail of their academic speciality, but are also freed to discover for themselves an understanding of how to "be" in an increasingly complex world.'[4] In a play concerned in no small part with the encounter with new spaces, whose opening line in many productions (with the first two scenes transposed) is 'What country, friends, is this?' (1.2.1), attention to the environments that shape learning and experience seems particularly essential.

Twelfth Night is one of the most popular plays on undergraduate level courses; in Neill Thew's 2006 report only *Hamlet* and *The Tempest* were more widely taught in UK institutions.[5] The literature on teaching Shakespeare is too extensive to be covered in full here, but approaches that involve performance are now *de rigueur*, particularly at school level. Volumes such as Ronald E. Salomone and James E. Davis's *Teaching Shakespeare into the Twenty-First Century*[6] and Edward L. Rocklin's *Performance Approaches to Teaching Shakespeare*[7] offer excellent Shakespeare-specific overviews of pedagogic practice and possibility. *Twelfth Night* itself comes up several times in Rex Gibson's seminal *Teaching Shakespeare*, where the play is particularly an example for the teaching of dramatic character and development, Gibson finding Malvolio's experience a useful means to open up the work of the play. A typical exercise which asks students to 'select a character and invent a succession of tableaux to show his or her emotional / physical progress through the play' illustrates the exercise with a series of images of Malvolio at various stages of empowerment and ridicule in various productions.[8] A similar process informs Tim Crouch's one-man show for young audiences, *I, Malvolio* (2010), which retells the play through Malvolio's eyes and draws young audiences into questions of their own complicity in bullying practices.

Character exploration occurs frequently throughout the pedagogic literature on *Twelfth Night*, with the play's unusually even distribution of roles and memorable personalities providing a straightforward way to engage younger students with the issues and dynamics of the play. James Stredder approaches *Twelfth Night* with the 'Excuse Me Dance' activity, in which students cast as Olivia, Orsino, Viola, Andrew, Malvolio and Sebastian are all given a 'love monologue' made up of lines from the play and determine which part of their body shall 'lead' them as they perform, before beginning an artificial dance.[9] The purpose is to foreground Sebastian as the resolving influence of the play, entering into the 'dance' of characters and allowing matches to be made. Alexander Leggatt, meanwhile, finds rich pedagogic possibility in answering questions without an answer, arguing that 'in the reunion of the twins in *Twelfth Night* we may be so concentrated on the story conventions [...] and the general sense of wonder and resolution that we may not notice the details, some of which should give us pause.'[10] He suggests that asking students to consider questions such as why Viola and Sebastian both refer to their birthday as *Viola*'s birthday and the creation for the first time of an identity called 'Viola' within the play help turn the scene on its head, allowing for genuinely open-ended discussion of the play's ambiguities.

Another key strand of pedagogy sees the play being used as an exemplar to open students' minds to questions about broader social issues. Stephen Orgel argues for the foregrounding of Renaissance attitudes to male–male flirtation as a productive means of opening up questions in the classroom about gender identity, early modern stage practice and the implications of transvestism. He prioritizes the importance of costume in creating shared identity and offers a fascinating overview of classroom responses to the masculinity of 'Cesario' in modern televised productions of *Twelfth Night*.[11] Mario DiGangi couples the play with Middleton and Dekker's *The Roaring Girl* to illustrate contemporary anxieties over cross-dressing, gender and social relations, drawing attention to problems of historicizing ideas about sexuality.[12] The familiarity of *Twelfth Night*'s characters allows for an accessible entry point to the wider early modern canon and the exploration of identities and types across a range of works.

'A common recreation' (2.3.132): Genre and Intertexts

The decision of what other works to group *Twelfth Night* with inevitably shapes approaches to the play. For example, in 2012 the Royal Shakespeare Company performed the play in repertory with *The Comedy of Errors* and *The Tempest* as 'Shakespeare's Shipwreck Trilogy', placing emphasis on the staging of encounters with new/undiscovered spaces. However, later in the same year, the all-male Propeller theatre company toured the play alongside *The Taming of the Shrew*, placing clear focus on gender issues. *Twelfth Night*, as with its protean central characters, shifts identity according to the context in which it is encountered, and the generic environment is perhaps the most important for shaping the play's role within the classroom.

As William C. Carroll explains, *Twelfth Night* surfaces most often as an exemplar of Shakespeare's 'Romantic Comedies',[13] and Carroll views *Twelfth Night* as the culmination of the genre throughout Shakespeare's middle career. Linking the play with *The Comedy of Errors*, *As You Like It* and *The Two Gentlemen of Verona*, Carroll offers an extended reading of the generic tropes which are revisited in *Twelfth Night*: twins, shipwrecks and reunions, self-love, cross-dressed heroines, song and bawdy. Carroll argues that the romantic comedy is fuelled by desire and defined by its happy endings, before looking at the ways in which Shakespeare subverts this, particularly in *Twelfth Night*'s melancholic closing song. Malvolio's final words, whether in Crouch's play or in Michael D. Bristol's theoretical reading of the Battle between Carnival and Lent,[14] are an important provocation for classrooms debating the purpose of comedy.

Alexander Leggatt in *Shakespeare's Comedy of Love* similarly treats *Twelfth Night* as the last of the 'romantic comedies',[15] devoting a full chapter of his study to the play.[16] Leggatt considers the play to be a reversal of the simplicity of *As You Like It*, drawing attention to its compartmentalized structure and tighter logic. He shows especial interest in the questions of disguise and deceit in complicating the love games. Leggatt's still-significant chapter informs Terence Hawkes's work on the play in 'Comedy, Orality and Duplicity: *Twelfth Night*', which sees the play as an accumulation and consolidation of the early comedies.[17] Hawkes draws on Northrop Frye's structuralist definition of comedy as a story working through to its own logical end and integrates this with a Bakhtinian reading of Malvolio as the denier of carnival. This reading is also central to Bristol's work on the play, where Malvolio's 'Parthian shot' ensures that the comedy is never allowed entirely to win.[18] Phebe Jensen's 'Teaching Drama as Festivity' uses the play as part of a module that 'allows students to discover for themselves how dramatic activities [...] both shape and reflect the social, economic, and dramatic culture in which they are performed', and offers the question over whether the Lord of Misrule challenges or upholds traditional authority as a productive classroom debate.[19]

More recently, Janet Clare's 'The "Complexion" of *Twelfth Night*' considers the play as the last gasp of romantic comedy at a time when satire was beginning to dominate comedy.[20] Relating the play to Jonson's *Every Man in His Humour*, she argues that the play asserts its self-conscious performativity in response to the literariness of satirical comedy, while continuing to expand and develop the generic convention of romantic comedy. The critical consensus has remained on *Twelfth Night* marking the end of a particular generic movement, but Clare's work broadens its focus from the Shakespeare canon in isolation to consider how *Twelfth Night* responds to wider generic shifts.

Emma Smith's volume on *Shakespeare's Comedies* gathers important materials related to a broader discussion of Shakespearean comedy, linking *Twelfth Night* to Shakespeare's other comedies throughout.[21] *Twelfth Night* features most prominently in Valerie Traub's reprinted chapter 'The Homoerotics of Shakespearian Comedy',[22] which analyzes the nature of desire in relation to the boy player in this play and *As You Like It*. A similar connection is prioritized by Barbara Hodgdon in 'Sexual Disguise and the Theatre of Gender', which adds *The Two Gentlemen of*

Verona and *The Merchant of Venice* to the discussion,[23] opening up
a nuanced discussion of the different kinds of sexual ambiguity
offered by each play's instances of cross-dressing.

Leggatt's 2002 *Cambridge Companion to Shakespearean Comedy*
includes several other essays of interest to the student of *Twelfth
Night* that deliberately integrate discussion of the comedies
into broader thematic essays, making this an ideal volume for
conveners of courses on the comedies. Edward Berry's 'Laughing
at "Others" ' links Malvolio to Caliban and the Falstaff of *Merry
Wives* as figures isolated by mockery,[24] while Catherine Bates
uses the play as the conclusion to her chapter on 'Love and
Courtship',[25] which sees the play as illustrative of comedy's
use of comic misrule to reinforce rules of courtship. The play
also features prominently – again, at the end of a discussion of
Shakespeare's comedies – in Michael Mangan's *A Preface to
Shakespeare's Comedies 1594–1603*,[26] a more traditional volume
that situates the play with Elizabethan cultural history, focusing
specifically on structure and wordplay in the play's battle between
Carnival and Lent.

'I will read politic authors' (2.5.157): Critical Trends in the Classroom

Considering *Twelfth Night*'s insistence on wilfully misreading,
on exchanging texts that are misinterpreted (one is reminded of
the unrecorded but essential performance business in 5.1 that
prompts Olivia to take Malvolio's letter from Feste and pass it
to Fabian for a less 'mad' interpretation) and on deliberately
misconstruing opinion, there is something to be said for adopting
a playful approach to the critical texts that attempt to pin down
the play. This section considers some of the important trends
that expand the discussion of genre and carnival above: character,
sources, gender/sexuality and text/language.

More than most of the comedies, *Twelfth Night* has consistently
lent itself to approaches that deal with character, at school level
as in the above examples and beyond. More recently, attempts

have been made to distinguish a newer form of character study integrated in socio-historical contexts from an older romantic model. Graham Atkin, for example, links the myriad characters of the play to theories of the carnivalesque, the language of love and the figure of the stage wit.[27] Character is also the focus of Emma Fielding's short book in the *Actors on Shakespeare* series.[28] Fielding discusses her experience of playing Viola in the RSC's 1994 production, with particular attention to the possibilities for fusing theatricality with psychological realism. Classroom approaches that 'hot-seat' the play's characters and attempt to rationalize actions may be well established but are still productive means of engagement that can then be challenged and complicated with regard to types and role playing. The value of character also informs Tracy Irish's approach to her edition of the play for *The Shorter Shakespeare*,[29] a heavily abridged version for young people which links sections of the original text using a narration by an older version of the Sea Captain, utilizing a minor character as a aid to interpretation of the play as a whole.

Since 2000, several important collections of essays on *Twelfth Night* have been published, the excellent work of which can only be briefly recapped here. Bruce R. Smith's mammoth compilation *Twelfth Night: Texts and Contexts* draws together an impressive range of Renaissance sources for the play, both direct and contextual.[30] The volume ranges from Aristotle to Augustine Phillips, covering romance, music, sexuality, clothing/disguise, household economics, Puritan probity and clowning/laughter, as well as a full text of the play edited by David Bevington. Sonia Massai's *William Shakespeare's Twelfth Night: A Sourcebook* has a similar remit, gathering useful materials for teaching and interpreting the play.[31] The section entitled 'Contexts' raises the key issues and pulls together relevant contemporary documents on the intellectual and social concerns of the play. A longer middle segment covers critical and theatrical interpretations, drawing on a wide range of critics from across the centuries and leading up to more recent work on carnival and gender, as well as reviews of the play in performance. A useful third subdivision selects key passages for glossing and longer discussion, an invaluable resource for close-reading work. Massai's compendium is contemporaneous with John R. Ford's sole-authored *Twelfth Night: A Guide to the Play*, which offers a general guide covering text, sources, structure, themes, critical approaches and performance, the last a detailed overview of the play's stage and screen history.[32] Ford places particular focus on the social and theatrical performances within the play, linking them with attention to language, identity, gender and status.

James Schiffer's 2011 volume *Twelfth Night: New Critical Essays* is a wide-ranging collection attempting to situate the play at the heart of critical, theoretical and historical debates, thus rendering it particularly useful for undergraduate-level teaching.[33] Schiffer's introductory essay, 'Taking the Long View: *Twelfth Night* Criticism and Performance', gives an important and timely overview of the play.[34] As the title of his prefatory material suggests, Schiffer uses performance history as a means of introducing criticism. Significantly, he notes how the play has become a site for cultural critics to consider early modern ideas about gender, sexuality, the body, identity, misrule, religion, class and hierarchy, and these issues are addressed within *Twelfth Night: New Critical Essays*. Schiffer's anthology highlights some recent priorities in criticism, including concern with the phenomenological nature of the play. Bruce R. Smith's ' "His Fancy's Queen": Sensing Sexual Strangeness in *Twelfth Night*' draws on the multi-sensory aspects of Shakespeare's comedy and relates them to early modern discourses surrounding sexual activity and fancy, including the ways in which Cesario and Sebastian are figured and experienced by others.[35] The sensory aspect is continued in David Schalkwyk's 'Music, Food, and Love in the Affective Landscapes of *Twelfth Night*.'[36] The play's unusually musical nature gives it prominence in discussions of early modern music, most notably David Lindley's monograph *Shakespeare and Music*, where a chapter is devoted to musical thematics in *Twelfth Night* and *The Tempest*.[37]

Discussions of gender and sexuality pervade critical responses to the play. Laurie E. Osborne approaches these through the prism of the play's central questions of doubling and mirroring, particularly in relation to the correspondence between amity and heterosexual love.[38] Osborne presents these as mutually dependent, creating a situation where 'the best male friend is a woman and the most desirable wife is the loving male friend.'[39] Chad Allen Thomas in 'On Queering *Twelfth Night*' (2010) draws on two modern all-male productions of the play to consider ways of integrating theatre practice and pedagogy to open up space for discussion of queer theatre,[40] while Jami Ake argues that the play subverts heterosexual discourses to offer 'a glimpse of a tentative "lesbian" poetics as one female character imagines and articulates the words that will seduce another.'[41] Penny Gay surveys the play in performance between the 1960s and 1980s.[42] She argues that it is particularly prone to nostalgic productions, yet that the sexual intrigues and gender bending of the 1970s gave way to more serious readings in the conservative atmosphere of the 1980s, repressing the play's own ability to disrupt.

Stanley Wells's 'Boys Should be Girls: Shakespeare's Female Roles and the Boy Players' takes a more historical focus in arguing against modern theatrical practice for the importance of recognizing that boys, and not adults, originated roles such as Viola.[43] In *Shakespeare, Sex, and Love*, Wells attempts to unpack the discourses of homosociality and homosexuality in Shakespeare's characters named Antonio, placing them on a continuum of affection probably best imagined as unrequited love, usefully re-integrating character study and historical attention to male–male relationships.[44] Adrian Kiernander, meanwhile, traces the play's recent performance history and argues that it is relatively recent shifts that have allowed Antonio's 'desire' to gain consequence, the play becoming revitalized in a rising regime of conservative/puritanical politics.[45]

As Keir Elam points out, 'the only authoritative text that we have of *Twelfth Night* is the one published in the 1623 Folio edition',[46] yet it continues to pose important textual questions. The commonplace observation that Viola's real name is *written* but not *spoken* until the play's end is a productive jumping off point for discussions of textuality and orality in relation to identity forming, for example. Patricia Parker's '*Twelfth Night*: Editing Puzzles and Eunuchs of All Kinds' surveys the textual issues of the play, including the insight that Viola's decision to become a 'eunuch' is not actually an inconsistency (long read as a loose end or unrealized plot point) but rather shows that 'eunuch', through intertextual glossing, can be read as a type of early modern flute that served to transmit artificially the voices of others – a metaphor for the enabling disguise of Cesario.[47] An earlier article by Parker, 'Altering the Letter of *Twelfth Night*', offers a useful re-examination of editorial procedures relating to the play, pointing out that the reading of all four Folios, 'Some are become great', is routinely emended to 'born great' in modern editions despite no textual warrant in this scene.[48] Parker raises the fascinating question of whether or not we consider the letter to be a fixed entity, and argues for the usefulness of this crux for students in opening up questions. In addressing this question with MA students, I found employment of the 1910 silent film – which rewrites and abbreviates the letter, while elevating it to the same prominence as an 'objective' title card – a stimulating example of the authority carried by this unstable missive.

While the play's early textual history is relatively uncompli-cated, Laurie E. Osborne's *The Trick of Singularity* makes a strong case for the significance of later performance editions of the play, introducing an editorial afterlife that traces a history of variation and rearrangement and provides raw material for discussions of appropriation and adaptation. The play's language and wordplay are a perennial focus for discussion, and Elam's edition opens up a range of points for discussion surrounding class distinction by looking at verse/prose, pronoun use, neologisms and idioms, and paradox.[49] David Crystal notes that the play has more prose than any other play in the canon excepting *Much Ado about Nothing* and *The Merry Wives of Windsor*, which allows for consid-erable flexibility and can be exploited to introduce students to the complexities of dramatic prose.[50] David Schalkwyk scruti-nizes *Twelfth Night*'s use of the word 'love' alongside four of the sonnets, arguing that the play demonstrates Shakespeare's use of the word to open up networks of meaning rather than close down interpretation.[51] Thomas Rist considers wordplay in terms of the importance of punning and intertextuality in Shakespearean comedy more generally.[52] He traces the Mary/marry/merry pun through its religious associations, and links this to the play's comic form, pointing out the contradictions between the connotations of the Virgin icon and discourses of romantic love. Meanwhile, Walter Nash's analysis is symptomatic of the employment of *Twelfth Night* to illustrate Shakespeare's punning while also considering decorum. He acknowledges C-U-T as an important pun but refers to 'mischievous spelling' and 'potentially obscene' before finally acknowledging the allusion to the 'female pudenda.'[53] The explicit nature of the pun (given, of course, the lack of Cs or Ps in the letter's address) offers an opportunity to confront Shakespeare's bawdy, while also addressing the problems of articulating it within a discourse often more concerned with the play's genteel aspects.

'Now Sir, what is your text?' (1.5.214): Editions

The glossing of rude words is only one of the fascinating points for discussion made available by the fact that the play has been frequently re-edited for a range of audiences, and this section offers an overview of the particular strengths of some of these. A useful starting edition for those interested in the mechanics of print and transmission is Nick de Somogyi's version for the *Shakespeare Folios* series,[54] which presents parallel texts of the play in Folio transcript and modernized script. A brief introduction introduces the play's material form in the Folio and textual questions. In a play with only one early witness, most editions are largely more focused on context and interpretation than textual questions.

The main scholarly series are typically reliable. Roger Warren and Stanley Wells's edition for Oxford is heavily annotated and has a strong theatrical leaning throughout, which places particular emphasis on the work done on stage by the play's language.[55] The introduction moves from original staging and the significance of Illyria through discussion of the nature of comedy to a largely character-oriented introduction to the play's themes and complexities. The Appendix includes a fully re-edited version of the music by James Walker. Based on the Oxford edition, The Norton Shakespeare's *Twelfth Night* is prefaced by Stephen Greenblatt's enabling essay.[56] Elizabeth Story Donno's New Cambridge Shakespeare text is similarly clear, though its larger print makes it more useful for practical classroom work.[57] Penny Gay's fine introduction devotes a third of its length to stage history and is particularly strong on the play's use of classical mythology. The most recent full-length scholarly edition is Keir Elam's 2008 volume for the third series of the Arden Shakespeare. Elam's attention to performance is consolidated in a list of 120 stage and screen productions, which inform his work throughout the edition. The lengthy section devoted to performance includes both overview and character-specific stage histories, and the rest of his articulate and playful introduction deals with questions of context and interpretation, semiotics and material history, spatial politics and questions of gender, making it particularly useful for advanced-level students.

Jonathan Bate and Eric Rasmussen's lightly edited text in the RSC Shakespeare series is designed with actors and students in mind and includes extensive glossing.[58] The brief introduction includes suggestions that the play responds to Jonson's comedies and discussion of the relationship between the lyrical language of the play and the Sonnets. Perhaps of more unique value are the separate stage histories and lengthy interviews with the directors Sam Mendes, Declan Donnellan and Neil Bartlett about their productions of *Twelfth Night*.

While supplanted by Elam's edition, J. M. Lothian and T. W. Craik's edition for the New Arden Shakespeare (Craik taking over after Lothian's death) remains a useful, systematic introduction to the play, surveying historical criticism with interesting discussion of the critical attempts to demonstrate the unity and relative lightness of the play, and a scene-by-scene critical analysis.[59] A selective stage history points up key performance traditions, and an appendix includes a reprinted version of relevant source passages from Barnaby Riche's *Farewell to Militarie Profession* (1581). From the same era, but recently reprinted with a new introduction by Michael Dobson,[60] is Molly Mahood's Penguin text. Mahood's own introduction in the first edition remains useful for its discussion of masques and festivities, and plotting of the play's inconsistencies and confusions. Dobson's introduction to the revised edition prioritizes the lyrical and musical nature of the play, linking this to the play's fairytale treatment of the passage of time, and the exploration of selfish and self-deluding forms of love. A separate section gives a brief overview of the play in performance.

Editions for young people and students include Barbara Mowat and Paul Werstine's Folger Shakespeare Library text (1993),[61] whose facing-page explanatory notes and suggestions for further reading are accompanied by a short essay on identity confusions in the play by Catherine Belsey. This edition is supported by a website of further resources from the Folger which includes lesson and workshop plans as well as explanatory materials about language, character and text. As with Tracy Irish's edition, John O'Connor's New Longman Shakespeare edition has a particular focus on characters and language, with extensive facing-page glossary notes and suggestions for classroom activities.[62] Rex Gibson's edition for the Cambridge School Shakespeare also includes extensive suggestions for classroom activities involving performance, debate and further exploration.[63] Gibson suggests discussion topics based around themes of love, fantastical space and genre that are easily transferable across levels. His companion volume for Cambridge Student Guides offers a more advanced walkthrough of the play, with commentary, discussion of historical contexts, language and a particularly useful undergraduate-level introduction to critical approaches including carnival, feminist theory and postmodernism.[64] A list of resources and a short essay-writing guide may provide further tools for teachers.

In addition to scholarly editions for young people, there exists a subgenre of more popular versions designed to tie the play into youth culture. Richard Appignanesi's abridged edition for the popular *Manga Shakespeare* series, illustrated by Nana Li, adopts a steampunk setting and angular, attractive characters living out a love triangle that, in this context, carries clear resonance to popular teen narratives such as the *Twilight* saga.[65] The dangers of cartoon adaptations are perhaps exemplified in the Saddleback's Illustrated Classics series, for which the opening frame features a reclining Orsino saying 'If music is the food of love, play on. If I am fed too much, maybe I'll lose my appetite** for both', the asterisks redundantly glossing appetite as 'desire for food.'[66] At the opposite end of the spectrum, Simon Greaves's' *Comic Book Shakespeare*, which includes a full edited text and modern text translation, squeezes huge blocks of text next to compressed illustrations, which rather defeats the edition's purpose.[67] While none of these publications provides a substitute for a scholarly edition, each acts as a useful introduction to the play's narrative and language, as well as in themselves acting as a case study for appropriation and audience-specific adaptation. The Manga edition is the most successful in its decision to embrace fully the chosen genre at the expense of a 'complete' text, re-performing *Twelfth Night* for a new audience while remaining close enough to the Shakespearean play to remain useful pedagogically. The website of the series offers a selection of resources including glossary, synopsis and lesson plans, though at the time of writing there is little specific to *Twelfth Night*. Abridged texts further provide potential for use in performance-based classes, and schools can sign up to the Shakespeare Schools Festival project to access a thirty-minute adaptation of *Twelfth Night* designed for young actors.

The play is frequently anthologized. Its inclusion in *The Norton Anthology of English Literature: The Major Authors* alongside Christopher Marlowe's *Dr Faustus* and a selection of the Sonnets isolates it from its usual context of comedies but

advocates study of the play within a much broader context of
literary and theatrical history.[68] At the University of Nottingham,
for example, the play has been taught from *The Norton Anthology
of English Literature* in a Level 1 'Introduction to Drama' module
(between the Wakefield *Second Shepherd's Play* and Aphra Behn's
The Rover [1677]) and on a Level 2 'Resistance and Obedience'
module that groups the comedy with, among others, Thomas
More's *Utopia* (1516), Edmund Spenser's *The Faerie Queene*
(1590–6), Marlowe's *Dr Faustus* (c. 1594), Shakespeare's *Sonnets*
(1609) and John Webster's *The Duchess of Malfi* (c. 1613–14). In
the former course, attention is paid to language and to developments in dramatic form and convention; in the latter, class and
gender politics come to the fore.

'You are now out of your text' (1.5.225): *Twelfth Night* in Production

Twelfth Night's ubiquity in the modern theatrical repertoire has
led to a plethora of print and electronic resources on performance
that expand the textual questions above for students to consider
their practical ramifications. Tim Carroll's 2002 production at
Middle Temple Hall offered one of the most important experi-
ments in 'original' staging practices of recent times, and Michael
Dobson's annual review of UK Shakespeare performances in
Shakespeare Survey begins with a useful, critical account of
Carroll's production that offers a primary source for classes on
the original staging of the play and problems of historical recre-
ation.[69] Carroll himself writes about the challenges of original
practice productions in Christie Carson and Farah Karim-
Cooper's *Shakespeare's Globe: A Theatrical Experiment*.[70] Indeed,
Shakespeare's Globe archives a selection of blogs and interviews
with participants in Carroll's 2002 *Twelfth Night* including Paul
Chahidi (Maria), Peter Hamilton Dyer (Feste), Michael Brown
(Viola) and Timothy Walker (Malvolio). The 2012 revival of this
production at the Globe (with Stephen Fry taking over the role of
Malvolio) will be available on DVD from 2013.

Several anthologies of essays deal with the play's performance history. The most comprehensive is Elizabeth Schafer's volume for the *Shakespeare in Production* series which offers an excellent, thorough performance history of the play and a fully edited text with performance-based glosses that list and explain key theatrical interpretations of lines.[71] Schafer's introduction pays attention not only to the on-stage developments, but also to the shifts in audience responses to the play in line with historical concerns, while also paying attention to the individual histories of certain characters. Shorter, but equally useful, is Paul Edmondson's volume for the *Shakespeare Handbooks* series, which focuses primarily on the play in performance.[72] Edmondson highlights major screen and stage productions and offers an overview of critical assessments of the play on stage. It includes a lengthy and detailed commentary which concentrates especially on the play's dramaturgy. Lois Potter's short book *Twelfth Night: Text and Performance* unpacks the play's issues with reference to four productions from the 1970s and early 1980s, and what it lacks in length it makes up for in accessibility, including in a more general introduction to the work.[73] Penny Gay, in 'Women and Shakespearean Performance', takes a different slant, tracing the development of approaches to playing Shakespeare's women, discussing Viola alongside Rosalind, Beatrice, Lady Macbeth and Cleopatra as some of the more totemic roles in the repertoire of historical actresses.[74]

Two essays in Schiffer's 2011 collection offer less-mainstream views on performance history. Jennifer C. Vaught's '*Twelfth Night* and the New Orleans Twelfth Night Revelers' links the carnivalesque to the second oldest Mardi Gras krewe in New Orleans, both of which feature a Lord of Misrule and 'cakes and ale', but she connects both in their display of folk traditions being used to suppress and guard against socially mobile individuals, as Toby does in the case of Malvolio.[75] Christa Jansohn's '"The Text Remains for Another Attempt": *Twelfth Night, or What You Will* on the German Stage' surveys the play's fortunes in German productions.[76] Another fascinating approach to the play is unpacked by Peter Novak, who describes the process of translating the play into American Sign Language for performance, which leads to discussion of the play's visual elements, use of architectural space and the cultural/linguistic differences between the early modern text and contemporary translation.[77]

From the practitioner standpoint, Emma Fielding's aforementioned book offers a route via character. Michael Pennington's *Twelfth Night: A User's Guide* is an anecdotal volume by the director based on experience of directing three productions of the play on three continents.[78] With the insight of applied stagecraft and discussion of how his productions reinterpreted the play over several years, Pennington walks through the action of Shakespeare's comedy in chronological order. In so doing, Pennington details the important decisions he made and their implications. The director's no-nonsense series of observations, with their focus on characterization, are particularly useful for students on practice-based drama modules.

Twelfth Night has been filmed for television on a number of occasions, and several adaptations are available on DVD. The oldest of these, recently re-released, is John Sichel's 1969 version starring Tommy Steele as Feste, Ralph Richardson as Sir Toby and Alec Guinness as Malvolio. John Gorrie's 1980 film for the BBC–Time–Life Complete Works of Shakespeare series is a period-dressed, studio-bound television version, useful as a pedagogic resource for its near-complete text and capable performances, but otherwise unremarkable. Rather more lively is Paul Kafno's 1988 version based on Kenneth Branagh's stage production for the Renaissance Theatre Company. In a wintry setting, the treatment of Richard Briers' Malvolio particularly stands out.

Tim Supple's 2003 version, broadcast on Channel 4, is currently obtainable from some outlets as a Region 1 DVD only. The multicultural cast and modern-day setting makes it particularly fitting for advanced secondary-level students confronting questions of race, class and sexual politics through Shakespeare. Channel 4 produced an important education pack for Key Stage

4 students that is currently freely available. Focusing on the structure of the play and the means by which Supple created meaning in this version, this pack is useful for examining film literacy and adaptation. Alfredo Michel Modenessi offers a scholarly discussion of Supple's adaptation and of the accompanying educational aids.[79] His article pays particular attention to the creation of an oppressive surveillance atmosphere and to Supple's interest in multiculturalism and violence.

Shakespeare's play is easily accessible in two big screen versions: the 1910 silent film directed by Charles Kent for the Vitagraph Company of America (found in the British Film Institute's *Silent Shakespeare* package)[80] and Trevor Nunn's all-star 1996 version. The surprisingly nuanced silent film provides an excellent introduction to this period of cinematic history, both in Kent's foregrounding of his own performance as Malvolio and in the fascinating use of title cards to compress and summarize action. This film offers the opportunity to discuss narrative and performative strategies in adaptation, and the cultural resonance of devices such as the yellow stockings, here presumed immediately apparent without the need for title cards. For advanced-level students, the 1910 *Twelfth Night* is supported by discussion in Judith Buchanan's *Shakespeare on Silent Film*.[81] Nunn's film, filmed on location in Cornwall and featuring Imogen Stubbs, Toby Stephens, Nigel Hawthorne, Richard E. Grant, Ben Kingsley and Helena Bonham Carter, is an accessible and elegiac take on the play with excellent music but few laughs. Inspired by classic Merchant Ivory productions, set in and around a high-Victorian country house and featuring a cast accustomed to performing in television period dramas, the film draws attention to its clichés of Englishness and invites critique as an example of what Katherine Eggert terms a 'British-Shakespearean minstrelsy',[82] proving helpful for beginning discussions of class identity, heritage approaches to Shakespeare and the clash between filmic naturalism and theatrical representation.

Similarly moderate in its success is Andy Fickman's 'teen Shakespeare' version of the play, *She's the Man* (2006). Amanda

Bynes' Viola disguises herself as her twin brother Sebastian (James Kirk) in order to play soccer with the local boys' high-school team. An attempt to draw on the popularity of cinematic reworkings of Shakespeare such as *10 Things I Hate About You* (1999) and *'O'* (2001), it is primarily interesting as a resource for courses on adaptation and appropriation, as well as offering some diverting comparisons between American elite high school social politics and *Twelfth Night*'s treatment of class. A half-hour stop-motion version directed by Stanislav Sokolov is included in the *Shakespeare: The Animated Tales* (1992–4) box set, with Leon Garfield's summary narration stringing together quotations and compressing the action, including the entire exclusion of the Malvolio plot after his appearance in yellow stockings.[83] This is one of the least successful of the animated films, conservative in both visual style and textual adaptation, but can consequently serve as an important case study for debate over the extent to which infantilizing narration and severe cutting serve the intended young audience. Nonetheless, the range and accessi-bility of adaptations of *Twelfth Night* makes the play an ideal case study for modules on screen adaptations of Shakespeare.

'Give me excess of it' (1.1.2): Electronic Resources

The proliferation of online databaseses in recent years has been tempered by ongoing debates over cost, accessibility and sustain-ability. The speed at which resources appear and disappear needs to be taken into account; however, the new possibilities opened up in the twenty-first century classroom equipped with technologi-cally proficient students have led to fresh and exciting approaches to *Twelfth Night*. It is this final set of environments for encoun-tering the play which perhaps offers the most difficulty for the teacher trying to stay abreast of them, but this overview notes some that have proven integral to pedagogical situations.

Early English Books Online (EEBO) offers photographic facsimiles of all of the early texts of *Twelfth Night*, in the Shakespeare Folios of 1623, 1632, 1663/4 and 1685. This allows for a number of useful exercises in classroom settings by allowing students to see typography (capitalization, italics, parentheses), character names and inconsistencies (e.g. the choice of speech prefixes for Viola, Orsino and Feste) and the original readings of cruxes such as those outlined by Parker, above. In introducing students to a semblance of an 'unedited' text, basic assumptions about characterization and coherence can begin to be challenged. EEBO also includes facsimiles of Barnaby Rich's *Rich his Farewell to Militarie Profession* (1581 and later editions) and an edition of William Warner's translation of Plautus' *Menaecmi: A Pleasant and Fine Conceited Comaedie* (1595), allowing easy access to the sources and intertexts that inform *Twelfth Night*. These materials are particularly useful if discussing the play in relation to early modern comic theory and form.

The companion database Eighteenth Century Collections Online (ECCO) is more chronologically focused, but includes a wealth of resources on the play, from John Boydell's *A Catalogue of the Pictures, &c. in the Shakspeare Gallery, Pall-Mall* (1790) to collections of quotation books and musical miscellanies, to the burgeoning editorial tradition beginning with Nicholas Rowe's edition (1709) and extending through Pope (1725), Theobald (1733), Capell (1768), Johnson (1733), Steevens (1773) and Malone (1790). The resource is most useful for advanced-level students working on textual and social cultures, but there are a few resources specifically useful to *Twelfth Night*, including acting editions such as the play as performed in Crow-Street, Dublin, 1759. The Text Creation Partnership (TCP) is currently working to transcribe and encode images from EEBO and ECCO for use as electronic texts in the public domain, making these essential resources more broadly available for educators.

Literature Online (LION) links to a wide array of full-text resources and its value as a dynamic hub for teaching materials is not to be underestimated. Currently, it collates two online texts and details of over 700 scholarly books and articles on the play.[84] There are full-text versions of student knowledge guides and, usefully, an embedded copy of the 2003 Arkangel audio recording of the play. It is perhaps the single most comprehensive hub of information for students of the play, although inexperienced users may require assistance distinguishing references to the play from the wealth of other material on *Twelfth Night* themes.

Internet Shakespeare Editions is a much newer resource that is still being updated at the time of going to press. David Carnegie and Mark Houlahan's good-length introduction focuses especially on space, dramaturgy and performance. It includes a comprehensive bibliography of over 175 academic books and articles on the play, a modernized text and a diplomatic transcription of the Folio, links to digital facsimiles of all four early witnesses (including two different copies of the 1623 Folio), and links to relevant pages elsewhere on the site. Perhaps most impressively, a list of over 100 modern theatrical productions includes details of cast and crew where available, and often reproductions of artifacts, images and reviews. While patchy and still incomplete, this promises to be one of the fullest and most accessible archives of performance related to the play freely available on the web.

For students of performance history, there are a number of resources. The Designing Shakespeare website sponsored by the Higher Education Authority links to a database of more than 1,000 productions with full details, and often images and interviews. Sixty-seven productions of *Twelfth Night* are included, from Peter Hall's 1960 Stratford Memorial Theatre production to Rachel Kavanaugh's version for the Open Air Theatre in Regent's Park in 1999. In addition to cast lists and excerpted reviews for each entry, several include production images with a focus on design, providing raw material for classroom discussions on interpretation and setting. Virtual reality models of major British theatres and recorded interviews with professional designers provide the intellectual context for the *Twelfth Night* material, though a lack of index to specific productions discussed within the interviews makes the collection rather less easy to navigate. The Royal Shakespeare Company and Shakespeare's Globe websites both include information on the play aimed at school-age audiences, and the RSC is continuing to develop education packs specific to its major productions that are particularly useful for teachers with access to the productions or wishing to connect to contemporary theatrical practice. For researchers, the RSC Performance Database hosted by the Shakespeare Birthplace Trust links to full production details of all performances of the play by the Stratford-upon-Avon company since the late nineteenth century.

Miscellaneous resources include the software package Kar2ouche, an interactive roleplay software designed for classroom use which allows students to create storyboards, video footage, movies and animations based around a text; *Twelfth Night* is one of the few Shakespeare plays currently available as a package. Shakespeare Navigators provides a basic annotated text of the play, with the novel feature of being able to navigate by character entrance/exit, a useful tool for amateur performance. On behalf of Propeller Theatre, Will Wollen has produced an Education Pack aimed at GCSE and A level students which is designed to augment Propeller's theatrical performances. The continued development of tablet-specific editions by companies such as Cambridge University Press and the Centre for Research Computing at the University of Notre Dame suggests, however, that limited packages such as these will soon be replaced by interactive hypertext editions that will serve both traditional and performance-centred classrooms, offering the ability to edit texts, listen to critical commentary and actors' readings, and link to further resources. While, at the time of writing, these next-generation projects are yet to announce specific versions of *Twelfth Night*, it is impossible to imagine that so protean a play, shifting easily to fit changing critical and pedagogic environments, will not be at the forefront of developments in the twenty-first century classroom.

Select Editions

Appignanesi, Richard (ed.), *Manga Shakespeare: Twelfth Night*, illustrated by Nana Li (New York: Amulet, 2009; 2nd edn. London: SelfMadeHero Publications, 2012).

Bate, Jonathan and Rasmussen, Eric (ed.), *Twelfth Night* (Basingstoke: Macmillan, 2010).

de Somogyi, Nick (ed.), *The Shakespeare Folios: Twelfth Night* (London: Nick Hern, 2001.

Story Donno, Elizabeth (ed.), *Twelfth Night*, 2nd edn. (Cambridge: Cambridge University Press, 2003).

Elam, Keir (ed.), *The Arden Shakespeare: Twelfth Night*, (London: Bloomsbury, 2008).

Gibson, Rex (ed.), *Twelfth Night* (Cambridge: Cambridge University Press, 1993).

Greaves, Simon (ed.), *The Comic Book Shakespeare: Twelfth Night* (Oswestry: Timber Frame, 2003).

Greenblatt, Stephen (gen. ed.), *The Norton Anthology of English Literature, The Major Authors*, 2 Vols (8th edn.) (New York: W. W. Norton, 2006).

Greenblatt, Stephen 'Twelfth Night', in *The Norton Shakespeare*, Stephen Greenblatt, Walter Cohen, Jean E. Howard and Katharine Eisaman Maus (ed.), 2nd edn. (New York: W. W. Norton, 2008), pp. 1785–1846.

Irish, Tracy (ed.), *The Shorter Shakespeare: Twelfth Night* (Carlisle: Carel Press, 2001).

Lothian, J. M. and Craik, T. W. (ed.), *The Arden Shakespeare: Twelfth Night* (London: Methuen, 1975).

Mahood, M. M. (ed.), *Twelfth Night* (London: Penguin, 1968; repr. 2005).

Mowat, Barbara A. and Werstine, Paul (ed.), *Twelfth Night* (Washington: Washington Square Press, 1993).

O'Connor, John (ed.), *New Longman Shakespeare: Twelfth Night* (London: Longman, 1999).

Schafer, Elizabeth (ed.), *Shakespeare in Production: Twelfth Night* (Cambridge: Cambridge University Press, 2009).

Warren, Roger and Wells, Stanley (ed.), *Twelfth Night, or What You Will* (Oxford: Oxford University Press, 1994).

Web Resources

Channel 4, Twelfth Night Resource Pack http://www.channel4.com/learning/programmenotes/english/bard21stcent01.htm
[accessed 20 June 2012]

The Complete Works of William Shakespeare
http://shakespeare.mit.edu/
[accessed 20 June 2012]

Designing Shakespeare
    http://www.english.heacademy.ac.uk/designshake/design/index.htm
    [accessed 20 June 2012]
Early English Books Online
    http://eebo.chadwyck.com
    [accessed 20 June 2012]
Eighteenth Century Collections Online
    http://mlr.com/DigitalCollections/products/ecco/
    [accessed 20 June 2012]
Folger Shakespeare Library, *Teaching Twelfth Night*
    http://www.folger.edu/template.cfm?cid=3890
    [accessed 7 October 2012]
Internet Shakespeare Editions 'Twelfth Night', ed. by David Carnegie and Mark
    Houlahan
    http://internetshakespeare.uvic.ca/Foyer/plays/TN.html# intro
    [accessed 20 June 2012]
Kar2ouche
    http://www.immersiveeducation.eu/index.php/kar2ouchepg
    [accessed 20 June 2012]
Literature Online
    http://lion.chadwyck.co.uk/
    [accessed 20 June 2012]
Manga Shakespeare Learning
    http://www.mangashakespeare.com/free_resources.html
    [accessed 7 October 2012]
Propeller Theatre, *Twelfth Night* Education Pack
    http://propeller.org.uk/current-productions/
    twelfth-night-and-the-taming-of-the-shrew/education
    [accessed 20 December 2012]
Royal Shakespeare Company Education
    http://www.rsc.org.uk/education/
    [accessed 20 June 2012]
Shakespeare Birthplace Trust, RSC Performance Database
    http://calm.shakespeare.org.uk/dserve/dserve.exe?dsqApp=Archive&dsqD
    b=Catalog&dsqCmd=SearchRSC.tcl
    [accessed 20 June 2012]
Shakespeare's Globe, *Twelfth Night*
    http://www.shakespearesglobe.com/education/discovery-space/
    previous-productions/twelfth-night-1
    [accessed 19 June 2012]

Shakespeare Navigators, *Twelfth Night*
    http://www.shakespeare-navigators.com/TN_Navigator/index.html
    [accessed 20 June 2012]
Shakespearean Prompt-Books of the Seventeenth Century
    http://etext.virginia.edu/bsuva/promptbook/ShaTweP.html
    [accessed 20 June 2012]
Shakespeare Schools Festival
    http://www.ssf.uk.com/allscripts
    [accessed 7 October 2012]
YouTube
    http://youtube.com
    [accessed 20 June 2012]

Screen Adaptations: Commercially Available

Twelfth Night, dir. Charles Kent, 1910. *Silent Shakespeare*, British Film Institute, 2004 [on DVD]
Twelfth Night, dir. John Sichel, 1969. Network, 2009 [on DVD]
Twelfth Night, dir. John Gorrie. BBC–Time–Life, 1980 [on DVD]
William Shakespeare's Twelfth Night, dir. Paul Kafno, 1988. Based on the stage production dir. Kenneth Branagh. Renaissance Theatre Company, 2004 [on DVD]
Twelfth Night, dir. Trevor Nunn. Fine Line Features, 1996 [on DVD]
Twelfth Night, or What You Will, dir. Tim Supple. Homevision, 2003 [on DVD, Region 1 only]
Shakespeare: The Animated Tales, dir. various, 1992. Metrodome, 2005 [on DVD]
She's the Man, dir. Andy Fickman. Lakeshore Entertainment/Dreamworks, 2006 [on DVD]

NOTES

Introduction

1   William Shakespeare's *Twelfth Night*, directed for the stage by Des McAnuff, produced and directed for film by Barry Avrich (Entertainment One Films Canada, Inc. 2012).

2   This production was originally performed at the Middle Temple in January 2002 to celebrate the quartercentenary of John Manningham's record of seeing of a play called 'Twelve night, or What You Will' at that venue on 2 February 1602. It was revived at the Globe in May 2002 and in 2012.

3   The other plays were *The Comedy of Errors* and *The Tempest*.

4   Gary Taylor, 'Theatrical Proximities: The Stratford Festival 1998', *Shakespeare Quarterly* 50:3 (1999): 334–54, 348. See further Linda Anderson's essay in this volume, pp. 52–70.

5   All quotations are from Keir Elam (ed.), *The Arden Shakespeare: Twelfth Night* (London: Bloomsbury, 2008).

6   Ibid., pp. 15–17.

7   Gary Taylor, *Reinventing Shakespeare: A Cultural History from the Restoration to the Present* (New York: Weidenfeld & Nicolson, 1989).

8   See further Peter Kirwan's essay in this volume, p. 193.

9   See further William C. Carroll's essay in this volume, p. 71–97

10 Stephen Greenblatt, 'Fiction and Friction', in Shakespearean Negotiations (Berkeley: University of California Press, 1988), pp. 66–93.

11 See further Carroll's essay in this volume, pp. 70–98.

12 Keir Elam, '"In What Chapter of His Bosom"? Reading Shakespeare's Bodies', in *Alternative Shakespeares*, Vol. 2, (ed.) Terence Hawkes (London: Routledge, 1996), pp. 140–63.

13 Ibid., p. 144.

14 Ibid., p. 145.

15 Ibid., pp. 145–6.

16 Maev Kennedy, 'Mark Rylance to Return to Shakespeare's Globe as Lady Olivia', *The Guardian*, 2 December 2011, http://www.guardian.co.uk/stage/2011/dec/02/mark-rylance-shakespeare-globe-olivia [accessed 20 January 2013].

17 Naomi West, 'Mark Rylance returns to the Globe as Shakespeare's Richard III', *The Telegraph*, 7 July 2012, http://www.telegraph.co.uk/culture/

theatre/william-shakespeare/9357279/Mark-Rylance-returns-to-the-Globe-as-Shakespeares-Richard-III.html [accessed 20 January 2013], para 8.

18   Kennedy, 'Mark Rylance to Return', para 6.

19   Stanley Wells, 'Boys Should be Girls: Shakespeare's Female Roles and the Boy Players', *New Theatre Quarterly* 25.2 (2009): 172–7, 174.

20   James Bulman, ' "Unsex Me Here": Male Cross-Dressing at the Globe', in *Shakespeare Re-Dressed: Cross-Gender Casting in Contemporary Performance*s, (ed.) James Bulman (Cranbury: Associated University Presses, 2008), pp. 231–45.

21   Louise Jury, 'I'll Need a Facelift to be Olivia Again: Mark Rylance Returns to the Globe', *London Evening Standard*, 2 December 2011, http://www.standard.co.uk/news/ill-need-a-facelift-to-be-olivia-again-mark-rylance-returns-to-the-globe-6374414.html [accessed 14 January 2013], para 3.

22   Charles Spencer, '*Richard III/ Twelfth Night*, Apollo theatre, review', *The Telegraph*, 19 November 2012, http://www.telegraph.co.uk/culture/theatre/theatre-reviews/9687579/Richard-III-Twelfth-Night-Apollo-theatre-review.html [accessed 14 January 2013], para 7.

23   Stephen Wilmot, 'Theatre Review*: Twelfth Night* @ Apollo Theatre', *Londonist*, 19 November 2012, http://londonist.com/2012/11/theatre-review-twelfth-night-apollo-theatre.php [accessed 21 January 2013], para 2.

24   Anon., '*Twelfth Night* – Shakespeare's Globe, Wednesday 3rd October 2012', 10 November 1012, http://notthewestendwhingers.blogspot.co.uk/2012/11/twelfth-night-shakespeares-globe.html [accessed 21 January 2013], para. 8.

25   See further Keir Elam's essay in this volume, p. 107.

26   Elam (ed.), *Twelfth Night*, p. 70.

27   Ibid., pp. 70, 72.

28   Nathalie Rivère de Carles, 'Staging the Exotic *in Twelfth Night*,' in *Twelfth Night: New Critical Essays*, (ed.) James Schiffer (London: Routledge, 2011), pp. 184–200, 184.

29   Steve Mentz, *At the Bottom of Shakespeare's Ocean* (London: Continuum, 2009).

30   Quoted in ibid., p. 51.

31   Ibid.

32   The production transferred to the Apollo theatre on 2 November 2012.

33   Charlie Cooper, 'All the World's a Stage – and All the Men and Women Merely Environmentalists who Hate BP', 3 October 2012, http://www.independent.co.uk/arts-entertainment/theatre-dance/news/all-the-worlds-a-stage--and-all-the-men-and-women-merely-

environmentalists-who-hate-bp-8194854.html [accessed 14 January 2013], paras 1–7.

34   *bp OR NOT bp* http://bp-or-not-bp.org/ [accessed 14 January 2013], para 1.

35   *bp OR NOT bp*, 'RSC Hit by Yet Another On-Stage Protest Over BP Sponsorship', http://bp-or-not-bp.org/news/twelfthnight/ [accessed 14 January 2013], para 8ff.

36   See further Linda Anderson's essay in this volume, p. 53.

37   Claire Jowitt, *The Culture of Piracy, 1580–1630: English Literature and Seaborne Crime* (Aldershot: Ashgate, 2010), p. 127.

38   Ibid., pp. 127–8.

39   Leslie Hotson, *The First Night of Twelfth Night* (London: Rupert Hart-Davis, 1954), p. 151.

40   *bp OR NOT bp*, 'We Strike Again, with Green and Yellow Melancholy', http://bp-or-not-bp.org/news/twelfthnight/ [accessed 14 January 2013], para 5.

41   Ibid., para 3.

42   Elam (ed.), *Twelfth Night*, n. 113.

43   In November 2012, the Royal Shakespeare Company ended its BP sponsorship. See *bp OR NOT bp*, 'RSC Backs Away from World's Biggest Corporate Criminal', http://bp-or-not-bp.org/news/rsc-backs-away-from-worlds-biggest-corporate-criminal/ [accessed 14 January 2013], para 2.

44   Interview with Reclaim Shakespeare Company performers, Stratford-upon-Avon, 25 April 2012, http://london.indymedia.org/videos/12135 [accessed 6 February 2013].

45   See further Tiffany Stern's essay in this volume, pp. 166–88.

46   Hotson, *The First Night*, p. 15.

47   Ibid., pp. 199, 189, 18, 181.

48   See D. Poulton, 'The Favourite Singer of Queen Elizabeth I', *The Consort* 14 (1957): 24–7; Diana Poulton, *John Dowland* (Berkeley: University of California Press, 1982), p. 408; David G. Price, *Patrons and Musicians of the English Renaissance* (Cambridge: Cambridge University Press, 1981), p. 105.

49   Hotson, *The First Night*, p. 201.

50   Richard Crewdston, *Apollo's Swan and Lyre: Five Hundred Years of the Musicians' Company* (Woodbridge: Boydell Press, 2000), p. 61

51   Hotson, *The First Night*, pp. 181, 202.

52   Ibid., p. 202.

53   See further Andrew Stott's essay in this volume, p. 148.

54   Elam (ed.) *Twelfth Night*, p. 24.

55   See further Tiffany Stern's essay in this volume, p. 187.

56 Christopher Marlowe, 'The Passionate Shepherd to His Love' and 'The Nymph's Reply to the Shepherd' (possibly by Walter Raleigh) from *England's Helicon* (London, 1600) in *Elizabethan Lyrics*, (ed.) Norman Ault (London: Faber and Faber, 1986), nos. 134–5.

57 See further Carroll's essay in this volume, p. 74.

58 See Randall Martin's essay in this volume, pp. 123–43.

59 See Elam's essay in this volume, p. 103.

60 Suzanne Penuel, 'Missing Fathers: *Twelfth Night* and the Reformation of Mourning', *Studies in Philology* 107:1 (2010), 74–96.

61 Roger-François Gauthier (ed.), *Hamlet, / La Nuit Des Rois: La Scene et Ses Miroirs, Théâtre Aujourd' Hui 6* (Paris: CNDP, 1998).

62 John Bucke, *Instructions for the Use of the Rosarie* (1589), p. 4.

63 Edward Bunny, *A Survey of the Popes Supremacie* (1595) p. 209.

64 Paul Dean, '"Nothing That is So is So": *Twelfth Night* and Transubstantiation', *Literature and Theology* 17 (2003): 281–97; Maurice Hunt, *Shakespeare's Religious Allusiveness: Its Play and Tolerance* (Burlington: Ashgate, 2004).

65 See Elam's essay in this volume, p. 108.

66 Penuel, 'Missing Fathers', p. 84.

67 Muriel Spark, *The Prime of Miss Jean Brodie* (Harmondsworth: Penguin Classics, 2000), p. 36.

68 *Twelfth Night*, dir. Sean Holmes (2007). Excerpts from the production are included in the film *What You Will: A Fly on the Wall, Behind the Scenes, Documentary Tragi-Comical Road Movie*, dir. Simon Reade (Fluidity Films, 2012).

69 Eleanor Findlay (aged 13), interview 25 July 2012.

70 Richard Appignanesi (ed.), *Manga Shakespeare: Twelfth Night*, illustrated by Nana Li, 2nd edn. (London: SelfMadeHero Publications, 2012).

71 Ibid., pp. 120, 81, 89.

72 Ibid., pp. 55, 69.

73 See Kirwan's essay in this volume, p. 191.

74 Rex Gibson, *Teaching Shakespeare* (Cambridge: Cambridge University Press, 1998).

75 This is by no means a new phenomenon as shown in Alan Sinfield, 'Give an account of Shakespeare and Education, showing why you think they are effective and what you have appreciated about them. Support your comments with precise references', in *Political Shakespeare: New Essays in Cultural Materialism*, Jonathan Dollimore and Alan Sinfield (eds) (Manchester: Manchester University Press, 1985), pp. 134–57.

76 Shakespeare Schools Festival http://www.ssf.uk.com/howitworks/primary [accessed 6 February 2013].

77 E-mail interview with Emily Hayton, after playing Viola in the Barwick-in-Elmet primary school's production of the thirty-minute text prepared

by the Shakespeare Schools Festival and performed at the West Yorkshire Playhouse, 17 October 2012.

1: The Critical Backstory

1   Line references and quotations are from Stanley Wells and Gary Taylor, (ed.), '*Twelfth Night, Or What You Will*', in *The Oxford Shakespeare: The Complete Works* (Oxford: Oxford University Press, 1988), pp. 691–714.

2   Edwin Wilson (ed.), *Shaw on Shakespeare* (Harmondsworth: Penguin Books, 1969), p. 25.

3   For textual conundrums see Laurie Osborne, 'Editing Frailty in *Twelfth Night*: "Where Lies Your Text?"', in *Reading Readings: Essays on Shakespeare Editing in the Eighteenth Century*, (ed.) Joanna Gondris (Madison: Fairleigh Dickinson Press, 1998), pp. 209–23; Roger Warren and Stanley Wells, (ed.), *Twelfth Night* (Oxford: Oxford University Press, 1994); Patricia Parker, '*Twelfth Night*: Editing Puzzles and Eunuchs of All Kinds' in *Twelfth Night: New Critical Essays*, (ed.) James Schiffer (London: Routledge, 2011), pp. 45–64; for problems of 'plotting' in the play, see Cynthia Lewis, 'Whodunit? Plot, Plotting, and Detection in *Twelfth Night*', in Schiffer (ed.), *Twelfth Night* pp. 273–72, and John Sutherland and Cedric Watts, 'What Happens to Viola's "Eunuch" Plan?' and 'Malvolio: Vengeful or Reconciled?' in *Henry V, War Criminal? And Other Shakespeare Puzzles* (Oxford: Oxford University Press, 2000), pp. 126–36.

4   Quoted from Geoffrey Bullough (ed.), *Narrative and Dramatic Sources of Shakespeare: The Comedies*, Vol. 2. (London: Routledge & Kegan Paul, 1958), p. 269.

5   Anthony Arlidge, *Shakespeare and the Prince of Love: The Feast of Misrule in the Middle Temple* (London: Giles de la Mare Publishers, 2000).

6   Roland Barthes, 'The Death of the Author,' in *Image, Music, Text*, trans. by Stephen Heath (London: Faber, 1977), p. 130.

7   Bullough, *Narrative and Dramatic Sources*, Vol. 2, pp. 269–85, 270.

8   See Simon Palfrey and Tiffany Stern, *Shakespeare in Parts* (Oxford: Oxford University Press, 2007).

9   See R. S. White, 'Estranging Word and Self in *Twelfth Night*', in *Word and Self Estranged in English Texts, 1550–1660*, Philippa Kelly and L. E. Semler (ed.) (Aldershot: Ashgate, 2010), pp. 107–20.

10   F. S. Boas, *Shakespeare and His Predecessors* (London: John Murray, 1896).

11   Quotations from Horace Howard Furness (ed.), *Twelfth Night, Or What You Will*, in *A New Variorum Edition*, repr. (Philadelphia: J. B. Lippincott, 1901), pp. 377–8.

12   Roy Porter, *English Society in the 18th Century* (Harmondsworth: Penguin Books, 1982), p. 231.

13 Fiona Ritchie, 'Shakespeare and the Eighteenth-Century Actress', *Borrowers and Lenders: The Journal of Shakespeare and Appropriation* 2.2 (2006) http://www.borrowers.uga.edu/7151/toc [accessed 11 February 2013].

14 Michael Dobson, *The Making of the National Poet: Shakespeare, Adaptation and Authorship, 1660–1769* (Oxford: Clarendon Press, 1992), p. 124.

15 See Elizabeth Pentland, 'Beyond the "Lyric" in Illyricum: Some Early Modern Backgrounds to *Twelfth Night*', in Schiffer (ed.), *Twelfth Night*, pp. 149–66.

16 See further R. S. White, *Keats as a Reader of Shakespeare* (Norman: University of Oklahoma Press, 1987).

17 Jonathan Bate (ed.), *The Romantics on Shakespeare* (Harmondsworth: Penguin Books, 1992), p. 550.

18 G. K. Hunter, *Shakespeare: The Later Comedies* (London: The British Council, Longmans, Green & Co., 1962), pp. 39–50.

19 Quotations from R. S. White (ed.), *Hazlitt's Criticism of Shakespeare: A Selection* (Lewiston: Edwin Mellen Press, 1996), pp. 168–71.

20 Quotations from Joan Coldwell (ed.), *Charles Lamb on Shakespeare* (Gerrards Cross: Colin Smythe, 1978), pp. 50–62.

21 For an authoritative account of Jameson's life and works, see Judith Johnston, *Anna Jameson: Victorian, Feminist, Woman of Letters* (Aldershot: Scolar Press, 1997).

22 Quotations from Anna Jameson, *Characteristics of Women: Moral, Poetical, and Historical* (London: Saunders and Otley, 1832).

23 George C. Gross, 'Mary Cowden Clarke, "The Girlhood of Shakespeare's Heroines," and the Sex Education of Victorian Women', *Victorian Studies* 16 (1972): 7–58, 40.

24 Furness (ed.), *Twelfth Night*, pp. 402–3.

25 Ibid., pp. 403–6.

26 A. C. Bradley, 'Feste the Jester [1916]', in *Twelfth Night: Critical Essays*, (ed.) Stanley Wells (New York: Garland Publishing, Inc. 1986), pp. 17–24.

27 See Karen Greif, 'A Star is Born: Feste on the Modern Stage', *Shakespeare Quarterly* 39 (1988): 61–78 and Andrew Stott's chapter in this volume.

28 L. G. Salingar, 'The Design of *Twelfth Night*', *Shakespeare Quarterly* 9 (1958): 117–39, 117.

29 Harley Granville-Barker, *Prefaces to Shakespeare*, 6 vols, repr. (London: B. T. Batsford Ltd, 1974), vol. VI, 'Preface to *Twelfth Night*.'

30 Wilson (ed.), *Shaw on Shakespeare*, pp. 205–7.

31 W. H. Auden, *Lectures on Shakespeare*, (ed.) Arthur C. Kirsch (Princeton: Princeton University Press, 2000), pp. 152–8, 154. Lecture dated 1946.

32 See Christopher R. Wilson and Michela Calore (ed.), *Music in Shakespeare: A Dictionary* (London: Thoemmes Continuum, 2005), references throughout.

33 Barbara Everett, "Or What You Will"', *Essays in Criticism* 35 (1985): 294–314.

34 Northrop Frye, *A Natural Perspective: The Development of Shakespearean Comedy and Romance* (New York: Columbia University Press, 1965).

35 Clifford Leech, *Twelfth Night and Shakespearian Comedy* (Toronto: University of Toronto Press, 1965).

36 C. L. Barber, *Shakespeare's Festive Comedy: A Study of Dramatic Form and its Relation to Social Custom* (Princeton: Princeton University Press, 1959).

37 Ibid., pp. 243, 251, 256.

38 Ibid., p. 245.

39 Carolyn Ruth Swift Lenz, Gayle Greene and Carol Thomas Neely (ed.), *The Woman's Part: Feminist Criticism of* Shakespeare (Urbana: University of Illinois Press, 1980).

40 Auden, *Lectures on Shakespeare*, pp. 152–8.

41 Elliot Krieger, *A Marxist Study of Shakespeare's Comedies* (London: Macmillan, 1979).

42 Thomas F. van Laan, *Role-Playing in Shakespeare* (Toronto: University of Toronto Press, 1978).

43 See, for example, Joseph Summers, 'The Masks of *Twelfth Night*', in *Shakespeare: Modern Essays in Criticism*, (ed.) Leonard F. Dean (New York: Oxford University Press, 1967), 133–43 and John Kerrigan, 'Secrecy and Gossip in *Twelfth Night*', *Shakespeare Survey* 50 (1997): 65–80.

44 Alexander Leggatt, *Shakespeare's Comedy of Love* (London: Methuen, 1974).

45 Leslie Hotson, *The First Night of 'Twelfth Night'* (New York: Macmillan, 1954).

46 John W. Draper, *The Twelfth Night of Shakespeare's Audience* (Stanford: Stanford University Press, 1950).

47 Ibid., p. 6.

48 Ibid., p. 250.

49 Ibid., p. 39.

50 Stephen Greenblatt, 'Fiction and Friction', *Shakespearean Negotiations* (Berkeley: University of California Press, 1988), pp. 66–93.

51 Barbara Freedman, 'Naming Loss: Mourning and Representation in *Twelfth Night*', in *Staging the Gaze: Postmodernism, Psychoanalysis, and Shakespearean Comedy* (Ithaca: Cornell University Press, 1991), pp. 192–236.

52 Ibid., pp. 2, 3.

53 Ibid., pp. 192–3, 203.

54 Ruth Nevo, 'Nature's Bias', in *Comic Transformations in Shakespeare* (London: Methuen, 1980), pp. 200–215.

55 Germaine Greer, *Shakespeare* (Oxford: Oxford University Press, 1986), p. 99.

56   Ibid., p. 113.

57   Germaine Greer, *Shakespeare's Wife* (London: Bloomsbury, 2007).

58   Juliet Dusinberre, *Shakespeare and the Nature of Women* (New York: Barnes and Noble, 1975).

59   See, for example, Carole McKewin, 'Counsels of Gall and Grace: Intimate Conversations between Women in Shakespeare's Plays', in Lenz, Greene and Neely (ed.), *The Woman's Part*, pp. 117–32.

60   Kathleen McLuskie, 'The Patriarchal Bard: Feminist Criticism and Shakespeare: *King Lear* and *Measure for Measure*', in *Political Shakespeare: New Essays in Cultural Materialism*, Jonathan Dollimore and Alan Sinfield (ed.) (Ithaca: Cornell University Press, 1985), pp. 88–108.

61   Dympna Callaghan, *Shakespeare Without Women: Representing Gender and Race on the Renaissance Stage* (London: Routledge, 1999).

62   David Margolies, 'Teaching the Handsaw to Fly: Shakespeare as a Hegemonic Instrument', in *The Shakespeare Myth*, (ed.) Graham Holderness (Manchester University Press, 1988), pp. 42–53.

63   Marianne Novy, '"An You Smile Not, He's Gagged": Mutuality in Shakespeare's Comedy', in *Love's Argument: Gender Relations in Shakespeare* (Chapel Hill: University of North Carolina Press, 1984), pp. 21–44.

64   Catherine Belsey, 'Disrupting Sexual Difference: Meaning and Gender in the Comedies', *Alternative Shakespeares*, (ed.) John Drakakis (London: Methuen, 1985), pp. 166–90, p. 189.

65   See Nicholas R. Jones's excellent account, 'Trevor Nunn's *Twelfth Night*: Contemporary Film and Classic British Theatre', *Early Modern Literary Studies* (2002): 1–38, http://extra.shu.ac.uk/emls/08-1/jonetwel.htm.

66   Jean E. Howard, 'Crossdressing, the Theatre, and Gender Struggle in Early Modern England', *Shakespeare Quarterly* 39 (1988): 418–40; Phyllis Rackin, 'Androgyny, Mimesis, and the Marriage of the Boy Heroine on the English Renaissance Stages', *Publications of the Modern Language Association* 102 (1987): 29–47; Valerie Wayne (ed.), *The Matter of Difference: Materialist Feminist Criticism of Shakespeare* (New York: Harvester-Wheatsheaf, 1992); Penny Gay, *As She Likes It: Shakespeare's Unruly Women* (London: Routledge, 1994).

67   Alison Findlay, *Women in Shakespeare: A Dictionary* (London: Continuum, 2010), references throughout.

68   Stephen Orgel, *Impersonations: The Performance of Gender in Shakespeare's England* (Cambridge: Cambridge University Press, 1996), pp. 53–60.

69   Marjorie Garber, *Vested Interests: Cross-Dressing and Cultural Anxiety* (New York: Routledge, 1991).

70   Madhavi Menon (ed.), *Shakesqueer: A Queer Companion to the Complete Works of Shakespeare* (Durham: Duke University Press, 2011).

71   Joseph Pequigney, 'The Two Antonios and Same-Sex Love in *Twelfth Night* and *The Merchant of Venice*', *English Literary Renaissance* 22 (1992): 41–54, and *Such is My Love: A Study of Shakespeare's Sonnets* (Chicago: University of Chicago Press, 1985).

72   Kate Chedgzoy, *Shakespeare's Queer Children: Sexual Politics and Contemporary Culture* (Manchester: Manchester University Press, 1996).

73   Jonathan Goldberg, *Queering the Renaissance* (Durham: Duke University Press, 1994) and *Sodometries: Renaissance Texts, Modern Sexualities* (Stanford: Stanford University Press, 1992).

74   Menon (ed.), *Shakesqueer*, pp. 386ff.

2: Performance and Adaptation

1   Quotations are from J. M. Lothian and T. W. Craik (ed.), *The Arden Shakespeare: Twelfth Night*, repr. (London: Thomson Learning, 2002).

2   Ralph Berry, *Changing Styles in Shakespeare* (London: George Allen & Unwin, 1981), p. 13; Gary Taylor, 'Theatrical Proximities: The Stratford Festival 1998', *Shakespeare Quarterly* 50:3 (1999): 334–54, 348.

3   Audrey Williamson, *Old Vic Drama: A Twelve Years' Study of Plays and Players* (London: Rockliff, 1948), p. 86; Michael Billington (ed.), *Approaches to Twelfth Night* (London: Nick Hern Books, 1990), p. 25; M. St Clare Byrne, 'The Shakespeare Season at The Old Vic, 1957–58 and Stratford-upon-Avon, 1958', *Shakespeare Quarterly* 9:4 (1958): 507–30, 523. Robert Speaight also refers to the play's 'perfection' in 'Shakespeare in Britain', *Shakespeare Quarterly* 22:4 (1971): 359–64, 359.

4   Billington, (ed.), *Approaches to Twelfth Night*, p. ix. Given the propensity of directors to rearrange, redefine and reinterpret nearly every aspect of the play, Billington's later comment seems more on point: 'The critic W. A. Darlington once said that there is a perfect production of *Twelfth Night* laid up for us in heaven. What is fascinating is how hard it was [following Granville Barker's 1912 production], to come by the perfect one on earth. Time and again, one finds one aspect of the play emphasised at the expense of another: usually prankish comedy at the expense of delicate melancholy.' Billington (ed.), *Approaches to Twelfth Night*, p. xvi.

5   Charles Lamb, 'On Some of the Old Actors' [1822], in *The Portable Charles Lamb*, (ed.) John Mason Brown, repr. (New York: Viking, 1969), p. 531.

6   George C. D. Odell, *Shakespeare – From Betterton to Irving*, 2 vols, repr. (New York: Benjamin Blom, 1963), vol. 1, p. 38. It is not certain, however, that the play Pepys saw was Shakespeare's; it may have been a version revised by Sir William Davenant or another writer.

7   Paul Sawyer, 'The Popularity of Shakespeare's Plays, 1720–21 through
     1732–33', *Shakespeare Quarterly* 29:3 (1978): 427–30, 428; see also
     Williamson, *Old Vic Drama*, p. 86.

8   Odell, *Shakespeare*, pp. 337, 338. It was not only a staple of the stage
     throughout the English-speaking world, but often chosen for special
     occasions: it was the play actor–manager Charles Kean chose to open
     the Princess's Theatre in 1850; it was one of the plays performed at the
     Shakespeare Tercentenary Festival at Stratford-upon-Avon in April 1864;
     it was the first play performed by William Poel's Elizabethan Stage Society
     in June 1895; it was the first play performed at the Repertory Theatre in
     Station Street in 1913; it was one of the three plays (the others being *The
     Winter's Tale* and *A Midsummer Night's Dream*) staged by Harley Granville-
     Barker at the Savoy shortly before the First World War, performances that
     are frequently described as having a revolutionary effect on Shakespearean
     production; and it was the play chosen to re-open Sadler's Wells on 6
     January 1931, with Gielgud playing Malvolio.
          Twelfth Night is also apparently assumed to travel well: it was one
     of the plays taken to the New Royal Opera House, Berlin, by Herbert
     Beerbohm Tree in 1907; to the Royal Opera House, Stockholm, in
     1915; to the Grosses Schauspielhaus, Rotterdam, and the Stadttheater,
     Amsterdam, in 1916. See Richard Foulkes, *Performing Shakespeare in the
     Age of Empire* (Cambridge: Cambridge University Press, 2002), pp. 136,
     187. *Twelfth Night* was one of the few Shakespearean plays the Old Vic
     chose to take on tour during the Second World War (see Williamson, *Old
     Vic Drama*, p. 213). '*Twelfth Night* was taken by the Oxford University
     Dramatic Society on a brief tour of French universities' and, by a group
     of graduates of Catholic University, on a tour of US Armed Forces bases
     in Korea and Japan in 1952 (Anon., 'Current Theatre Notes', *Shakespeare
     Quarterly* 4:1 (1953): 61–75, 61–2, 75). It was also the first Shakespearean
     play performed by the Irish Theatre Company, Ireland's national touring
     company (Christopher Murray, 'Shakespeare in Ireland', *Shakespeare
     Quarterly* 33:2 (1982): 197–9, 197).

9   Billington (ed.), *Approaches to Twelfth Night*, p. xii; J. L. Styan, *The
     Shakespeare Revolution: Criticism and Performance in the Twentieth Century*
     (Cambridge: Cambridge University Press, 1977), pp. 11, 18.

10   Gamini Salgādo, (ed.), *Eyewitnesses of Shakespeare: First Hand Accounts of
     Performances 1590–1890* (London: Sussex University Press, 1975), p. 207.
     Salgādo also notes that 'The play has always been vulnerable to musical
     prettification and this tendency increased alarmingly throughout the 19th
     century' (p. 202).

11   Styan, *The Shakespeare Revolution*, p. 28.

12   Billington (ed.), *Approaches to Twelfth Night*, p. xii.

13   Ibid., p. xiii.

14   Foulkes, *Performing Shakespeare*, p. 3.

15   Sir John Gielgud describes Irving's production as 'disastrous' and states that Irving was booed (John Gielgud, *An Actor and His Time* [London: Sidgwick & Jackson, 1979], p. 228). On the other hand, Edward Gordon Craig, who as a boy walked on in *Twelfth Night*, among other plays, during an 1884 US tour starring his mother Ellen Terry and Irving, liked Irving's Malvolio, writing in his memoir: 'I recall much of this production. In it Irving was remarkable in the guise of Malvolio – not playing the buffoon, but solemnly comic, with great distinction, calm and dark' (Edward Gordon Craig, *Index to the Story of My Days: Some Memoirs of Edward Gordon Craig, 1872–1907* [New York: Viking, 1957], p. 59). On Tree, see Billington (ed.), *Approaches to Twelfth Night*, p. xiii; Williamson, *Old Vic Drama*, p. 87.

16   Styan, *The Shakespeare Revolution*, pp. 59, 60; Billington (ed.), *Approaches to Twelfth Night*, p. xiii.

17   See Foulkes, *Performing Shakespeare*, p. 3; Gielgud, *An Actor and His Time*, p. 233; Cary M. Mazer, *Shakespeare Refashioned: Elizabethan Plays on Edwardian Stages* (Ann Arbor: UMI Research Press, 1981), p. 123; and Styan, *The Shakespeare Revolution*, p. 224.

18   Williamson, *Old Vic Drama*, pp. 86–8.

19   Gielgud, *An Actor and His Time*, pp. 176, 178; see also J. C. Trewin, *Shakespeare on the English Stage 1900–1964: A Survey from Productions* (London: Barrie and Rockliff, 1964), pp. 234–5.

20   Billington (ed.), *Approaches to Twelfth Night*, pp. xvii, xxi. Lois Potter, however, states that 'the Barton production was initially criticised for being too melancholy', although she adds that 'it got funnier in successive revivals' (Lois Potter, *Twelfth Night: Text and Performance* [Basingstoke: Macmillan, 1985], p. 67).

21   Berry, *Changing Styles in Shakespeare*, p. 115; Billington (ed.), *Approaches to Twelfth Night*, p. xxiii; Potter, *Twelfth Night*, p. 68. In contrast, the *Twelfth Night* presented at the Colorado Shakespeare Festival in the summer of 1984 was played for every possible laugh, for which it was savaged by the critics, though very popular with the audiences. Michael Mullin, 'The Colorado Shakespeare Festival', *Shakespeare Quarterly* 36:4 (1985): 470–2, 472.

22   Roger Warren, 'Shakespeare in England, 1983', *Shakespeare Quarterly* 34:4 (1983): 451–60, 454.

23   Douglas Brode, *Shakespeare in the Movies: From the Silent Era to Shakespeare in Love* (Oxford: Oxford University Press, 2000), p. 96; Judith Buchanan, *Shakespeare on Silent Film: An Excellent Dumb Discourse* (Cambridge: Cambridge University Press, 2009), p. 108.

24   Robert Hamilton Ball, *Shakespeare on Silent Film: A Strange Eventful
      History* (New York: Theatre Arts Books 1968), p. 56.

25   Kenneth S. Rothwell, *A History of Shakespeare on Screen: A Century of Film
      and Television*, 2nd edn (Cambridge: Cambridge University Press, 2004),
      p. 7. In 1911, the English Co-operative Cinematograph Company announced
      that it would film *Twelfth Night* as part of a series of Shakespearean
      productions by the F. R. Benson Company, but this film was never made
      (Ball, *Shakespeare on Silent Film*, pp. 82–4).

26   Kenneth S. Rothwell and Annabelle Henkin Melzer, *Shakespeare on Screen:
      An International Filmography and Videography* (New York: Neal-Schuman,
      1990), pp. 302, 303, 305.

27   Roger Manvell, *Shakespeare and the Film* (New York: Praeger, 1971),
      p. 77; Eddie Sammons, *Shakespeare: A Hundred Years on Film* (Lanham:
      Scarecrow Press, 2004), pp. 160–1.

28   See Michael Anderegg, *Cinematic Shakespeare – Genre and Beyond: A
      Film Studies Series* (Lanham: Rowman & Littlefield, 2004), pp. 152, 156–8;
      Rothwell and Melzer, *Shakespeare on Screen*, pp. 306, 307.

29   Sammons, *Shakespeare*, pp. 161, 162. Rothwell and Melzer indicate that
      the West Germans released their version of *Was ihr Wollt* in 1962 and
      the East Germans released their version – with the same title – in 1963
      (Rothwell and Melzer, *Shakespeare on Screen*, p. 305).

30   On Nunn's film, see Anderegg, *Cinematic Shakespeare*, pp. 141–2; Brode,
      Shakespeare in the Movies, pp. 97–8; and Rothwell, who summarizes: 'in
      its world-weariness and rather fashionable despair it ironically repli-
      cates the *fin-de-siècle* mood of the late nineteenth century' (*A History of
      Shakespeare on Screen*, pp. 226–7). In 1985, the Stratford Shakespeare
      Festival of Ontario, Canada, released a thirty-minute cassette featuring
      excerpts from *Twelfth Night* as part of a series of educational materials
      on several plays (Rothwell and Melzer, *Shakespeare on Screen*, p. 308).
      Twelfth Night is one of twelve Shakespeare plays produced in half-hour
      animated versions for BBC2 between 1992 and 1994; 'complete
      with study guides', *The Animated Tales* (alternate title *The Animated
      Shakespeare*) were 'geared to the needs of teenagers confronted with
      a Shakespeare play on their exam syllabus' (Michèle Willems, 'Video
      and its Paradoxes', in *The Cambridge Companion to Shakespeare on Film*,
      (ed.) Russell Jackson [Cambridge: Cambridge University Press, 2000],
      pp. 35–46, 35). Susanne Greenhalgh and Robert Shaughnessy note that
      'Tim Supple's (2003) made-for-TV production of *Twelfth Night* was
      commissioned by Channel 4 Learning predominantly for the educa-
      tional market with an avowed intention of its being "multicultural"'
      (Susan Greenhalgh and Robert Shaughnessy, 'Our Shakespeares:
      British Television and the Strains of Multiculturalism', in *Screening*

Shakespeare in the Twenty-First Century, Mark Thornton Burnett and Ramona Wray (ed.) [Edinburgh: Edinburgh University Press, 2006], pp. 90–112, 99).

31 Odell, *Shakespeare* vol. 1, pp. 71, 81–3.

32 Brode, *Shakespeare*, p. 96; Rothwell and Melzer describe Lucia's production as 'elusive' (Rothwell and Melzer, *Shakespeare on Screen*, p. 302). For *Nichts Als Sünde*, see Sammons, *Shakespeare*, p. 162.

33 Sammons, *Shakespeare*, p. 161.

34 H. R. Coursen, 'Cinderella's *Twelfth Night*', *Marlowe Society of America Newsletter* X:1 (1990): 5–6.

35 Alfred Weiss, 'The Edinburgh International Festival, 1990', *Shakespeare Quarterly* 42:4 (1991): 470.

36 Sammons, *Shakespeare*, p. 161.

37 Buchanan, *Shakespeare on Silent Film*, pp. 30–1.

38 Michael Anderegg, *Orson Welles, Shakespeare, and Popular Culture* (New York: Columbia University Press, 1999), p. 39. Anderegg notes that Welles and Hill had 'codirected the play [...] earlier at Todd School for the Chicago Drama League competition. (This production, of which some photos and a short film survive, had been based on a 1930 New York production by Kenneth McGowan)', p. 44.

39 Sammons, *Shakespeare*, p. 222.

40 Katharine Davies, *A Good Voyage* (London: Chatto & Windus, 2004) and *The Madness of Love* (London: Vintage, 2005).

41 Foulkes, *Performing Shakespeare*, pp. 148–9.

42 Sammons, *Shakespeare*, p. 217.

43 Rothwell and Melzer, *Shakespeare on Screen*, p. 302; Sammons, *Shakespeare*, p. 160.

44 Sammons, *Shakespeare*, p. 192.

45 Ibid., pp. 214, 228.

46 *Wicker Park*, dir. by Paul McGuigan (2004).

47 In addition to the preceding, most of which were commercial productions, there have also been a host of educational materials containing excerpts from the play, including, for example, 'Shakespeare's Theater: The Globe Playhouse', a 1954 documentary produced by the UCLA Department of Theatre Arts and narrated by Ronald Coleman, which featured brief excerpts from several plays including *Twelfth Night*, and the 'Fair Adventure Series', a series of short films produced in 1964 by the University of Southern California, including an abbreviated version of *Twelfth Night* (Sammons, *Shakespeare*, pp. 222, 225).

48 Billington (ed.), *Approaches to Twelfth Night*, p. xii; Arthur Colby Sprague, *Shakespeare and the Actors: The Stage Business in His Plays (1660–1905)*, repr. (New York: Russell & Russell, 1963), p. 354, n. 22.

49   Arthur Colby Sprague and J. C. Trewin, *Shakespeare's Plays Today: Some Customs and Conventions of the Stage*, repr. (Columbia: University of South Carolina Press, 1971), p. 49; Billington (ed.), *Approaches to Twelfth Night*, pp. xvii, 22–3.

50   Berry, *Changing Styles in Shakespeare*, pp. 111–12.

51   Billington (ed.), *Approaches to Twelfth Night*, pp. xv–xvi.

52   Louis A. DeCatur, 'West German Shakespeare as Seen by a Teacher Abroad', *Shakespeare Quarterly* 33:4 (1982): 515–18, 517.

53   Director Terry Hands asserts that 'If you look at the nineteenth century, you'll find the play is cut down finally to five scenes' (Billington (ed.), *Approaches to Twelfth Night*, p. 25).

54   Ishrat Lindblad, 'Shakespeare on the Swedish Stage', *Shakespeare Quarterly* 33:4 (Winter 1982): 524–8, 526; Lindblad states that 'this precedent (for transposing the first two scenes) was set by Kemble in 1815' (527).

55   In 1977 J. L. Styan quoted Norman Marshall eloquently lamenting 'the transposition of scenes to fit the scenery': 'Imagine a conductor beginning his performance of a Beethoven symphony by transposing the first and second subjects of the opening movement. Yet this seems to me no worse than what was done to *Twelfth Night* when it was produced at Stratford in 1948 with the first and second scenes transposed. The opening lines of Scene One ('If music be the food of love, play on') announce the theme of the play. Musically the verse is exquisitely attuned to its purpose, which is to establish a mood. Begin instead with the deliberately utilitarian verse of the second scene and the musical structure is at once shattered' (Styan, *The Shakespeare Revolution*, pp. 19–20).

56   Arthur Colby Sprague and J. C. Trewin suggest that this bit of business has been 'perpetuated from the Kembles' time to ours' (Sprague and Trewin, *Shakespeare's Plays Today*, p. 28). This convention carried over to the first film of *Twelfth Night*, the 1910 Vitagraph production, in which the rescued Viola arrives with a trunk.

57   Sprague (who wrote this chapter) writes 'It is hard for me to imagine Malvolio without his staff of office – the staff from the end of which he contemptuously drops the ring for Cesario. But although Shakespeare mentions such ceremonial wands more than once, it is not in connection with Malvolio [...]' (Sprague and Trewin, *Shakespeare's Plays Today*, p. 87). This common stage business was also used in the 1910 Vitagraph film.

58   Sprague and Trewin report that 'Beerbohm Tree was blamed and defended for introducing the night-shirt in 1907. There is a possibility, however, that he may have been anticipated a good while before. For in a promptbook of the performance at the Academy of Music, Brooklyn, 23 April 1864, is the illuminating note referring to this scene: "Mal. Wears long white night gown, white conical cap, leg fleshings and slippers"' (Sprague and Trewin,

Shakespeare's Plays Today, p. 84), see also p. 17, and Trewin, *Shakespeare on the English Stage 1900–1964*, pp. 165–6.

59   Gielgud, *An Actor and His Time*, p. 178.

60   Mazer, *Shakespeare Refashioned*, p. 24. Mazer notes that 'This interpolation carried with it the implication that the life of the great household, in which the play is set, goes on around the clock' (p. 24).

61   Billington poses the question 'To what extent is Illyria a state of mind or a real Mediterranean locale?' in *Approaches to Twelfth Night*, p. xxix.

62   Ibid., pp. xxviii, 8–9; Berry, *Changing Styles in Shakespeare*, p. 115. Directors Barton, Caird and Hands all say that the sea was an important element in their productions (Billington (ed.), *Approaches to Twelfth Night*, pp. 1, 2, 6–7). It was also a prominent feature in a 1980 production at the Royal Theatre in Copenhagen (Ingeborg Nixon, 'Shakespeare in Denmark', *Shakespeare Quarterly* 32:3 [1981]: 374–5, 375).

63   Gerald M. Berkowitz, 'Shakespeare at the 1988 Edinburgh Festival', *Shakespeare Quarterly* 40:1 (1989): 75–83, 79; H. R. Coursen, 'Refuting the Reviews: Two D.C. Tickets', *Marlowe Society of America Newsletter* X:1 (1990): 6; Miranda Johnson Haddad, 'The Shakespeare Theatre at the Folger, 1989–90', *Shakespeare Quarterly* 41:4 (1990): 507–20, 508–11.

64   Elizabeth Schafer, 'Introduction', *Twelfth Night: Shakespeare in Production*, (ed.) Elizabeth Schafer (Cambridge: Cambridge University Press, 2009), pp. 1–79, 2–4. Of Barton's 1969 RSC production Berry comments: 'this is a directorial statement that rests solidly on the title: *Twelfth Night*. It is curious that this has been so widely interpreted as an unequivocal call to revelry. In fact, most people understand perfectly well that the *last* day of the Christmas festivities finds one sated. One more party, and then thank God for work' (Berry, *Changing Styles in Shakespeare*, pp. 113–14). Two Czechoslovakian productions in 1980 and 1981 were set during Carnival season because 'in Czechoslovakia, there is no tradition of feasting on Twelfth Night, whereas Carnival is generally associated here, as elsewhere on the Continent, with the kind of winter feasting and frolicking that in England went on from St. Andrew's Day though the twelve days of Christmas to Shrovetide' (Zdeněk Stříbrný, 'Shakespeare in Czechoslovakia', *Shakespeare Quarterly* 33:4 [1982]: 502–5, 503–4). Hands' 1979 RSC production began in winter and moved into spring. Alexander's production was set in summer – as was, apparently, Robin Phillips's 1988 production for the Stratford Ontario Young Company – but emphasized different times of day.

65   Barton says that his production was 'autumnal in mood' (as Peter Hall's famous RSC production is said to have been) (Billington (ed.), *Approaches to Twelfth Night*, pp. 4, 7). See also Adrian Kiernander, 'Shakespeare in New Zealand', *Shakespeare Quarterly* 31:3 (1980): 400–2, 401; Jeanne

Addison Roberts, 'Shakespeare in The Nation's Capital', *Shakespeare Quarterly* 32:2 (1981): 206–10, 207; and Daniel J. Watermeier, 'Shakespeare in Canada: The Stratford Season, 1988', *Shakespeare Quarterly* 40:2 (1989): 212–17, 214–15. Trevor Nunn has described the play as 'the most autumnal of Shakespeare's comedies' (Sammons, *Shakespeare*, p. 161).

66 Berry, *Changing Styles in Shakespeare*, p. 112; Michael Benthall's Old Vic production that same year was also set in the Cavalier period (Alice Griffin, 'Current Theatre Notes, 1958–59', *Shakespeare Quarterly* 11:1 (1960): 97–115, 113).

67 Watermeier, 'Shakespeare in Canada', p. 214; Alan C. Dessen, 'Exciting Shakespeare in 1988', *Shakespeare Quarterly* 40:2 (1989): 198–207, 198; Haddad, 'The Shakespeare Theatre at the Folger, 1989–90', p. 508; Griffin, 'Current Theatre Notes, 1958–59', pp. 113, 114; Gerald M. Berkowitz, 'Shakespeare at the Edinburgh Festival, 1991', *Shakespeare Quarterly* 43:2 (1992): 227–32, 230.

68 Billington (ed.), *Approaches to Twelfth Night*, pp. xxix–xxx.

69 See ibid., p. ix and John W. Draper, *Twelfth Night of Shakespeare's Audience*, repr. (New York: Octagon Books, 1975), p. 221. Draper proposes that Sir Toby is another 'star part', Billington suggests that he 'is the motor that drives the plot', and Thomas Betterton played the role in the seventeenth century (Schafer, 'Introduction', p. 4). As Billington discusses, Caird argues that an actor cast as Toby quickly realizes 'that the other characters get all the laughs, and constantly he's being undercut by Ague-Cheek or Malvolio or Feste', and Billington agrees that Sir Andrew's 'is the part that often yields up the most surprising comedy', but notes that 'the temptation of lead actors is always to go for Malvolio' (Billington (ed.), *Approaches to Twelfth Night*, pp. 22, xvi).

70 Lamb, 'On Some of the Old Actors', pp. 527–31; J. C. Trewin, *Going to Shakespeare* (London: Allen & Unwin, 1978), p. 164.

71 Henry Morley, *The Journal of a London Playgoer, From 1851 to 1866* (London: George Routledge & Sons, 1891), p. 139. Lamb, of course, had compared Bensley's Malvolio to 'an old Castilian' and 'the hero of La Mancha': 'Some of the Old Actors, p. 530. (1822, p. 530).

72 Edward Aveling, in his July 1884 review of Irving's production, quoted in Salgado, *Eyewitnesses of Shakespeare*, p. 214; Williamson, *Old Vic Drama*, p. 87.

73 Williamson, *Old Vic Drama*, p. 88; Arthur Colby Sprague and J. C. Trewin, *Shakespeare's Plays Today: Some Customs and Conventions of the Stage*, repr. (Columbia: University of South Carolina Press, 1971), pp. 94–5; Billington (ed.), *Approaches to Twelfth Night*, pp. xxiv, xxvii; Potter, *Twelfth Night*, p. 68.

74 Watermeier, 'Shakespeare in Canada', p. 215.

75 Berry, *Changing Styles in Shakespeare*, p. 115 (the critic alluded to was B. A. Young, *The Financial Times*, 23 August 1974); Robert Speaight, 'Shakespeare in Britain', *Shakespeare Quarterly* 28:2 (1977): 184–90, 185; DeCatur, 'West German Shakespeare as Seen by a Teacher Abroad', p. 518.

76 Billington (ed.), *Approaches to Twelfth Night*, pp. xvii, xxix, xxx, 48, 54; Murray, 'Shakespeare in Ireland', p. 198; Sprague and Trewin, *Shakespeare's Plays Today*, pp. 95–6; Trewin, *Going to Shakespeare*, p. 163; Williamson, *Old Vic Drama*, pp. 87–8.

77 On Sir Toby, see Berry, *Changing Styles in Shakespeare*, pp. 111, 113, 115; Billington (ed.), *Approaches to Twelfth Night*, pp. xxiii, xxvii, xxx, 56; DeCatur, 'West German Shakespeare', p. 517; Potter, *Twelfth Night*, pp. 68, 70; Warren, 'Shakespeare in England, 1983', p. 454; Watermeier, 'Shakespeare in Canada', p. 215; Williamson, *Old Vic Drama*, p. 88. On Viola, see Billington (ed.), *Approaches to Twelfth Night*, p. 37; Williamson, *Old Vic Drama*, p. 87.

78 On Maria, see Berry, *Changing Styles in Shakespeare*, pp. 114, 115; Billington (ed.), *Approaches to Twelfth Night*, pp. xxiii, xxvii, xxx; Potter, *Twelfth Night*, p. 68; Sprague and Trewin, *Shakespeare's Plays Today*, pp. 92–3; Trewin, *Going to Shakespeare*, p. 164; Watermeier, 'Shakespeare in Canada', p. 215; and Williamson, *Old Vic Drama*, p. 88. On Feste, see Berkowitz, 'Shakespeare at the Edinburgh Festival, 1991', p. 230; Berry, *Changing Styles in Shakespeare*, p. 113; Billington (ed.), *Approaches to Twelfth Night*, pp. xiv, xix, xxiv, 69; John Spalding Gatton, 'Shakespeare in Central Park, Louisville', *Shakespeare Quarterly* 33:3 (1982): 353–5, 353; Potter, *Twelfth Night*, pp. 63, 68; Sprague and Trewin, *Shakespeare's Plays Today*, pp. 96–7, 113n. 18; and Williamson, *Old Vic Drama*, p. 87. Feste has, on occasion, been played by a woman. See Billington (ed.), *Approaches to Twelfth Night*, p. xii; Styan *The Shakespeare Revolution*, pp. 11, 18.

79 Russell Jackson, 'Shakespeare in Gdansk, August 2006', *Shakespeare Quarterly* 58:1 (2007): 93–108, 104, 106, 108.

80 Stephen Booth, 'Shakespeare in the San Francisco Bay Area', *Shakespeare Quarterly* 29:2 (1978): 267–8, 268.

81 References to Chekhov are so common as to risk becoming a cliché. Nunn has said that Peter Hall's 1958 *Twelfth Night* was 'definitively right. He had touched a Chekhov-like centre in the play; it was unarguable' (quoted in Berry, *Changing Styles in Shakespeare*, p. 113); Billington praises Barton's 1969 RSC production by concluding that 'It was the most Chekhovian *Twelfth Night* most of us had ever seen' (Billington, (ed.), *Approaches to Twelfth Night*, p. xxi); and Branagh describes his Renaissance Theatre production of the play as 'close to Chekhov' (Rothwell, *A History of Shakespeare on Screen*, p. 227). The ultimate Chekhovian *Twelfth Night* was intended to be a 1981 production of the

play in Los Angeles, where it was to be paired with a production of *Chekhov in Yalta* as 'Shakespeare interpreted by the Moscow Art Theatre company'; however, the concept does not seem to have developed beyond the setting, costumes, and music (Lillian Wilds, 'Shakespeare in Southern California', *Shakespeare Quarterly* 33:3 (1982): 380–93, 381). *Cheek by Jowl*'s all-male production of *Twelfth Night* in Russian, which opened in Moscow in 2003, was produced in association with The Chekhov Festival Theatre.

3: The State of the Art

1   C. L. Barber, *Shakespeare's Festive Comedy: A Study of Dramatic Form and Its Relation to Social Custom* (Princeton: Princeton University Press, 1959).

2   Keir Elam (ed.), *The Arden Shakespeare: Twelfth Night* (London: Bloomsbury, 2008).

3   Keir Elam, 'The Fertile Eunuch: *Twelfth Night*, Early Modern Intercourse and the Fruits of Castration', *Shakespeare Quarterly* 47 (1996): 1–36.

4   Elam (ed.), *Twelfth Night*, p. 2.

5   Ibid., p. 3.

6   Ibid., p. 40.

7   Ibid., pp. 80, 81.

8   Ibid., pp. 11, 24.

9   Ibid., pp. 11, 15.

10 Ibid., p. 16.

11 Ibid., p. 24.

12 Arthur F. Kinney, 'The Unity of *Twelfth Night*', in *Shakespeare's Comedies of Love: Essays in Honour of Alexander Leggatt*, Karen Bamford and Ric Knowles (ed.) (Toronto: University of Toronto Press, 2008), pp. 155–74, 161.

13 Ibid., pp. 161, 171.

14 Stephen Greenblatt, 'Fiction and Friction', in *Reconstructing Individualism: Autonomy, Individuality, and the Self in Western Thoughts*, Thomas C. Heller, Morton Sosna and David E. Wellberg (ed.) (Stanford: Stanford University Press, 1986).

15 Thomas Laqueur, *Making Sex: Body and Gender from the Greeks to Freud* (Cambridge: Harvard University Press, 1990).

16 Janet Adelman, 'Making Defect Perfection: Shakespeare and the One-Sex Model', in *Enacting Gender on the English Renaissance Stage*, Viviana Comensoli and Anne Russell (ed.) (Urbana: University of Illinois Press, 1999), pp. 23–52.

17 R. W. Maslen, '*Twelfth Night*, Gender, and Comedy', in *Early Modern English Drama: A Critical Companion*, Garrett A. Sullivan Jr., Patrick

Cheney and Andrew Hadfield (ed.) (Oxford: Oxford University Press, 2006), pp. 130–9, 138.

18   Stephen Orgel, *Impersonations: The Performance of Gender in Shakespeare's England* (Cambridge: Cambridge University Press, 1996).

19   Robin Headlam Wells, '*Twelfth Night*, Puritanism, and the Myth of Gender Anxiety', in *The Shakespearean International Yearbook Volume 3*, Graham Bradshaw, John M. Mucciolo and Angus Fletcher (ed.) (Aldershot: Ashgate, 2003), pp. 79–103.

20   Wells, '*Twelfth Night*', p. 81.

21   Laurie J. Shannon, 'Nature's Bias: Renaissance Homonormativity and Elizabethan Comic Likeness', *Modern Philology* 98 (2000–1): 183–210, 185.

22   Ibid., p. 187.

23   Ibid., p. 207.

24   Ibid., p. 208.

25   Valerie Traub, *The Renaissance of Lesbianism in Early Modern England* (Cambridge: Cambridge University Press, 2002), p. 56.

26   Ibid., p. 57.

27   Denise A. Walen, *Construction of Female Homoeroticism in Early Modern Drama* (New York: Palgrave Macmillan, 2005), p. 60.

28   Jami Ake, 'Glimpsing a "Lesbian" Poetics in *Twelfth Night*', *Studies in English Literature 1500–1900* 43.2 (2003): 375–94, 375.

29   Ibid., pp. 375–6.

30   Ibid., p. 380.

31   Chad Allen Thomas, 'On Queering *Twelfth Night*', *Theatre Topics* 20.2 (2010): 101–11, 103.

32   Bruce R. Smith, '"His Fancy's Queen": Sensing Sexual Strangeness in *Twelfth Night*', in *Twelfth Night: New Critical Essays*, (ed.) James Schiffer (London: Routledge, 2011), pp. 65–80, 79.

33   Goran V. Stanivukovic, 'Masculine Plots in *Twelfth Night*', in Schiffer (ed.), *Twelfth Night*, pp. 114–30, 114.

34   Stanivukovic, 'Masculine Plots in *Twelfth Night*', p. 116.

35   Ibid., pp. 118, 121, 126.

36   Laurie E. Osborne, '"The Marriage of True Minds": Amity, Twinning, and Comic Closure in *Twelfth Night*', in Schiffer (ed.), *Twelfth Night*, pp. 99–113, 112.

37   David Schalkwyk, 'The Discourses of Friendship and the Structural Imagination of Shakespeare's Theater: Montaigne, *Twelfth Night*, De Gournay', *Renaissance Drama* 38 (2010): 141–71, 142.

38   Ibid., p. 146.

39   Ibid., p. 151.

40   Ibid., p. 151.

41   Ibid., pp. 152, 152–3.

42   Tom MacFaul, *Male Friendship in Shakespeare and His Contemporaries*
      (Cambridge: Cambridge University Press, 2007), p. 176.

43   Ibid., p. 181.

44   Lesel Dawson, *Lovesickness and Gender in Early Modern English Literature*
      (Oxford: Oxford University Press, 2008), pp. 92–3.

45   Amy L. Smith and Elizabeth Hodgson, ' "A Cypress, Not a Bosom, Hides
      my Heart": Olivia's Veiled Conversions', *Early Modern Literary Studies*
      15.1 (2009–10) http://purl.oclc.org/emls/15-1/olivveil.htm [accessed
      28 April 2012], para 5.

46   Ibid.

47   Ibid., para 8.

48   See further Brinda Charry, ' "[T]he Beauteous Scarf": Shakespeare and
      the "Veil Question"', *Shakespeare* 4 (2008): 112–26.

49   Loreen L. Giese, 'Malvolio's Yellow Stockings: Coding Illicit Sexuality in
      Early Modern London', *Medieval and Renaissance Drama in England* 19
      (2006): 235–46.

50   Ibid., p. 235.

51   Ibid., p. 241.

52   Elam, (ed.), *Twelfth Night*, p. 71.

53   Anne Blake, 'Location, Imagination, and Heterotopia in *Twelfth Night*',
      Litteraria Pragensia 12.23 (2002): 66–79, 69, 71.

54   Francois Laroque, 'Shakespeare's Imaginary Geography', in *Shakespeare
      and Renaissance Europe*, Andrew Hadfield and Paul Hammond (ed.)
      (London: Thomson, 2005), pp. 193–219, 211.

55   Patricia Parker, 'Was Illyria as Mysterious and Foreign as We Think?', in
      The Mysterious and the Foreign in Early Modern England, Helen Ostovich,
      Mary V. Silcox and Graham Roebuck (ed.) (Newark: University of
      Delaware Press, 2008), pp. 209–33, 224. See further: Sara Hanna, 'From
      Illyria to Elysium: Geographical Fantasy in *Twelfth Night*', *Litteraria
      Pragensia* 12.23 (2002): 21–45; Elizabeth Pentland, 'Beyond the "Lyric" in
      Illyricum: Some Early Modern Backgrounds to *Twelfth Night*', in Schiffer
      (ed.), *Twelfth Night*, pp. 149–66; Goran V. Stanivukovic, ' "What Country,
      Friends, is This?": The Geographies of Illyria in Early Modern England',
      Litteraria Pragensia 12.23 (2002): 5–20; and 'Illyria Revisited: Shakespeare
      and the Eastern Adriatic', in *Shakespeare and the Mediterranean: The
      Selected Proceedings of the International Shakespeare Association World
      Congress, Valencia, 2001*, Thomas Clayton, Susan Brock and Vincente
      Forés (ed.) (Newark: University of Delaware Press, 2004), pp. 400–15.

56   Pentland, 'Beyond the "Lyric" in Illyricum', p. 163.

57   Parker, 'Was Illyria as Mysterious?', p. 215.

58   Stanivukovic, 'Illyria Revisited', pp. 405, 412.

59 Catherine Lisak, 'Domesticating Strangeness in *Twelfth Night*', in Schiffer (ed.), *Twelfth Night* pp. 167–83, 169.

60 Lisak, 'Domesticating Strangeness in *Twelfth Night*', pp. 169, 172.

61 Peter Milward, 'The Religious Dimension of Shakespeare's Illyria', *Litteraria Pragensia* 12.23 (2002): 59–65, 63.

62 Richard Wilson, 'Making Men of Monsters: Shakespeare in the Company of Strangers', *Shakespeare* 1 (2005): 8–28, 18–19.

63 Timothy Billings, 'Caterwauling Cataians: The Genealogy of a Gloss', *Shakespeare Quarterly*, 54 (2003): 1–28, 7.

64 Carol Thomas Neely, *Distracted Subjects: Madness and Gender in Shakespeare and Early Modern Culture* (Ithaca: Cornell University Press, 2004), pp. 151–2.

65 Ibid., p. 154.

66 Kathleen R. Sands, *Demon Possession in Elizabethan England* (London: Praeger, 2004).

67 Marion Gibson, *Possession, Puritanism and Print: Darrell, Harsnett, Shakespeare and the Elizabethan Exorcism Controversy* (London: Pickering & Chatto, 2006).

68 Mihoko Suzuki, 'Gender, Class, and the Ideology of Comic Form: *Much Ado about Nothing* and *Twelfth Night*', in *A Feminist Companion to Shakespeare*, (ed.) Dympna C. Callaghan (Oxford: Blackwell, 2000), pp. 121–43, 137.

69 Ibid., p. 130.

70 Ibid., p. 139.

71 Ibid.

72 Ibid., p. 138.

73 Ivo Kamps, 'Madness and Social Mobility in *Twelfth Night*', in Schiffer (ed.), *Twelfth Night*, pp. 229–43, 239.

74 Ibid., p. 231.

75 Ibid., pp. 235–6.

76 Ibid., p. 238.

77 Ibid., p. 240.

78 Elam (ed.), *Twelfth Night*, p. 19.

79 Ibid., p. 21.

80 Ann Lecercle, 'Country House, Catholicity, and the Crypt(ic) in *Twelfth Night*', in *Region, Religion, and Patronage: Lancastrian Shakespeare*, Richard Dutton, Alison Findlay and Richard Wilson (ed.) (Manchester: Manchester University Press, 2003), pp. 84–100, 96.

81 Phebe Jensen, *Religion and Revelry in Shakespeare's Festive World* (Cambridge: Cambridge University Press, 2008), p. 5.

82 Ibid., p. 20.

83 Ibid., p. 149.

84 Smith, Bruce R. (ed.), *Twelfth Night: Texts and Contexts* (New York: Bedford/St Martin's, 2001), p. 320.

85 G. P. Jones, 'Malvolio Flouted and Abused', *English Language Notes* 42.1 (2004): 20–6, 22–3. Kristen Poole, *Radical Religion from Shakespeare to Milton* (Cambridge: Cambridge University Press, 2000), p. 192, n.28.

86 Brett D. Hirsch, 'Rousing the Night Owl: Malvolio, *Twelfth Night*, and Anti-Puritan Satire', *Notes and Queries* 56.1 (2009): 53–5.

87 Paul Yachnin, 'Reversal of Fortune: Shakespeare, Middleton, and the Puritans', *English Literary History* 70 (2003): 757–86, 758.

88 William Kerwin, *Beyond the Body: The Boundaries of Medicine and English Renaissance Drama* (Amherst: University of Massachusetts Press, 2005), p. 194.

89 Ibid., pp. 195–6.

90 Ibid., 198.

91 Ibid., p. 207.

92 Ibid., p. 214.

93 Ibid., p. 222.

94 Ibid., p. 13.

95 Darryl Chalk, ' "To Creep in at Mine Eyes": Theatre and Secret Contagion in *Twelfth Night*', in *'Rapt in Secret Studies': Emerging Shakespeares*, Michael Neill, Darryl Chalk and Laurie Johnson (ed.) (Newcastle upon Tyne: Cambridge Scholars, 2010), pp. 171–93, 174.

96 Becky Kemper, 'A Clown in the Dark House: Reclaiming the Humor in Malvolio's Downfall', *Journal of the Wooden O Symposium*, 7 (2007), 42–50, 48.

97 Indira Ghose, 'Licence to Laugh: Festive Laughter in *Twelfth Night*', in *A History of English Laughter: Laughter from Beowulf to Beckett and Beyond*, (ed.) Manfred Pfister (Amsterdam: Rodopi, 2002), pp. 35–46.

98 Jensen, *Religion and Revelry*, p. 174.

99 Ibid., p. 171.

100 Ibid., p. 173.

101 Ibid., p. 176.

102 Ibid., p. 193.

103 Ibid., p. 178

104 Ibid., p. 177.

105 Paul Dean, ' "Nothing That is So is So": *Twelfth Night* and Transubstantiation', *Literature and Theology* 17 (2003): 281–97; Maurice Hunt, *Shakespeare's Religious Allusiveness: Its Play and Tolerance* (Burlington: Ashgate, 2004).

106 Thomas Rist, 'Merry, Marry, Mary: Shakespearian Wordplay and *Twelfth Night*', *Shakespeare Survey* 62 (2009): 81–91.

107 Ibid., p. 85.

108 Ibid.

109 Suzanne Penuel, 'Missing Fathers: *Twelfth Night* and the Reformation of Mourning', *Studies in Philology* 107.1 (2010): 74–96, 75.

110 Ibid., p. 79.

111 Ibid., p. 84.

112 Ibid., p. 87.

113 Ibid., p. 90.

114 Janet Clare, 'The "Complexion" of *Twelfth Night*', *Shakespeare Survey* 58 (2005): 199–207, 202.

115 Ibid., p. 207.

116 James P. Bednarz, *Shakespeare and the Poets' War* (New York: Columbia University Press, 2001).

117 Ibid., p. 180.

118 Ibid., p. 179.

119 Ibid.

120 Charlotte Coffin, 'An Echo Chamber for Narcissus: Mythological Rewritings in *Twelfth Night*', *Cahiers Élisabéthains* 66 (2004): 23–8, 23.

121 Ibid., p. 23.

122 Ibid., p. 26.

123 Mark Houlahan, '"Like to th'Egyptian Thief": Shakespeare Sampling Heliodorus in *Twelfth Night*', in Neill, Chalk and Johnson (ed.), *'Rapt in Secret Studies'*, pp. 305–15, 313.

124 Robert Appelbaum, 'Aguecheek's Beef', *Textual Practice* 14.2 (2000): 327–41, 'Belch's Hiccup', *Textus* 13 (2000), 231–62.

125 'Beef', p. 338.

126 Richard Wilson, *Shakespeare in French Theory: King of Shadows* (New York: Routledge-Taylor and Francis, 2007), p. 210.

127 Ibid., p. 223.

128 Ibid., p. 222.

129 Nancy Lindheim, 'Rethinking Sexuality and Class in *Twelfth Night*', *University of Toronto Quarterly* 76.2 (2007): 679–713, 696.

130 Ibid., p. 696.

131 Ibid.

132 Stephanie Chamberlain, '"Rings and Things" in *Twelfth Night*: Gift Exchange, Debt, and the Early Modern Matrimonial Economy', *Journal of the Wooden O Symposium* 7 (2007): 1–12; Alan W. Powers, '"What He Wills": Early Modern Rings and Vows in *Twelfth Night*', in Schiffer (ed.), *Twelfth Night*, pp. 217–28.

133 Chamberlain, '"Rings and Things", p. 5.

134 Ibid., p. 11.

135 Ibid., p. 11.

136 Lisa Marciano, 'The Serious Comedy of *Twelfth Night*: Dark Didacticism in Illyria', *Renascence* 56:1 (2003): 3–19, 3.

137   Ibid., p. 17.
138   Valerie Forman, *Tragicomic Redemptions: Global Economics and the Early Modern English Stage* (Philadelphia: University of Pennsylvania Press, 2008), p. 47.
139   Ibid., p. 52.
140   Ibid., p. 53.
141   Michelle M. Dowd, 'Labours of Love: Women, Marriage and Service in *Twelfth Night* and *The Compleat Servant-Maid*', in *Shakespearean International Yearbook Volume 5*, William R. Elton, John M. Mucciolo and Michael Neill (ed.) (Aldershot: Ashgate, 2005), pp. 103–26, 108–9.
142   Ibid., p. 111.
143   David Schalkwyk, 'Love and Service in *Twelfth Night* and the Sonnets', *Shakespeare Quarterly* 56.1 (2005): 76–100.
144   Ibid., p. 87.
145   Ibid., p. 89.
146   Ibid.
147   Ibid., p. 90.
148   Ibid., p. 91.
149   Schalkwyk, David, 'Music, Food, and Love in the Affective Landscapes of *Twelfth Night*', in Schiffer (ed.), *Twelfth Night*, pp. 81–98, 87.
150   Ibid., p. 95.
151   Elam (ed.), *Twelfth Night*, p. 15.
152   Cynthia Lewis, 'Whodunit?: Plot, Plotting, and Detection in *Twelfth Night*', in Schiffer (ed.), *Twelfth Night*, 258–72, 267.
153   Benson, Sean, ' "Perverse Fantasies"?: Rehabilitating Malvolio's Reading', *Papers on Language and Literature* 45:3 (2009): 261–86, 262.
154   Ibid., p. 263.
155   Ibid., p. 276.
156   Peter J. Smith, ' "M. O. A. I: What Should that Alphabetical Position Portend?" An Answer to the Metaphoric Malvolio', *Renaissance Quarterly* 51 (1998): 1129–224.
157   Lin Kelsey, ' "Many Sorts of Music": Musical Genre in *Twelfth Night* and *The Tempest*', *John Donne Journal* 25 (2006): 129–81, 154–5.
158   Patricia Parker, 'Altering the Letter of *Twelfth Night*: "Some are Born Great" and the Missing Signature', *Shakespeare Survey* 59 (2006): 49–62 and '*Twelfth Night*: Editing Puzzles and Eunuchs of All Kinds', in Schiffer (ed.), *Twelfth Night* pp. 45–64.
159   Elam (ed.), *Twelfth Night*, p. 246.
160   Parker, '*Twelfth Night*', p. 56. Parker is quoting from Edward W. Naylor, *The Poets and the Music* (London: J. M. Dent, 1928).
161   Elam (ed.), *Twelfth Night*, p. 383.
162   Kerwin, *Beyond the Body*, p. 215.

163 David Lindley, *Shakespeare and Music* (London: Thomson Learning, 2006), p. 201.
164 Ibid., p. 201.
165 Ibid., p. 203.
166 Ibid., p. 215.
167 Ibid., p. 216.
168 Ibid., p. 217.
169 Kelsey, ' "Many Sorts of Music" ', p. 133.
170 Ibid., p. 141.
171 Ibid., p. 138.
172 Ibid., p. 143.
173 Ibid., pp. 142–3, 143.
174 Penny Gay, '*Twelfth Night:* "The Babbling Gossip of the Air" ', in *A Companion to Shakespeare's Works*, Richard Dutton and Jean E. Howard (ed.) (Oxford: Blackwell, 2003), pp. 429–46, 430, 432.
175 R. S. White, 'Estranging Word and Self in *Twelfth Night*', in *Word and Self Estranged in English Texts, 1550–1660*, Philippa Kelly and L. E. Semler (ed.) (Burlington: Ashgate, 2010), pp. 107–20, 108, 107
176 Paul Edmondson, *Twelfth Night* (Basingstoke: Macmillan, 2005); Emma Fielding, *Actors on Shakespeare: Twelfth Night* (London: Faber, 2002); John R. Ford, *Twelfth Night: A Guide to the Play* (Westport: Greenwood, 2006); Rex Gibson, *Twelfth Night* (Cambridge: Cambridge University Press, 2002); Sonia Massai (ed.), *William Shakespeare's Twelfth Night: A Sourcebook* (London: Routledge, 2007); Michael Pennington, *Twelfth Night: A User's Guide* (London: Hern, 2000); Bruce R. Smith, *Twelfth Night*.

4: New Directions: 'Ready to distrust mine eyes': Optics and Graphics in *Twelfth Night*

1 All quotations are from Keir Elam (ed.), *The Arden Shakespeare: Twelfth Night* (London: Bloomsbury, 2008). Unless stated, all other references to Shakespeare's plays are from Stephen Greenblatt, gen. (ed.), *The Norton Shakespeare*, 2nd edn. (New York: W. W. Norton, 2008).
2 One of the earliest uses of the term cited by the *OED* is in the Wycliffite Bible (1382, Acts 19.29), where the term 'teatre' is glossed 'or comune biholdyng place.'
3 Andrew Gurr and Mariko Ichikawa, *Staging in Shakespeare's Theatres* (Oxford: Oxford University Press, 2000), p. 6. For a rebuttal of this hypothesis, see Tim Fitzpatrick, *Playwright, Space and Place in Early Modern Performance: Shakespeare and Company* (Farnham: Ashgate, 2011), pp. 181–214.

4   Philip Henslowe, *Henslowe's Diary*, (ed.) R. A. Foakes, 2nd edn (Cambridge:
      Cambridge University Press, 2002), p. 319.

5   See Douglas Bruster and Robert Weimann, *Prologues to Shakespeare's
      Theatre: Performance and Liminality in Early Modern Drama* (London:
      Routledge, 2004), p. 24.

6   Accademici degli Intronati di Siena, *Gl'Ingannati*, (ed.) Marzia Pieri
      (Corazzano: Titivillus, 2009), p. 51.

7   Ibid., pp. 168–9.

8   Curzio Gonzaga, *Gli inganni*, (ed.) Anna Maria Razzoli Roio (Cerrina
      Alessandria: Verso l'arte, 2006), pp. 96–7.

9   Frances Teague, *Shakespeare's Speaking Properties* (London: Associated
      University Presses, 1991), p. 30.

10   Nicholas Hilliard, *A Treatise Concerning the Arte of Limning*, R. K. R. Thornton
      and T. G. S. Cain (ed.) (Ashington: Carcanet New Press, 1981), p. 23.

11   Ibid., p. 16.

12   Henry Constable, 'To Mr Hilliard, upon occasion of a picture he made of
      my Lady Rich', in Ibid., p. v. On the subject of portrait painting, compare
      Constable's *Diana* (1592) Sonnet 2: 'So Loue too weake by force thy hart
      to taint, / within my hart thy heauenly shape doth paint: / suffring therein
      his arrowes to abide, / onelie to th'end he might by witches art, / within
      my hart pierce through thy pictures side, / and through thy pictures side
      might wound my hart'.

13   John Buxton, *Elizabethan Taste* (London: Macmillan, 1966), p. 36.

14   See W. J. T. Mitchell, *Picture Theory* (Chicago and London: University of
      Chicago Press, 1994).

15   See Liliane Louvel, *Poetics of the Iconotext*, trans. by Laurence Petit, (ed.)
      Karen Jacobs (Aldershot: Ashgate, 2011).

16   Mitchell, *Picture Theory*, p. 91.

17   See David Norbrook, 'The Reformation of the Masque', in *The Court
      Masque*, (ed.) David Lindley (Manchester: Manchester University Press,
      1984), pp. 94–110.

18   Thomas Heywood, *An Apology for Actors* (1612), Sig. B3ᵛ.

19   Ibid.

20   Ibid.

21   Jacques Derrida, *Of Grammatology*, trans. by Gayatri Chakrovorty Spivak,
      corrected edn. (Baltimore and London: The Johns Hopkins University
      Press, 1974), p. 46.

22   Reginald Scot, *The Discovery of Witchcraft* (1584), p. 316.

23   See Huber Damisch, *The Origin of Perspective*, trans. John Goodman
      (Cambridge, MA: MIT Press, 1995,) pp. 144–7 and Vincent Ilardi,
      Renaissance Vision: From Spectacles to Telescopes (Philadelphia, American
      Philosophical Society, 2007), pp. 188–9.

24   On Renaissance anamorphic effects, see Jurgis Baltrusaitis, *Anamorphoses ou perspectives curieuses* (Paris: Vrin, 1957). See also Stephen Greenblatt, 'At the Table of the Great: More's Self-Fashioning and Self-Cancellation', in *Renaissance Self-Fashioning: From More to Shakespeare* (Chicago: University of Chicago Press, 1984), pp. 11–73

25   Andrew Gurr (ed.), *King Henry V*, updated edn (Cambridge: Cambridge University Press, 2005), p. 215, n. 286.

26   T. W. Craik (ed.), *The Arden Shakespeare: King Henry V* (London: Routledge, 1995), p. 366n. 316–17.

27   John Shute, *The First and Chief Groundes of Architecture Used in All the Auncient and Famous Monymentes* (1563), Sig. ii^r–iii^v.

28   Sebastiano Serlio, *The second Booke of Architecture, made by Sebastian Serly, Entreating of Perspectiue* (1611), f. 25^r.

29   Marzia Pieri, 'Introduzione', in Accademici degli Intronati di Siena, *Gl'Ingannati*, pp. 24–5.

30   Accademici degli Intronati di Siena, *Gl'Ingannati*, pp. 168–9.

31   Curzio Gonzaga, *Gli inganni*, p. 47.

32   Giovanni Paolo Lomazzo, *A Tracte Concerning the Artes of Curious Paintings Carvinge and Buildinge*, trans. by Richard Haydocke (1598), p. 185.

33   Ibid., p. 207.

34   Ibid., p. 188.

35   Martin Banham, *The Cambridge Guide to Theatre*, 2nd edn (Cambridge: Cambridge University Press 1995), p. 1093.

36   Reported by William Drummond of Hawthornden (R. F. Patterson (ed.), *Ben Jonson's Conversations with William Drummond of Hawthornden* [London: Blackie, 1923], p. 37).

37   Heywood, *An Apology for Actors*, Sig. E4^v.

5: New Directions: Shipwreck and the Hermeneutics of Transience in *Twelfth Night*

1   The final discovery scene complicates the play's shadowed festivity in several ways. Bloodied from head wounds, the injured Toby and Andrew call for help from a surgeon who has passed out from drink. Yet Toby unexpectedly and improbably marries Maria. Viola and Sebastian are reunited, but Viola defers physical contact with her brother until she can retrieve her 'maiden weeds' and resume her identity as woman. Orsino asks for Viola's hand in betrothal, yet also requests her change in appearance before their 'golden time' is fulfilled. Comic convention proposes that Olivia will be as happily married with Sebastian as she would have been with his twin sister. But we remember how particularly Olivia responded

to Cesario's wooing, which was uniquely informed by Viola's knowledge of desire as a woman, just as we remember the mutual trust and devotion generated by Antonio's courageous but now hopeless passion for Sebastian. Viola's all-important clothes are in the keeping of the off-stage Captain, but he is in prison as a result of a mysterious legal action Malvolio has brought against him. Malvolio's vow to be revenged against everyone who has gulled him seems like a genuine threat because Olivia promises he will be 'both the plaintiff and the judge / Of [his] own cause' (5.1.345–6).

2   C. L. Barber, *Shakespeare's Festive Comedy: A Study of Dramatic Form and its Relation to Social Custom* (Princeton: Princeton University Press, 1959); Northrup Frye, *A Natural Perspective: The Development of Shakespeare's Comedies and Romances* (New York: Columbia University Press, 1965); François Laroque, *Shakespeare's Festive World*, trans. by Janet Lloyd (Cambridge: Cambridge University Press, 1992). A notable exception to this tradition is Steve Mentz's 'Beachcombing: *Twelfth Night*' in *At the Bottom of Shakespeare's Ocean* (London: Continuum, 2009), pp. 50–62, which takes the critical presence of shipwreck seriously.

3   Hans Blumenberg, *Shipwreck with Spectator: Paradigm of a Metaphor for Existence*, trans. by Steven Rendell (Cambridge, MA: MIT, 1997), p. 14 and throughout.

4   Josiah Blackmore, *Manifest Perdition: Shipwreck Narrative and the Disruption of Empire* (Minneapolis: University of Minneapolis Press, 2002), p. 29.

5   Not coincidentally Blumenberg's and Blackmore's terms relate the survivor's experience emblematically to the biblical figure of Paul. Conversion and shipwreck were the two iconic events of Paul's life: respectively, on the road to Damascus (Acts of the Apostles 9) and off the coast of Malta (Acts 27–28). The second event recapitulated the first, since Paul's survival on Malta led to the conversion of what the Geneva Bible calls the island's 'natives.' Together these events became an archetype of early modern overseas colonization, which Shakespeare alludes to in *The Tempest*.

6   Frank Kermode, *The Sense of an Ending: Studies in the Theory of Fiction* (New York: Oxford University Press, 1967).

7   Giorgio Agamben, *The Time That Remains: A Commentary on the Letter to the Romans*, trans. by Patricia Daley (Stanford: Stanford University Press, 2005), p. 1 and *throughout*.

8   And in later-written New Testament texts. For example, Luke, the second-century author of the Acts of the Apostles, refigured the earlier period of eschatological time as a precise moment of positive *peripeteia* in his narrative of Paul's shipwreck off Malta. This move reflected the fact that time had not ended and the messianic event had to be reconciled with on-going diachronic history.

9   As Kermode observes (citing the work of Rudolph Bultmann, *History and Eschatology* [1957]), already at some points in Paul's letters there is an emerging awareness that the end-of-times is not imminent. Paul's ecclesiastical successors seized on these tendencies to redefine messianic transience as an internal condition corresponding with the believer's personal life and death. Eschatology thereby changed from being a collective historical event to an eternal condition played out at the level of the individual human soul. This de-escalation of eschatology by the Christian church merged with rituals of festive release and return to discipline in pre-Christian holidays such as the Roman Saturnalia, evolving eventually into the oscillating temporalities of Carnival and Lent. See Kermode, *The Sense of an Ending*, p. 25.

10   Mikhail Bakhtin, 'Forms of Time and of the Chronotope in the Novel', in *The Dialogic Imagination: Four Essays*, trans. by Caryl Emerson and Michael Holquist, (ed.) M. Holquist (Austin: University of Texas Press, 1981), pp. 84–258.

11   All quotations are from Roger Warren and Stanley Wells (ed.), *Twelfth Night, or What You Will* (Oxford: Oxford University Press, 1994).

12   Blackmore, *Manifest Perdition*, pp. xxvi, 54.

13   Marina adopts similar performative rhetoric, including ecstatic song, dance and 'other virtues which I'll keep from boast', to liberate herself from the sexual degradation of the Mytilene brothel in *Pericles*, 19.228–20.4 ((ed.) Roger Warren [Oxford: Oxford University Press, 2003]).

14   Goran V. Stanovukovic, 'Illyria Revisited: Shakespeare and the Eastern Adriatic', in *Shakespeare and the Mediterranean: The Selected Proceedings of the International Shakespeare Association World Congress, Valencia, 2001*, Tom Clayton, Susan Brock and Vicente Forés (ed.) (Newark: University of Delaware Press, 2004), pp. 400–15.

15   In *Twelfth Night* Antonio's association with piracy similarly renders his past behaviour and present motives ethically and sexually ambiguous from an Elizabethan perspective.

16   For example, R. Chris Hassel, *Faith and Folly in Shakespeare's Romantic Comedies* (Athens: University of Georgia Press, 1980); Peter Milward, 'Wise Fools in Shakespeare', *Christianity and Literature* 33 (1984): 21–7; Helen M. Whall, 'Divining Paul in Shakespeare's Comedies', *Hellas: A journal of Poetry and the Humanities* 7 (1996): 29–37; Jeffrey Knapp, *Shakespeare's Tribe: Church, Nation and Theatre in Renaissance England* (Chicago: University of Chicago Press, 2002). A related article is D. J. Palmer, 'Bottom, St. Paul, and Erasmus's *Praise of Folly*', *KM 80: A Birthday Album for Kenneth Muir*, Philip Edwards, Vincent Newey and Ann Thompson (ed.) (Liverpool: Liverpool University Press, 1987), pp. 112–13. Recent departures from this tradition include Lisa Lampert, *Gender and Jewish Difference*

from Paul to Shakespeare (Philadelphia: University of Pennsylvania Press, 2004) and Julia Reinhard Lupton, *Citizen-Saints: Shakespeare and Political Theology* (Chicago: University of Chicago Press, 2005).

17 For empirical evidence of the exchange between dramatic representation and audience interpretation in English early modern theatres see Charles Whitney, *Early Responses to Renaissance Drama* (Cambridge: Cambridge University Press, 2006).

18 Linda Hutcheon, *Irony's Edge: The Theory and Politics of Irony* (London: Routledge, 1995), pp. 3–4, 64–5 and *A Theory of Adaptation* (London: Routledge, 2006), pp. 113–39 and throughout.

19 Daniel Boyarin, 'Circumcision, Allegory, and Universal "Man"', in *A Radical Jew: Paul and the Politics of Identity* (Berkeley: University of California Press, 1994), pp. 13–38; Agamben, *The Time That Remains*, pp. 23–7; Reinhard Lupton, *Citizen-Saints*. Universalist and typological readings have long been central to received interpretations of plays such as *The Merchant of Venice* and *Measure for Measure*. In their imperial missionary forms they provided ideological justification for early modern epic narratives of overseas exploration and conquest that Josiah Blackmore analyses in *Manifest Perdition*.

20 See Randall Martin, 'Shakespearian Biography, Biblical Allusion, and Early Modern Practices of Reading Scripture', *Shakespeare Survey* 63 (2010): 212–24.

21 Millar Maclure, *Marlowe: The Critical Inheritance* (London: Routledge & Kegan Paul, 1970), pp. 35, 37. Marlowe's statements are based on Richard Baines's testimony about the playwright's alleged 'atheism.'

22 One possible moment of unspoken recognition occurs during the following exchange:

> FESTE   Now Jove in his next commodity of hair send thee a beard.
>
> VIOLA   By my troth I'll tell thee, I am almost sick for one, though I would not have it grow on *my* chin. (3.1.43–6, editorial italics)

23 John S. Coolidge, *The Pauline Renaissance in England* (Oxford: Oxford University Press, 1970).

24 Warren and Wells (ed.), *Twelfth Night*, pp. 58–60.

25 'The *Opalus* is a pretious stone which hath in it the bright fiery flame of a *Carbuncle*, the pure refulgent purple of an *Amethyst*, and a whole sea of the *Emeraulds* spring glory, or virescency, and every one of them shining with an incredible mixture, and very much pleasure' (Thomas Nicols, *A Lapidary, or, The History of Pretious Stones* [1653], N3ᵛ). We now know that the opal is not only visually but also physically watery. Its natural water content ranges between 2–21 per cent. This reflects the ambient light and

gives the opal its harlequin character, whose symbolism has been interpreted ambiguously. The opal was associated with both good fortune (the
sense of Feste's veiled sarcasm directed at Orsino) and the evil eye www.
gemstone.org [accessed 11 February 2013]. A third watery jewel is the pearl
which Olivia gives to Sebastian (as Cesario): 4.3.2.

26 Elisabeth Schüssler Fiorenza, *Rhetoric and Ethic: The Politics of Biblical
Studies* (Minneapolis: Fortress Press, 1999), pp. 31–55.

27 Erasmus, *The Seconde Tome or Volume of the Paraphrase of Erasmus vpon
the Newe Testamente* (1549). Tudor governments beginning with Edward
VI had required a copy of Erasmus's New Testament *Paraphrases* to
be accessible to lay-readers in every English parish church. See John
Craig, 'Forming a Protestant Consciousness? Erasmus' *Paraphrases* in
English Parishes, 1547–1666', in *Holy Scripture Speaks: The Production
and Reception of Erasmus' Paraphrases on the New Testament*, Hilmar M.
Pabel and Mark Vessey (ed.) (Toronto: University of Toronto Press, 2002),
pp. 313–59.

28 The idea of equality of Christian public participation was another point that
Erasmus commented on in his preface to *Paraphrases on First Corinthians*.

29 G. A. Kennedy, *New Testament Interpretation through Rhetorical Criticism*
(Chapel Hill: University of North Carolina, 1984); Jerome Murphy-
O'Connor, *Paul the Letter-Writer: His World, His Options, His Skills*
(Collegeville: The Liturgical Press, 1995), especially ch. 2, 'Organizing a
Letter', pp. 42–113; Fiorenza, *Rhetoric and Ethic*.

30 For example, Anne Dowriche, 'Preface', *The French History* (1589);
Dorothy Leigh, *The Mother's Blessing* (1616); Rachel Speght, *A Dream*, in
Mortality's Memorandum (1621).

31 Editors support this reading by citing *Richard II* – 'perspectives, which,
rightly gazed upon, / Show nothing but confusion; eyed awry, / Distinguish
form' (2.2.18–20; Oxford edition, Anthony B. Dawson and Paul Yachnin
(ed.) [2011]), or *All's Well That Ends Well* ('scornful perspective [...] Which
warp'd the line of every other favour' (5.3.48–49; Arden 2 edition, (ed.)
G. K. Hunter [1967]). Shakespeare's other use of the word besides *Twelfth
Night* occurs in *Henry V* (as an adverb). There its meaning is positive:
King Henry: '[I] cannot see many a fair French city for one fair French
maid that stands in the way. King Charles: Yes, my lord, you may see them
perspectively' (5.3.306–8, (ed.) Gary Taylor [Oxford: Oxford University
Press, 1982]). Northrup Frye's influential study of cycles of nature in
Shakespearian comedy and romance was entitled *A Natural Perspective*
(New York: Columbia University Press, 1965).

32 Reginald Scot, *A Discovery of Witchcraft* (1584), Bbvi^v, p. 316, quoted by
Keir Elam in his Arden 3 edition of *Twelfth Night* (London: Bloomsbury,
2008), p. 338. *OED* entries confirm that 'perspective' signifies optical

glasses that could magnify, telescope, clarify, refract, distort and create multiple points of view (*OED* 2a, 3, 8, 9). See also Elam's essay in this volume.

33   I am very grateful to Madeline Bassnett and Julia Reinhard Lupton for reading earlier versions of this essay and offering improving suggestions. One version was presented in a 2012 Shakespeare Association of America seminar, 'Oceanic Shakespeares.' I'd like to thank the organizer, Steve Mentz, and seminar participants for their helpful comments as well.

6: New Directions: 'Let them use their talents': *Twelfth Night* and the Professional Comedian

1   C. L. Barber, *Shakespeare's Festive Comedy: A Study of Dramatic Form and its Relation to Social Custom* (Princeton: Princeton University Press, 1959), pp. 291, 292.

2   See, for example, Michael D. Bristol, *Carnival and Theatre: Plebian Culture and the Structure of Authority in Early Modern England* (London: Methuen, 1985); Stephen Greenblatt, 'Fiction and Friction', in *Reconstructing Individualism: Autonomy, Individuality, and the Self in Western Thought,* Thomas C. Heller et al. (ed.) (Stanford: Stanford University Press, 1986), pp. 30–52; Francois Laroque, *Shakespeare's Festive World: Elizabethan Entertainment and the Professional Stage*, trans. by Janet Lloyd (Cambridge: Cambridge University Press, 1993).

3   Marjorie Garber, *Shakespeare After All* (New York: Anchor, 2005), p. 534.

4   Laroque, *Shakespeare's Festive World*, p. 227.

5   Quotations are from Roger Warren and Stanley Wells (ed.), *Twelfth Night, or What You Will* (Oxford: Oxford University Press, 2008).

6   See, for example, Robert H. Bell, 'Motley to the View: The Shakespearean Performance of Folly', *Southwest Review* 95:1/2 (2010): 44–62, and Lisa Marciano, who writes that, 'Though he clearly enjoys merriment [...] he also sees the defects in his society and attempts to correct them by wisely pointing out the inevitability of death and the importance, therefore, of a life well-lived.' (Lisa Marciano, 'The Serious Comedy of *Twelfth Night*: Dark Didacticism in Illyria', *Renascence* 56:1 (2003): 3–19, 14.

7   Erasmus, *Praise of Folly*, trans. by Betty Radice (Harmondsworth: Penguin, 1993), p. 35.

8   Ibid., pp. 56–7.

9   On the representation of religion in *Twelfth Night* see Phebe Jensen, *Religion and Revelry in Shakespeare's Festive World* (Cambridge: Cambridge University Press, 2008), pp. 151–3.

10   Karin S. Coddon, ' "Slander in an Allow'd Fool": *Twelfth Night*'s Crisis of the Aristocracy', *Studies in English Literature, 1500–1900* 33:2 (1993): 309–25, 318. See also Jensen, *Religion and Revelry*, pp. 188–9.

11   Beatrice K. Otto, *Fools are Everywhere: The Court Jester Around the World* (Chicago: University of Chicago Press, 2001), p. xxii.

12   Barbara D. Palmer, 'Early Modern Mobility: Players, Payments, and Patrons', *Shakespeare Quarterly* 56:3 (2005): 259–305, 292. For the particular benefits of provincial houses for clowns and fools, see pp. 285–6.

13   Bristol, *Carnival and Theatre*, p. 126.

14   Nora Johnson, *The Actor as Playwright in Early Modern Drama* (Cambridge: Cambridge University Press, 2003), p. 21.

15   Quoted in Tom Rutter, *Work and Play on the Shakespearean Stage* (Cambridge: Cambridge University Press, 2008), p. 28.

16   Quoted in Wilfred Prest, 'Introduction: The Professions and Society in Early Modern England', in *The Professions in Early Modern England*, (ed.) Wilfred Prest (London: Croom Helm, 1987), pp. 1–24, 13.

17   See Alexandra Shepard, 'Manhood, Credit and Patriarchy in Early Modern England, c. 1580–1640', *Past and Present* 167:1 (2000): 75–106.

18   Robert Armin, *Quips Upon Questions* (1600), frontispiece.

19   Jean Howard, 'Afterword: Early Modern Work and the Work of Representation', in *Working Subjects in Early Modern English Drama*, (ed.) Michelle M. Dowd and Natasha Korda (Farnham: Ashgate, 2011), pp. 243–50, 248.

20   Rutter, *Work and Play*, p. 29.

21   Ibid., p. 37.

22   David Kathman, 'Grocers, Goldsmiths, and Drapers: Freemen and Apprentices in the Elizabethan Theater', *Shakespeare Quarterly* 55:1 (2004): 1–49, 2.

23   This is a status Shakespeare never attained, unlike many of his collaborators who had at one time or another been apprenticed to trades before becoming players. See John Astington, *Actors and Acting in Shakespeare's Time: The Art of Stage Playing* (Cambridge: Cambridge University Press, 2010), p. 77.

24   See Mary Edmond, 'Heminges, John (*bap.* 1566, *d.* 1630)', *Oxford Dictionary of National Biography* (Oxford: Oxford University Press, 2004); online edn, January 2009 http://www.oxforddnb.com.gate.lib.buffalo. edu/view/article/12890 [accessed 11 April 2012], paras 3–4; Kathman, 'Grocers, Goldsmiths, and Drapers', p. 8.

25   Peter Thomson, 'Tarlton, Richard (*d.* 1588)', *ODNB*, online edn, January 2012 http://www.oxforddnb.com.gate.lib.buffalo.edu/view/article/26971 [accessed 4 April 2012], paras 6–7.

26   Martin Butler, 'Armin, Robert (1563–1615)', *ODNB*, online edn, January
     2012   http://www.oxforddnb.com.gate.lib.buffalo.edu/view/article/647
     [accessed 30 March 2012], para 1.

27   See Butler, 'Armin', *ODNB*.

28   Richard Helgerson, *Forms of Nationhood: The Elizabethan Writing of
     England* (Chicago: University of Chicago Press, 1992), p. 223.

29   Ibid., p. 198.

30   Johnson, *The Actor as Playwright*, p. 155.

31   See David Wiles, *Shakespeare's Clown: Actor and Text in the Elizabethan
     Playhouse* (Cambridge: Cambridge University Press, 1987), p. 65.

32   Enid Welsford, *The Fool: His Social and Literary History* (London: Faber,
     1935), p. 119. See also Robert Hornback, *The English Clown Tradition
     from the Middle Ages to Shakespeare* (Cambridge: D. S. Brewer, 2009),
     pp. 150–55.

33   For more on this, see my ' "The Fondness, the Filthiness:" Deformity and
     Laughter in Early-Modern Comedy', *The Upstart Crow* 24, 2004: 15–24.

34   These points are well made by Peter Crockett, 'Performing Natural Folly:
     the Jests of Lean Leanard and the Touchstones of Robert Armin and David
     Tennant', *New Theatre Quarterly* 22:2 (2006): 141–54, 144.

35   Robert Armin, *Quips Upon Questions* (1600), f.C, verso.

36   See Hornback, *The English Clown Tradition*, p. 2.

37   See Ronda Arab, 'Will Kempe's Work: Performing the Player's Masculinity
     in *Kempe's Nine Daies Wonder*', in *Working Subjects in Early Modern English
     Drama*, Michelle M. Dowd and Natasha Korda (ed.) (Farnham: Ashgate,
     2011), pp. 101–14.

38   Robert Armin, *A Nest of Ninnies* (1608).

39   Keir Elam (ed.), *The Shakespeare Arden: Twelfth Night* (London:
     Bloomsbury, 2008), p. 80. See also Coddon, ' "Slander in an Allow'd
     Fool" ', and Barber, *Shakespeare's Festive Comedy*, p. 259.

40   Keith Thomas, 'The Place of Laughter in Tudor and Stuart England',
     Times Literary Supplement, 21 January 1977, p. 77.

41   See the footnote on Chris Holcomb, *Mirth Making: The Rhetorical
     Discourse on Jesting in Early Modern England* (Columbia: University of
     South Carolina Press, 2001), p. 101.

42   Jason Scott-Warren, 'When Theaters Were Bear-Gardens; or, What's
     at Stake in the Comedy of Humors', *Shakespeare Quarterly* 54:1 (2003):
     63–82, 65.

43   David Schalkwyk, 'Love and Service in *Twelfth Night*', *Shakespeare
     Quarterly* 56.1 (2005): 76–100, 90.

44   Ibid., p. 88.

45   In his *Treatise on Laughter* (1560), French physician Laurent Joubert
     offered numerous illustrations of laughter's important physiological worth,

including three detailed stories concerning the healthful benefits of placing laughter-provoking monkeys at the bedsides of the dangerously ill, before concluding 'the dignity and excellence of laughter is [...] very great inasmuch as it reinforces the spirit so much that it can suddenly change the state of the patient, and from his deathbed render him curable.' Laurent Joubert, *Treatise on Laughter*, trans. Gregory David De Rocher (Alabama: University of Alabama Press, 1980), p. 128.

46   See Kenneth J. Tiller, 'The Fool as Physician in Shakespeare's Play', in *Shakespeare's Theory of Blood, Character, and Class: A Festschrift in Honor of David Shelley Berkeley*, Peter C. Rollins and Alan Smith (ed.) (New York: Peter Lang, 2001), pp. 43–60, pp. 51–2.

7: New Directions: Inverted Commas around the 'Fun': Music in *Twelfth Night*

1   Sir Richard Baker, *A Chronicle of the Kings of England* (1643), p. 15.

2   Thomas Heywood, *The Life of Merlin* (1641), p. 277.

3   Thomas Campion, *The Discription of a Maske* (1607), title page.

4   *The Maske of Flowers* (1614), title page.

5   Ben Jonson, *Time Vindicated to Himselfe* (1622), title page.

6   Ben Jonson, *Neptune's Triumph* (1623), title page.

7   Leslie Hotson, *The First Night of Twelfth Night* (London: R. Hart-Davis, 1954), p. 202.

8   John Manningham, *The Diary* (ed.) Robert Parker Sorlien (Hannover: University of New Haven, 1976), p. 48.

9   Roger Warren and Stanley Wells (ed.), *Twelfth Night, or What You Will* (Oxford: Oxford University Press, 1994). Quotations are from this edition.

10   See Ross W. Duffin, *Shakespeare's Songbook* (New York: W. W. Norton, 2004), pp. 384–91.

11   The song settings are reproduced in Warren and Wells (ed.), *Twelfth Night*, pp. 227–8.

12   Tiffany Stern, 'Songs and Masques', in *Documents of Performance in Early Modern England* (Cambridge: Cambridge University Press, 2009), pp. 120–73.

13   William Chappell and G. A. Macfarren, *The Ballad Literature and Popular Music of the Olden Time*, 2 vols (London: Chappell & Co., 1855), Vol. 1, p. 209.

14   Howard Staunton (ed.), *The Plays of Shakespeare with the Poems*, 3 vols (London: Routledge, Warnes and Routledge, 1859), Vol. 2, p. 279.

15   *The Plays of William Shakspeare* [...] *To which are added, notes by Samuel Johnson and George Steevens*, 15 vols (1793), Vol. 4, p. 173.

16   John R. Ford, *Twelfth Night: A Guide to the Play* (Westport: Greenwood Press, 2006), p. 53.

17 David Lindley, *Shakespeare and Music* (London: Thomson Learning, 2006), p. 210.

18 W. H. Auden, *Lectures on Shakespeare*, (ed.) Arthur C. Kirsch (Princeton: Princeton University Press, 2000), p. 155.

19 John Hollander, 'Musica Mundana and *Twelfth Night*', in *Sound and Poetry*, (ed.) Northrop Frye (New York: Columbia University Press, 1957), pp. 55–82, 78.

20 Auden, *Lectures on Shakespeare*, p. 157.

21 Howard Staunton in his Shakespeare edition of 1858–60, quoted in Peter Seng, *The Vocal Songs in the Plays of Shakespeare: A Critical History* (Cambridge, MA: Harvard University Press, 1967), p. 124.

22 Richmond Samuel Howe Noble, *Shakespeare's Use of Song* (London: Oxford University Press, 1923), p. 85.

23 See Hollander, 'Musica Mundana', p. 236.

24 Cyril Tourneur, *Laugh and Lie Downe* (1605), B4^v.

25 David Schalkwyk, 'Music, Food, and Love in the Affective Landscapes of *Twelfth Night*', *Twelfth Night: New Critical Essays*, (ed.) James Schiffer (London: Routledge, 2011), pp. 81–98, 85.

26 E. W. Naylor, *Shakespeare and Music* (London: Dent, 1896), p. 105.

27 Philip Gordon, 'Shakespeare – with Music', *English Journal* 31 (1942): 433–8, 435.

28 Peter Thomson, *Shakespeare's Theatre* (London: Routledge, 1983), p. 90.

29 Sydney Beck, 'The Case of "O Mistresse Mine"', *Renaissance News* 6 (1953): 19–23; Philip Gordon, 'The Morley–Shakespeare Myth', *Music and Letters* 28 (1947): 121–5.

30 See Brydan N. S. Gooch and David Thatcher (ed.), *A Shakespeare Music Catalogue*, 5 Vols (Oxford: Clarendon Press, 1991), Vol. 3, p. 1834.

31 Vincent Duckles, 'New Light on "O Mistresse Mine"', *Renaissance News* 7 (1954): 98–100, 98.

32 A version that that uses musical rather than textual repetition is provided in Duffin, *Shakespeare's Songbook*, pp. 286–7.

33 Bruce R. Smith (ed.), *William Shakespeare, Twelfth Night: Texts and Contexts* (New York: Palgrave, 2001), p. 157.

34 R. T., *A Prettie Newe Ballad, intityled: The Crowe Sits Upon the Wall, Please One and Please All* (1592).

35 Katharine Garvin, 'A Speculation about *Twelfth Night*', *Notes and Queries* 170 (1936): 326–8.

36 See Willa McClung Evans, *Ben Jonson and Elizabethan Music* (New York: Da Capo Press, 1965), pp. 51, 97.

37 Noble, *Shakespeare's Use of Song*, p. 110.

38 Roger Warren (ed.), *Cymbeline* (Oxford: Oxford University Press, 1998).

39   John Dover Wilson, (ed.), *Twelfth Night* (Cambridge: Cambridge University Press, 1949), pp. 91–3; W. W. Greg, *The Shakespeare First Folio* (Oxford: Clarendon Press, 1955), p. 297.

40   Robert Armin, *A Nest of Ninnies* (1608), A2v; Robert Armin, *Foole upon Foole* (1605), A1v.

41   Auden, *Lectures on Shakespeare*, p. 152.

8: Learning and Teaching Resources

1   Keir Elam (ed.), *The Arden Shakespeare: Twelfth Night* (London: Bloomsbury, 2008). All references to the play are taken from this edition.

2   Jane Hwang Degenhardt, 'Foreign Worlds', in *The Oxford Handbook to Shakespeare* (ed.) Arthur F. Kinney (Oxford: Oxford University Press, 2012), pp. 433–57, 450.

3   David L. Norton, 'On Teaching What Students Already Know', *The School Review* 82:1 (1973): 45–56, 45.

4   Nicholas Monk with Carol Chillington Rutter, Jonothan Neelands and Jonothan Heron, *Open-space Learning: A Study in Transdisciplinary Pedagogy* (London: Bloomsbury, 2011), p. 3.

5   Neill Thew, 'Teaching Shakespeare: A Survey of the Undergraduate Level in Higher Education', *Reports to the Higher Education Academy English Subject Centre* 13 (2006): 29.

6   Ronald E. M. Salomone and James E. Davis, *Teaching Shakespeare into the Twenty-First Century* (Athens: Ohio University Press, 1997).

7   Edward L. Rocklin, *Performance Approaches to Teaching Shakespeare* (Urbana: National Council of Teachers of English, 2005).

8   Rex Gibson, *Teaching Shakespeare* (Cambridge: Cambridge University Press, 1998), p. 123.

9   James Stredder, *The North Face of Shakespeare* (Cambridge: Cambridge University Press, 2009), pp. 177–9.

10   Alexander Leggatt, 'Questions that Have no Answers', in *Teaching Shakespeare: Passing It On*, (ed.) G. B. Shand (Malden: Blackwell, 2009), pp. 61–72, 67.

11   Stephen Orgel, 'Why Did the English Stage Take Boys for Women?', in *Teaching Shakespeare through Performance* (ed.) Milla Cozart Riggio (New York: Modern Language Association of America, 1999), pp. 102–13.

12   Mario DiGangi, 'Sex Matters', in *Approaches to Teaching English Renaissance Drama*, (ed.) Karen Bamford and Alexander Leggatt (New York: Modern Language Association of America, 2002), pp. 150–57.

13   William C. Carroll, 'Romantic Comedies', in *Shakespeare: An Oxford Guide*, Stanley Wells (ed.) (Oxford: Oxford University Press, 2003), pp. 175–92.

14   Michael D. Bristol, *Carnival and Theater: Plebeian Culture and the Structure of Authority in Renaissance England* (London: Methuen, 1985).

15   Alexander Leggatt, *Shakespeare's Comedy of Love* (London: Methuen, 1974), p. xiii.

16   Ibid., pp. 221–54.

17   Terence Hawkes, 'Comedy, Orality and Duplicity: *Twelfth Night*', in *Shakespeare's Comedies*, (ed.) Gary Waller (New York: Longman, 1991), pp. 168–74.

18   Bristol, *Carnival and Theater*, p. 202.

19   Phebe Jansen, 'Teaching Drama as Festivity: Dekker's *The Shoemaker's Holiday* and Beaumont's *The Knight of the Burning Pestle*', in Bamford and Leggatt (ed.), *Approaches to Teaching English Renaissance, Drama* pp. 158–64, 158.

20   Janet Clare, 'The "Complexion" of *Twelfth Night*', *Shakespeare Survey* 58 (2005): 199–207.

21   Smith, Emma (ed.) *Shakespeare's Comedies* (Malden: Blackwell, 2004).

22   Valerie Traub, 'The Homoerotics of Shakespearian Comedy', in Smith (ed.), pp. 164–91.

23   Barbara Hodgdon, 'Sexual Disguise and the Theatre of Gender', in *The Cambridge Companion to Shakespeare's Comedies*, (ed.) Alexander Leggatt (Cambridge: Cambridge University Press, 2002), pp. 179–97.

24   Edward Berry, 'Laughing at "Others"', in Leggatt (ed.), *The Cambridge Companion to Shakespeare's Comedies*, pp. 123–38.

25   Catherine Bates, 'Love and Courtship', in Leggatt (ed.), *The Cambridge Companion to Shakespeare's Comedies*, pp. 102–21.

26   Michael Mangen, *A Preface to Shakespeare's Comedies 1594–1603* (London: Longman, 1996).

27   Graham Atkin, *Twelfth Night: Character Studies* (London: Continuum, 2008).

28   Emma Fielding, *Actors on Shakespeare: Twelfth Night* (London: Faber, 2002).

29   Tracey Irish (ed.), *The Shorter Shakespeare: Twelfth Night* (Carlisle: Carel Press, 2001).

30   Bruce R. Smith (ed.), *Twelfth Night: Texts and Contexts* (Boston: Bedford/St Martin's, 2001).

31   Sonia Massai (ed.), *William Shakespeare's Twelfth Night: A Sourcebook* (London: Routledge, 2007).

32   John R. Ford, *Twelfth Night: A Guide to the Play* (Westport: Greenwood Press, 2006).

33   James Schiffer (ed.), *Twelfth Night: New Critical Essays* (London: Routledge, 2011).

34   James Schiffer, 'Taking the Long View: *Twelfth Night* Criticism and Performance', in Schiffer (ed.), *Twelfth Night*, pp. 1–44.

35 Bruce R. Smith, ' "His Fancy's Queen": Sensing Sexual Strangeness in *Twelfth Night*', in Schiffer (ed.), *Twelfth Night*, pp. 65–80.

36 David Schalkwyk, 'Love and Service in *Twelfth Night* and the Sonnets', *Shakespeare Quarterly* 56.1 (2005): 76–100, 81–98.

37 David Lindley, *Shakespeare and Music* (London: Thomson Learning, 2006), pp. 199–234.

38 Laurie E. Osborne, ' "The Marriage of True Minds": Amity, Twinning, and Comic Closure', in Schiffer (ed.), *Twelfth Night*, pp. 99–113.

39 Ibid., p. 112.

40 Chad Thomas Allen, 'On Queering *Twelfth Night*', *Theatre Topics* 20.2 (2010): 101–11.

41 Jami Ake, 'Glimpsing a "Lesbian" Poetics in *Twelfth Night*', *Studies in English Literature 1500–1900* 43.2 (2003): 375–94, 376.

42 Penny Gay, *As She Likes It: Shakespeare's Unruly Women* (London: Routledge, 1994).

43 Stanley Wells, 'Boys Should be Girls: Shakespeare's Female Roles and the Boy Players', *New Theatre Quarterly* 25.2 (2009): 172–7.

44 Stanley Wells, *Shakespeare, Sex, and Love* (Oxford: Oxford University Press, 2010).

45 Adrian Kiernander, ' "You'll Be the Man": Homophobia and the Present in Performances of *Twelfth Night* and *Romeo and Juliet*', in *Presentism, Gender, and Sexuality in Shakespeare*, (ed.) Evelyn Gajowski (Basingstoke: Palgrave, 2009), pp. 125–42, 128.

46 Elam (ed.), *Twelfth Night*, p. 356

47 Patricia Parker, '*Twelfth Night*: Editing Puzzles and Eunuchs of All Kinds', in Schiffer (ed.), *Twelfth Night*, pp. 45–64.

48 Patricia Parker, 'Altering the Letter of *Twelfth Night*: "Some are Born Great" and the Missing Signature', *Shakespeare Survey* 59 (2006): 49–62.

49 Elam (ed.), *Twelfth Night*, pp. 78–87.

50 David Crystal, *'Think On My Words': Exploring Shakespeare's Language* (Cambridge: Cambridge University Press, 2008), p. 211.

51 Schalkwyk, 'Love and Service', pp. 76–100.

52 Thomas Rist, 'Merry, Marry, Mary: Shakespearian Wordplay and *Twelfth Night*', *Shakespeare Survey* 62 (2009): 81–91.

53 Walter Nash, 'Puns and Parody', in *Reading Shakespeare's Dramatic Language: A Guide*, Sylvia Adamson, Lynette Hunter, Lynne Magnusson, Ann Thompson and Katie Wales (ed.) (London: Arden Shakespeare, 2001), pp. 71–88, 77.

54 Nick de Somogyi, *Twelfth Night* (London: Nick Hern, 2001).

55 Roger Warren and Stanley Wells (ed.), *Twelfth Night* (Oxford: Oxford University Press, 1994).

56   Stephen Greenblatt, 'Twelfth Night', in *The Norton Shakespeare*, Stephen
      Greenblatt, Walter Cohen, Jean E. Howard and Katharine Eisaman Maus
      (ed.), 2nd edn (New York: W. W. Norton, 2008), pp. 1785–92.

57   Elizabeth Story Donno (ed.), *Twelfth Night*, 2nd edn. (Cambridge:
      Cambridge University Press, 2003).

58   Jonathan Bate and Eric Rasmussen (ed.), *Twelfth Night*. Basingstoke:
      Macmillan, 2010.

59   J. M. Lothian and T. W. Craik (ed.) *Twelfth Night* (London: Methuen, 1975).

60   M. M. Mahood (ed.), *Twelfth Night* (London: Penguin, 1968; repr. 2005).

61   Barbara A. Mowat and Paul Werstine (ed.), *Twelfth Night* (Washington:
      Washington Square Press, 1993).

62   John O'Connor (ed.), *New Longman Shakespeare: Twelfth Night* (London:
      Longman, 1999).

63   Rex Gibson (ed.), *Twelfth Night* (Cambridge: Cambridge University Press,
      1993).

64   Rex Gibson, *Twelfth Night: Cambridge Student Guide* (Cambridge:
      Cambridge University Press, 2002).

65   Richard Appignanesi (ed.), *Manga Shakespeare: Twelfth Night*, illustrated
      by Nana Li (New York: Amulet, 2009; 2nd edn, London: SelfMadeHero
      Publications, 2012).

66   William Shakespeare, *Twelfth Night* (Three Watson, IR: Saddleback
      Educational, 2009), p. 9.

67   Simon Greaves (ed.), *The Comic Book Shakespeare: Twelfth Night*
      (Oswestry: Timber Frame, 2003).

68   Stephen Greenblatt, (gen. ed.), *The Norton Anthology of English Literature:
      The Major Authors*, 2 Vols, (8th edn) (New York: W. W. Norton, 2006).

69   Michael Dobson, 'Shakespeare Performances in England, 2002',
      Shakespeare Survey 56 (2003): 256–86.

70   Tim Carroll, '"Practising Behaviour to His Own Shadow"', in
      Shakespeare's Globe: A Theatrical Experiment, Christie Carson and Farah
      Karim-Cooper (ed.) (Cambridge: Cambridge University Press, 2008),
      pp. 37–44.

71   Elizabeth Schafer (ed.), *Shakespeare in Production: Twelfth Night*
      (Cambridge: Cambridge University Press, 2009).

72   Paul Edmondson, *Twelfth Night* (Basingstoke: Palgrave, 2005).

73   Lois Potter, *Twelfth Night: Text and Performance* (Basingstoke: Macmillan,
      1985).

74   Penny Gay, 'Women and Shakespearean Performance', in *The Cambridge
      Companion to Shakespeare on Stage*, Stanley Wells and Sarah Stanton (ed.)
      (Cambridge: Cambridge University Press, 2002), pp. 155–73.

75   Jennifer C. Vaught, '*Twelfth Night* and the New Orleans Twelfth Night
      Revelers', in Schiffer (ed.), *Twelfth Night* pp. 244–54.

76   Christa Jansohn, '"The Text Remains for Another Attempt": *Twelfth Night, or What You Will* on the German Stage', in Schiffer (ed.), *Twelfth Night* pp. 201–16.

77   Peter Novak, '"Where Lies Your Text?": *Twelfth Night* in American Sign Language Translation', *Shakespeare Survey* 61 (2008): 74–90.

78   Michael Pennington, *Twelfth Night: A User's Guide* (London: Nick Hern, 2000).

79   Alfredo Michel Modenessi, '"This Uncivil and Unjust Extent Against Thy Peace": Tim Supple's *Twelfth Night*, or What Violence Will', *Shakespeare Survey* 61 (2008): 91–103.

80   The complete collection contains: *King John* (UK, 1899), *The Tempest* (UK, 1908), *A Midsummer Night's Dream* (USA, 1909), *King Lear* (Italy, 1910), *Twelfth Night* (USA, 1910), *The Merchant of Venice* (Italy, 1910) and *Richard III* (UK, 1911).

81   Judith Buchanan, *Shakespeare on Silent Film: An Excellent Dumb Discourse* (Cambridge: Cambridge University Press, 2009).

82   Katherine Eggert, 'Sure Can Sing and Dance: Minstrelsy, the Star System, and the Post-Postcoloniality of Kenneth Branagh's *Love's Labour's Lost* and Trevor Nunn's *Twelfth Night*', in *Shakespeare: The Movie II*, Richard Burt and Lynda E. Boose (ed.) (London: Routledge, 2003), pp. 72–88, 82.

83   The other animated tales are *The Taming of the Shrew*, *Romeo and Juliet*, *Julius Caesar*, *Hamlet*, *Othello*, *Macbeth*, *The Winter's Tale* and *The Tempest*.

84   The online texts are those available at http://shakespeare.mit.edu and W. J. Craig's 1914 Oxford text, transcribed at www.bartleby.com. [Accessed 5 May 2013]

SELECT BIBLIOGRAPHY

Anon., 'Current Theatre Notes', *Shakespeare Quarterly* 4:1 (1953): 61–75.

Accademici degli Intronati di Siena, *Gl'Ingannati*, (ed.) Marzia Pieri (Corazzano: Titivillus, 2009).

Adelman, Janet, 'Making Defect Perfection: Shakespeare and the One-Sex Model', *Enacting Gender on the English Renaissance Stage*, (ed.) Viviana Comensoli and Anne Russell (Urbana: University of Illinois Press, 1999), pp. 23–52.

Agamben, Giogio, *The Time That Remains: A Commentary on the Letter to the Romans*, trans. by Patricia Daley (Stanford: Stanford University Press, 2005).

Ake, Jami, 'Glimpsing a "Lesbian" Poetics in *Twelfth Night*', *Studies in English Literature 1500–1900* 43:2 (2003): 375–94.

Allen, Chad Thomas, 'On Queering *Twelfth Night*', *Theatre Topics* 20:2 (2010): 101–11.

Anderegg, Michael, *Orson Welles, Shakespeare, and Popular Culture* (New York: Columbia University Press, 1999).

—*Cinematic Shakespeare. Genre and Beyond: A Film Studies Series* (Lanham: Rowman & Littlefield, 2004).

Appelbaum, Robert, 'Aguecheek's Beef', *Textual Practice* 14:2 (2000): 327–41.

—'Belch's Hiccup', *Textus* 13 (2000): 231–62.

Arab, Ronda, 'Will Kempe's Work: Performing the Player's Masculinity in *Kempe's Nine Daies Wonder*', in *Working Subjects in Early Modern English Drama*, Michelle M. Dowd and Natasha Korda (ed.) (Farnham: Ashgate, 2011), pp.101–14.

Arlidge, Anthony, *Shakespeare and the Prince of Love: The Feast of Misrule in the Middle Temple* (London: Giles de la Mare Publishers, 2000).

Armin, Robert, *Quips Upon Questions* (1600).

—*Foole upon Foole* (1605).

—*A Nest of Ninnies* (1608).

Astington, John, *Actors and Acting in Shakespeare's Time: The Art of Stage Playing* (Cambridge: Cambridge University Press, 2010).

Atkin, Graham, *Twelfth Night: Character Studies* (London: Continuum, 2008).

Auden, W. H., *Lectures on Shakespeare*, (ed.) Arthur C. Kirsch (Princeton, New Jersey: Princeton University Press, 2000).

Ault, Norman (ed.), *Elizabethan Lyrics* (London: Faber and Faber, 1986).

Bakhtin, Mikhail, 'Forms of Time and of the Chronotope in the Novel', in *The Dialogic Imagination: Four Essays*, trans. by Caryl Emerson and Michael Holquist, (ed.) M. Holquist (Austin: University of Texas Press, 1981).

Ball, Robert Hamilton, *Shakespeare on Silent Film: A Strange Eventful History* (New York: Theatre Arts Books, 1968).

Banham, Martin, *The Cambridge Guide to Theatre*, 2nd edn, (Cambridge: Cambridge University Press, 1995).

Barber, C. L., *Shakespeare's Festive Comedy: A Study of Dramatic Form and its Relation to Social Custom* (Princeton: Princeton University Press, 1959).

Barthes, Roland, 'The Death of the Author,' in *Image, Music, Text*, trans. by Stephen Heath (London: Faber, 1977).

Bate, Jonathan (ed.), *The Romantics on Shakespeare* (Harmondsworth: Penguin Books, 1992).

Bates, Catherine, 'Love and Courtship', in *The Cambridge Companion to Shakespeare's Comedies*, (ed.) Alexander Leggatt (Cambridge: Cambridge University Press, 2002), pp. 102–21.

Beck, Sydney, 'The Case of "O Mistresse Mine"', *Renaissance News* 6 (1953): 19–23.

Bednarz, James P., *Shakespeare and the Poets' War* (New York: Columbia University Press, 2001).

Beier, Lucinda, *Sufferers and Healers: The Experience of Illness in Seventeenth-Century England* (London: Routledge, 1987).

Bell, Robert H., 'Motley to the View: The Shakespearean Performance of Folly', *Southwest Review* 95:1/2 (2010): 44–62.

Belsey, Catherine, 'Disrupting Sexual Difference: Meaning and Gender in the Comedies', *Alternative Shakespeares*, (ed.) John Drakakis (London: Methuen, 1985), pp. 166–90.

Benson, Sean, '"Perverse Fantasies"? Rehabilitating Malvolio's Reading', *Papers on Language and Literature* 45:3 (2009): 261–86.

Berkowitz, Gerald M., 'Shakespeare at the 1988 Edinburgh Festival', *Shakespeare Quarterly* 40:1 (1989): 75–83.

—'Shakespeare at the Edinburgh Festival, 1991', *Shakespeare Quarterly* 43:2 (1992): 227–32.

Berry, Edward, 'Laughing at "Others"', in *The Cambridge Companion to Shakespeare's Comedies*, (ed.) Alexander Leggatt (Cambridge: Cambridge University Press, 2002).

Berry, Ralph, *Changing Styles in Shakespeare* (London: George Allen & Unwin, 1981).

Billings, Timothy, 'Caterwauling Cataians: The Genealogy of a Gloss', *Shakespeare Quarterly* 54 (2003): 1–28.

Billington, Michael (ed.), *Approaches to Twelfth Night* (London: Nick Hern Books, 1990).

Blackmore, Josiah, *Manifest Perdition: Shipwreck Narrative and the Disruption of Empire* (Minneapolis: University of Minneapolis Press, 2002).

Blake, Ann, 'Location, Imagination, and Heterotopia in *Twelfth Night*', *Litteraria Pragensia* 12:23 (2002): 66–79.

Blumenberg, Hans, *Shipwreck with Spectator: Paradigm of a Metaphor for Existence*, trans. by Steven Rendell (Cambridge: MIT Press, 1997).

Boas, F. S., *Shakespeare and His Predecessors* (London: John Murray, 1896).

Booth, Stephen, 'Shakespeare in the San Francisco Bay Area', *Shakespeare Quarterly* 29:2 (1978): 267–8.

Boyarin, Daniel, 'Circumcision, Allegory, and Universal "Man"', in *A Radical Jew: Paul and the Politics of Identity* (Berkeley: University of California Press, 1994), pp. 13–38.

bp OR NOT bp http://bp-or-not-bp.org/ [accessed 14 January 2013].

Bradley, A. C., 'Feste the Jester [1916]', in *Twelfth Night: Critical Essays*, (ed.) Stanley Wells (Garland: New York, 1986), pp. 17–24.

Bray, Alan, *The Friend* (Chicago: University of Chicago Press, 2003).

Bristol, Michael D., *Carnival and Theater: Plebeian Culture and the Structure of Authority in Renaissance England* (London: Methuen, 1985).

Brode, Douglas, *Shakespeare in the Movies: From the Silent Era to 'Shakespeare in Love'* (Oxford: Oxford University Press, 2000).

Bruster, Douglas, and Robert Weimann, *Prologues to Shakespeare's Theatre: Performance and Liminality in Early Modern Drama* (London: Routledge, 2004).

Buchanan, Judith, *Shakespeare on Silent Film: An Excellent Dumb Discourse* (Cambridge: Cambridge University Press, 2009).

Bucke, John, *Instructions for the Use of the Rosarie* (1589).

Bullough, Geoffrey (ed.), *Narrative and Dramatic Sources of Shakespeare: The Comedies*, Vol. 2 (London: Routledge & Kegan Paul, 1958).

Bulman, James C., '"Unsex Me Here": Male Cross-Dressing at the Globe', in *Shakespeare Re-Dressed: Cross-Gender Casting in Contemporary Performances*, (ed.) James C. Bulman (Cranbury: Associated University Presses, 2008), pp. 231–45.

Bunny, Edward, *A Survey of the Popes Supremacie* (1595).

Buxton, John, *Elizabethan Taste* (London: Macmillan, 1966).

Callaghan, Dympna, *Shakespeare Without Women: Representing Gender and Race on the Renaissance Stage* (London: Routledge, 1999).

Carnegie, David, '"Maluolio Within": Performance Perspectives on the Dark House', *Shakespeare Quarterly* 52:3 (2001): 393–414.

Carroll, Tim, '"Practising Behaviour to His Own Shadow"', in *Shakespeare's Globe: A Theatrical Experiment*, Christie Carson and Farah Karim-Cooper (ed.) (Cambridge: Cambridge University Press, 2008), pp. 37–44.

Carroll, William C., 'Romantic Comedies', in *Shakespeare: An Oxford Guide*,

Stanley Wells and Lena Cowen Orlin (ed.) (Oxford: Oxford University Press, 2003), pp. 175–92.

Chalk, Darryl, ' "To Creep in at Mine Eyes": Theatre and Secret Contagion in *Twelfth Night*', in *'Rapt in Secret Studies': Emerging Shakespeares*, Michael Neill, Darryl Chalk and Laurie Johnson (ed.) (Newcastle upon Tyne: Cambridge Scholars, 2010), pp. 171–93.

Chamberlain, Stephanie, ' "Rings and Things" in *Twelfth Night:* Gift Exchange, Debt, and the Early Modern Matrimonial Economy', *Journal of the Wooden O Symposium* 7 (2007): 1–12.

Chappell, William and G. A. Macfarren, *The Ballad Literature and Popular Music of the Olden Time*, 2 vols (London: Chappell and Co., 1855).

Charry, Brinda, ' "[T]he Beauteous Scarf": Shakespeare and the "Veil Question" ', *Shakespeare* 4 (2008): 112–26.

Chedgzoy, Kate, *Shakespeare's Queer Children: Sexual Politics and Contemporary Culture* (Manchester: Manchester University Press, 1996).

Clare, Janet, 'The "Complexion" of *Twelfth Night*', *Shakespeare Survey* 58 (2005): 199–207.

Coddon, Karin S.,' "Slander in an Allow'd Fool": *Twelfth Night*'s Crisis of the Aristocracy', *Studies in English Literature, 1500–1900* 33:2 (1993): 309–25.

Coffin, Charlotte, 'An Echo Chamber for Narcissus: Mythological Rewritings in *Twelfth Night*', *Cahiers Élisabéthains* 66 (2004): 23–8.

Coldwell, Joan (ed.), *Charles Lamb on Shakespeare* (Gerrards Cross: Colin Smythe, 1978).

Coolidge, John S., *The Pauline Renaissance in England* (Oxford: Oxford University Press, 1970).

Coursen, H. R., 'Cinderella's *Twelfth Night*', *Marlowe Society of America Newsletter* X:1 (1990): 5–6.

—'Refuting the Reviews: Two D.C. Tickets', *Marlowe Society of America Newsletter* X:1 (1990): 6.

Craig, Edward Gordon, *Index to the Story of My Days: Some Memoirs of Edward Gordon Craig, 1872–1907* (New York: Viking, 1957).

Craig, John, 'Forming a Protestant Consciousness? Erasmus' *Paraphrases* in English Parishes, 1547–1666', in *Holy Scripture Speaks: The Production and Reception of Erasmus' Paraphrases on the New Testament*, Hilmar M. Pabel and Mark Vessey (ed.) (Toronto: University of Toronto Press, 2002), pp. 313–59.

Crewdston, Richard, *Apollo's Swan and Lyre: Five Hundred Years of the Musicians' Company* (Woodbridge: Boydell Press, 2000).

Crockett, Peter, 'Performing Natural Folly: The Jests of Lean Leanard and the Touchstones of Robert Armin and David Tennant', *New Theatre Quarterly* 22:2 (2006): 141–54

Crouch, Tim, *I Shakespeare* (London: Oberon, 2011).

Crystal, David, *'Think On My Words': Exploring Shakespeare's Language* (Cambridge: Cambridge University Press, 2008).

Damisch, Huber, *The Origin of Perspective*, trans. by John Goodman (Cambridge: MIT Press, 1995).

Dawson, Lesel, *Lovesickness and Gender in Early Modern English Literature* (Oxford: Oxford University Press, 2008).

De Carles, Nathalie Rivère, 'Staging the exotic in *Twelfth Night*', in *Twelfth Night: New Critical Essays*, (ed.) James Schiffer (London: Routledge, 2011), pp. 184–200.

De Catur, Louis A., 'West German Shakespeare as Seen by a Teacher Abroad', *Shakespeare Quarterly* 33:4 (1982): 515–18.

De Somogyi, Nick, *Twelfth Night* (London: Nick Hern, 2001).

Dean, Paul, ' "Nothing That is So is So": *Twelfth Night* and Transubstantiation', *Literature and Theology* 17 (2003): 281–97.

Degenhardt, Jane Hwang, 'Foreign Worlds', in *The Oxford Handbook to Shakespeare*, (ed.) Arthur F. Kinney (Oxford: Oxford University Press, 2012), pp. 433–57.

Derrida, Jacques, *Of Grammatology*, trans. by Gayatri Chakrovorty Spivak, corrected edn (Baltimore: The Johns Hopkins University Press, 1974).

Dessen, Alan C., 'Exciting Shakespeare in 1988', *Shakespeare Quarterly* 40:2 (1989): 198–207.

DiGangi, Mario, 'Sex Matters', in *Approaches to Teaching English Renaissance Drama*, Karen Bamford and Alexander Leggatt (ed.) (New York: Modern Language Association of America, 2002), pp. 150–7.

Dobson, Michael, *The Making of the National Poet: Shakespeare, Adaptation and Authorship, 1660–1769* (Oxford: Clarendon Press, 1992).

—'Shakespeare Performances in England, 2002', *Shakespeare Survey* 56 (2003): 256–86.

Donno, Elizabeth Story (ed.), *Twelfth Night*, 2nd edn (Cambridge: Cambridge University Press, 2003).

Dowd, Michelle M., 'Labours of Love: Women, Marriage and Service in *Twelfth Night* and *The Compleat Servant-Maid*', in *Shakespearean International Yearbook Volume 5*, William R. Elton, John M. Mucciolo and Michael Neill (ed.) (Aldershot: Ashgate, 2005), pp. 103–26.

Draper, John W., *The Twelfth Night of Shakespeare's Audience* (New York: Octagon Books, 1975).

Duckles, Vincent, 'New Light on "O Mistresse Mine" ', *Renaissance News* 7 (1954): 98–100.

Duffin, Ross W., *Shakespeare's Songbook* (New York: W. W. Norton, 2004).

Dusinberre, Juliet, *Shakespeare and the Nature of Women* (New York: Barnes and Noble, 1975).

Edmondson, Paul, *Twelfth Night* (Basingstoke: Palgrave, 2005).

Eggert, Katherine, 'Sure Can Sing and Dance: Minstrelsy, the Star System, and the Post-Postcoloniality of Kenneth Branagh's *Love's Labour's Lost* and Trevor Nunn's *Twelfth Night*', in *Shakespeare: The Movie II*, Richard Burt and Lynda E. Boose (ed.) (London: Routledge, 2003), pp. 72–88.

Elam, Keir 'The Fertile Eunuch: *Twelfth Night*, Early Modern Intercourse and the Fruits of Castration', *Shakespeare Quarterly* 47 (1996): 1–36.

—'"In What Chapter of his Bosom"? Reading Shakespeare's Bodies', in *Alternative Shakespeares Vol. 2*, (ed.) Terence Hawkes (London: Routledge, 1996), pp. 140–63.

—(ed.), *The Arden Shakespeare: Twelfth Night* (London: Bloomsbury, 2008).

Erasmus, *In Praise of Folly*, trans. by Betty Radice (Harmondsworth: Penguin, 1993).

Everett, Barbara, 'Or What You Will', *Essays in Criticism* 35 (1985): 294–314.

Fielding, Emma, *Actors on Shakespeare: Twelfth Night* (London: Faber, 2002).

Findlay, Alison, *Women in Shakespeare: A Dictionary* (London: Continuum, 2010).

Fiorenza, Elisabeth Schüssler, *Rhetoric and Ethic: The Politics of Biblical Studies* (Minneapolis: Fortress Press, 1999).

Fitzpatrick, Tim, *Playwright, Space and Place in Early Modern Performance: Shakespeare and Company* (Farnham: Ashgate, 2011).

Ford, John R., *Twelfth Night: A Guide to the Play* (Westport: Greenwood Press, 2006).

Forman, Valerie, *Tragicomic Redemptions: Global Economics and the Early Modern English Stage* (Philadelphia: University of Pennsylvania Press, 2008).

Foulkes, Richard, *Performing Shakespeare in the Age of Empire* (Cambridge: Cambridge University Press, 2002).

Freedman, Barbara, 'Naming Loss: Mourning and representation in *Twelfth Night*' in *Staging the Gaze: Postmodernism, Psychoanalysis, and Shakespearean Comedy* (Ithaca: Cornell University Press, 1991).

Frye, Northrop, *A Natural Perspective: the Development of Shakespeare's Comedies and Romances* (New York: Columbia University Press, 1965).

Furness, Horace Howard (ed.), *Twelfth Night*, in *A New Variorum Edition*, repr. (Philadelphia: J. B. Lippincott, 1901).

Garber, Marjorie, *Vested Interests: Cross-Dressing and Cultural Anxiety* (New York: Routledge, 1991).

—*Shakespeare After All* (New York: Anchor, 2005).

Garvin, Katharine, 'A Speculation about *Twelfth Night*', *Notes and Queries* 170 (1936): 326–8.

Gatton, John Spalding, 'Shakespeare in Central Park, Louisville', *Shakespeare Quarterly* 33:3 (1982): 353–5.

Gauthier, Roger-François (ed.), *Hamlet, / La Nuit Des Rois: La Scene et Ses Miroirs, Théâtre Aujourd' Hui 6* (Paris: CNDP, 1998).

Gay, Penny, *As She Likes It: Shakespeare's Unruly Women* (London: Routledge, 1994).

—'Women and Shakespearean Performance', *The Cambridge Companion to Shakespeare on Stage*, Stanley Wells and Sarah Stanton (ed.) (Cambridge: Cambridge University Press, 2002), pp. 155–73.

—'*Twelfth Night:* "The Babbling Gossip of the Air"', *A Companion to Shakespeare's Works*, Richard Dutton and Jean E. Howard (ed.) (Oxford: Blackwell, 2003), pp. 429–46.

Ghose, Indira, 'Licence to Laugh: Festive Laughter in *Twelfth Night*', *A History of English Laughter: Laughter from Beowulf to Beckett and Beyond*, (ed.) Manfred Pfister (Amsterdam: Rodopi, 2002), pp. 35–46.

Gibson, Marion, *Possession, Puritanism and Print: Darrell, Harsnett, Shakespeare and the Elizabethan Exorcism Controversy* (London: Pickering & Chatto, 2006).

Gibson, Rex (ed.), *Twelfth Night* (Cambridge: Cambridge University Press, 1993).

—*Teaching Shakespeare* (Cambridge: Cambridge University Press, 1998).

Gielgud, John, *An Actor and His Time* (London: Sidgwick & Jackson, 1979).

Giese, Loreen L., 'Malvolio's Yellow Stockings: Coding Illicit Sexuality in Early Modern London', *Medieval and Renaissance Drama in England* 19 (2006): 235–46.

Goldberg, Jonathan, *Sodometries: Renaissance Texts, Modern Sexualities* (Stanford: Stanford University Press, 1992).

—*Queering the Renaissance* (Durham: Duke University Press, 1994).

Gonzaga, Curzio, *Gli inganni*, (ed.) Anna Maria Razzoli Roio (Cerrina Alessandria: Verso l'arte, 2006).

Gooch, Brydan N. S., and David Thatcher (ed.), *A Shakespeare Music Catalogue*, 5 vols (Oxford: Clarendon Press, 1991).

Gordon, Philip, 'Shakespeare – with Music', *English Journal* 31 (1942): 433–8.
—'The Morley-Shakespeare Myth', *Music and Letters* 28 (1947): 121–5.

Granville-Barker, Harley, *Prefaces to Shakespeare*, 6 vols, repr. (London: B.T. Batsford, 1974).

Greaves, Simon (ed.), *The Comic Book Shakespeare: Twelfth Night* (Oswestry: Timber Frame, 2003).

Greenblatt, Stephen, *Renaissance Self-Fashioning: From More to Shakespeare* (Chicago: University of Chicago Press, 1980).

—'Fiction and Friction', in *Reconstructing Individualism: Autonomy, Individuality, and the Self in Western Thought*, Thomas C. Helle, Morton Sosner and David E. Wellerby (ed.) (Stanford: Stanford University Press, 1986), pp. 30–52.

—*Shakespearean Negotiations* (Berkeley: University of California Press, 1988).

—(ed.) 'Twelfth Night', in *The Norton Shakespeare*, Stephen Greenblatt, Walter

Cohen, Jean E. Howard and Katharine Eisaman Maus (ed.), 2nd edn (New York: W. W. Norton, 2008), pp. 1785–1846.

Greenhalgh, Susanne, and Robert Shaughnessy, 'Our Shakespeares: British Television and the Strains of Multiculturalism', in *Screening Shakespeare in the Twenty-First Century*, Mark Thornton Burnett and Ramona Wray (ed.) (Edinburgh: Edinburgh University Press, 2006), pp. 90–112.

Greer, Germaine, *Shakespeare* (Oxford: Oxford University Press, 1986).

—*Shakespeare's Wife* (London: Bloomsbury, 2007).

Greg, W. W., *The Shakespeare First Folio* (Oxford: Clarendon Press, 1955).

Greif, Karen, 'A Star is Born: Feste on the Modern Stage', *Shakespeare Quarterly* 39 (1988): 61–78.

Griffin, Alice, 'Current Theatre Notes, 1958–59', *Shakespeare Quarterly* 11:1 (1960): 97–115.

Gross, George C., 'Mary Cowden Clarke, "The Girlhood of Shakespeare's Heroines," and the Sex Education of Victorian Women', *Victorian Studies* 16 (1972): 7–58.

Gurr, Andrew, and Mariko Ichikawa, *Staging in Shakespeare's Theatres* (Oxford: Oxford University Press, 2000).

Haddad, Miranda Johnson, 'The Shakespeare Theatre at the Folger, 1989–90', *Shakespeare Quarterly* 41:4 (1990): 507–20.

Hammond, Paul, *Figuring Sex Between Men from Shakespeare to Rochester* (Oxford: Clarendon Press, 2002).

Hanna, Sara, 'From Illyria to Elysium: Geographical Fantasy in *Twelfth Night*', *Litteraria Pragensia* 12.23 (2002): 21–45.

Hassel, R. Chris, *Faith and Folly in Shakespeare's Romantic Comedies* (Athens: University of Georgia Press, 1980).

Hawkes, Terence, 'Comedy, Orality and Duplicity: *Twelfth Night*', in *Shakespeare's Comedies*, (ed.) Gary Waller (New York: Longman, 1991), pp. 168–74.

Helgerson, Richard, *Forms of Nationhood: The Elizabethan Writing of England* (Chicago: University of Chicago Press, 1992).

Henslowe, Philip, *Henslowe's Diary*, (ed.) R. A. Foakes, 2nd edn (Cambridge: Cambridge University Press, 2002).

Hirsch, Brett D., 'Rousing the Night Owl: Malvolio, *Twelfth Night*, and Anti-Puritan Satire', *Notes and Queries* 56.1 (2009): 53–5.

Hodgdon, Barbara, 'Sexual Disguise and the Theatre of Gender', in *The Cambridge Companion to Shakespeare's Comedies*, (ed.) Alexander Leggatt (Cambridge: Cambridge University Press, 2002), pp. 179–97.

Holcomb, Chris, *Mirth Making: The Rhetorical Discourse on Jesting in Early Modern England* (Columbia: University of South Carolina Press, 2001).

Hollander, John, 'Musica Mundana and *Twelfth Night*', in *Sound and Poetry*, (ed.) Northrop Frye (New York: Columbia University Press, 1957).

Honigmann, E. A. J., *Shakespeare: The 'Lost Years'* (Totowa: Barnes & Noble, 1985).

Hornback, Robert, *The English Clown Tradition from the Middle Ages to Shakespeare* (Cambridge: D. S. Brewer, 2009).

Hotson, Leslie, *The First Night of Twelfth Night* (London: Rupert Hart-Davis, 1954).

Houlahan, Mark, '"Like to th'Egyptian Thief": Shakespeare Sampling Heliodorus in *Twelfth Night*', in *'Rapt in Secret Studies': Emerging Shakespeares*, Michael Neill, Darryl Chalk and Laurie Johnson (ed.) (Newcastle upon Tyne: Cambridge Scholars, 2010), pp. 305–15.

Howard, Jean E., 'Crossdressing, the Theatre, and Gender Struggle in Early Modern England', *Shakespeare Quarterly* 39 (1988): 418–40.

—'Afterword: Early Modern Work and the Work of Representation', in *Working Subjects in Early Modern English Drama*, Michelle M. Dowd and Natasha Korda (ed.) (Farnham: Ashgate, 2011), pp. 243–50.

Hunt, Maurice, *Shakespeare's Religious Allusiveness: Its Play and Tolerance*, (Burlington: Ashgate, 2004).

Hunter, G. K., *Shakespeare: The Later Comedies* (London: Longmans Green, 1962).

Hutcheon, Linda, *Irony's Edge: The Theory and Politics of Irony* (London: Routledge, 1995).

—*A Theory of Adaptation* (London: Routledge, 2006).

Irish, Tracy (ed.), *The Shorter Shakespeare: Twelfth Night* (Carlisle: Carel Press, 2001).

Jackson, Russell, 'Shakespeare in Gdansk, August 2006', *Shakespeare Quarterly* 58:1 (2007): 93–108.

Jameson, Anna, *Characteristics of Women: Moral, Poetical, and Historical* (London Saunders and Otley, 1832).

Jansohn, Christa, '"The Text Remains for Another Attempt": *Twelfth Night, or What You Will* on the German Stage', in *Twelfth Night: New Critical Essays*, (ed.) James Schiffer (London: Routledge, 2011), pp. 201–16.

Jensen, Phebe, 'Teaching Drama as Festivity: Dekker's *The Shoemaker's Holiday* and Beaumont's *The Knight of the Burning Pestle*', *Approaches to Teaching English Renaissance Drama*, Karen Bamford and Alexander Leggatt (ed.) (New York: Modern Language Association of America, 2002), pp. 158–64.

—*Religion and Revelry in Shakespeare's Festive World* (Cambridge: Cambridge University Press, 2008).

Johnson, Nora, *The Actor As Playwright in Early Modern Drama* (Cambridge: Cambridge University Press, 2003).

Johnston, Judith, *Anna Jameson: Victorian, Feminist, Woman of Letters* (Aldershot: Scolar Press, 1997).

Jones, G. P., 'Malvolio Flouted and Abused', *English Language Notes* 42.1 (2004): 20–6.

Jones, Nicholas R., 'Trevor Nunn's *Twelfth Night*: Contemporary Film and Classic British Theatre', *Early Modern Literary Studies* (2002): 1–38.

Joubert, Laurent, *Treatise on Laughter*, trans. by Gregory David De Rocher (Alabama: University of Alabama Press, 1980).

Jowitt, Claire, *The Culture of Piracy, 1580–1630: English Literature and Seaborne Crime* (Aldershot: Ashgate, 2010).

Kamps, Ivo, 'Madness and Social Mobility in *Twelfth Night*', in *Twelfth Night: New Critical Essays*, (ed.) James Schiffer (London: Routledge, 2011), pp. 229–43.

Kathman, David, 'Grocers, Goldsmiths, and Drapers: Freemen and Apprentices in the Elizabethan Theater', *Shakespeare Quarterly* 55:1 (2004): 1–49.

Kelsey, Lin, ' "Many Sorts of Music": Musical Genre in *Twelfth Night* and *The Tempest*', *John Donne Journal* 25 (2006): 129–81.

Kemper, Becky, 'A Clown in the Dark House: Reclaiming the Humor in Malvolio's Downfall', *Journal of the Wooden O Symposium* 7 (2007): 42–50.

Kermode, Frank, *The Sense of an Ending: Studies in the Theory of Fiction* (New York: Oxford University Press, 1967).

Kerrigan, John, 'Secrecy and Gossip in *Twelfth Night*', *Shakespeare Survey* 50 (1997): 65–80.

Kerwin, William, *Beyond the Body: The Boundaries of Medicine and English Renaissance Drama* (Amherst: University of Massachusetts Press, 2005).

Kiernander, Adrian, 'Shakespeare in New Zealand', *Shakespeare Quarterly* 31:3 (1980): 400–2.

—' "You'll be the Man": Homophobia and the Present in Performances of *Twelfth Night* and *Romeo and Juliet*', *Presentism, Gender, and Sexuality in Shakespeare*, (ed.) Evelyn Gajowski (Basingstoke: Palgrave, 2009), pp. 125–42.

Kinney, Arthur F., 'The Unity of *Twelfth Night*', *Shakespeare's Comedies of Love: Essays in Honour of Alexander Leggatt*, Karen Bamford and Ric Knowles (ed.) (Toronto: University of Toronto Press, 2008), pp. 155–74.

Knapp, Jeffrey, *Shakespeare's Tribe: Church, Nation and Theatre in Renaissance England* (Chicago: University of Chicago Press, 2002).

Krieger, Elliot, *A Marxist Study of Shakespeare's Comedies* (London: Macmillan, 1979).

Lamb, Charles, 'On Some of the Old Actors [1822]', in *The Portable Charles Lamb*, (ed.) John Mason Brown, repr. (New York: Viking, 1969).

Lampert, Lisa, *Gender and Jewish Difference from Paul to Shakespeare* (Philadelphia: University of Pennsylvania Press, 2004).

Laqueur, Thomas, *Making Sex: Body and Gender from the Greeks to Freud* (Cambridge: Harvard University Press, 1990).

Select Bibliography

Laroque, François, *Shakespeare's Festive World: Elizabethan Entertainment and the Professional Stage*, trans. by Janet Lloyd (Cambridge: Cambridge University Press, 1993).
—'Shakespeare's Imaginary Geography', in *Shakespeare and Renaissance Europe*, Andrew Hadfield and Paul Hammond (ed.) (London: Thomson, 2005), pp. 193–219.
Lecercle, Ann, 'Country House, Catholicity, and the Crypt(ic) in *Twelfth Night*', *Region, Religion, and Patronage: Lancastrian Shakespeare,* Richard Dutton, Alison Findlay and Richard Wilson (ed.) (Manchester: Manchester University Press, 2003), pp. 84–100.
Leech, Clifford, *Twelfth Night and Shakespearian Comedy* (Toronto: University of Toronto Press, 1965).
Leggatt, Alexander, *Shakespeare's Comedy of Love* (London: Methuen, 1974).
—(ed.), *The Cambridge Companion to Shakespeare's Comedies* (Cambridge: Cambridge University Press, 2002).
—'Questions that Have No Answers', *Teaching Shakespeare: Passing it On*, (ed.) G. B. Shand (Malden: Blackwell, 2009), pp. 61–72.
Lenz, Carolyn Ruth Swift, Gayle Greene and Carol Thomas Neely (ed.), *The Woman's Part: Feminist Criticism of* Shakespeare (Urbana: University of Illinois Press, 1980).
Lewis, Cynthia, 'Whodunit? Plot, Plotting, and Detection in *Twelfth Night*', in *Twelfth Night: New Critical Essays*, (ed.) James Schiffer (London: Routledge, 2011), pp. 258–72.
Lindblad, Ishrat, 'Shakespeare on the Swedish Stage', *Shakespeare Quarterly* 33:4 (1982): 524–8.
Lindheim, Nancy, 'Rethinking Sexuality and Class in *Twelfth Night*', *University of Toronto Quarterly* 76.2 (2007): 679–713.
Lindley, David, *Shakespeare and Music* (London: Thomson Learning, 2006).
Lisak, Catherine, 'Domesticating Strangeness in *Twelfth Night*', in *Twelfth Night: New Critical Essays*, (ed.) James Schiffer (London: Routledge, 2011), pp. 167–83.
Louvel, Liliane, *Poetics of the Iconotext*, trans. by Laurence Petit, (ed.) Karen Jacobs (Aldershot: Ashgate, 2011).
MacFaul, Tom, *Male Friendship in Shakespeare and His Contemporaries* (Cambridge: Cambridge University Press, 2007).
Maclure, Millar, *Marlowe: The Critical Inheritance* (London: Routledge & Kegan Paul, 1970).
Mangen, Michael, *A Preface to Shakespeare's Comedies 1594–1603* (London: Longman, 1996).
Manningham, John, *The Diary*, (ed.) Robert Parker Sorlien (Hannover: University of New Haven, 1976).
Manvell, Roger, *Shakespeare and the Film* (New York: Praeger, 1971).

Marciano, Lisa, 'The Serious Comedy of *Twelfth Night*: Dark Didacticism in Illyria', *Renascence* 56:1, (2003): 3–19.

Margolies, David, 'Teaching the Handsaw to Fly: Shakespeare as a Hegemonic Instrument', in *The Shakespeare Myth*, (ed.) Graham Holderness (Manchester University Press, 1988), pp. 42–53.

Martin, Randall, 'Shakespearian Biography, Biblical Allusion, and Early Modern Practices of Reading Scripture,' *Shakespeare Survey* 63 (2010): 212–24.

Maslen, R. W., '*Twelfth Night*, Gender, and Comedy', in *Early Modern English Drama: A Critical Companion*, Garrett A. Sullivan Jr., Patrick Cheney and Andrew Hadfield (ed.) (Oxford: Oxford University Press, 2006), pp. 130–39.

Massai, Sonia (ed.) *William Shakespeare's Twelfth Night: A Sourcebook* (London: Routledge, 2007).

Mazer, Cary M., *Shakespeare Refashioned: Elizabethan Plays on Edwardian Stages* (Ann Arbor: UMI Research Press, 1981).

McClung Evans, Willa, *Ben Jonson and Elizabethan Music* (New York: Da Capo Press, 1965).

McKewin, Carole, 'Counsels of Gall and Grace: Intimate Conversations between Women in Shakespeare's Plays', in *The Woman's Part*, Carolyn Ruth Swift Lenz, Gayle Greene and Carol Thomas Neely (ed.) (Urbana: University of Illinois Press, 1980), pp. 117–32.

McLuskie, Kathleen, 'The Patriarchal Bard: Feminist Criticism and Shakespeare: *King Lear* and *Measure for Measure*', in *Political Shakespeare: New Essays in Cultural Materialism*, Jonathan Dollimore and Alan Sinfield (ed.) (Ithaca: Cornell University Press, 1985), pp. 88–108.

Menon, Madhavi (ed.), *Shakesqueer: A Queer Companion to the Complete Works of Shakespeare* (Durham: Duke University Press, 2011).

Mentz, Steve, *At the Bottom of Shakespeare's Ocean* (London: Continuum, 2009).

Milward, Peter, 'Wise Fools in Shakespeare,' *Christianity and Literature* 33 (1984): 21–7.

—'The Religious Dimension of Shakespeare's Illyria', *Litteraria Pragensia* 12:23 (2002): 59–65.

Mitchell, W. J. T., *Picture Theory* (Chicago and London: University of Chicago Press, 1994).

Modenessi, Alfredo Michel, ' "This Uncivil and Unjust Extent Against Thy Peace": Tim Supple's *Twelfth Night*, or What Violence Will', *Shakespeare Survey* 61 (2008): 91–103.

Monk, Nicholas with Carol Chillington Rutter, Jonothan Neelands and Jonathan Heron, *Open-space Learning: A Study in Transdisciplinary Pedagogy* (London: Bloomsbury, 2011).

Mullin, Michael, 'The Colorado Shakespeare Festival', *Shakespeare Quarterly* 36:4 (1985): 470–2.

Murray, Christopher, 'Shakespeare in Ireland', *Shakespeare Quarterly* 33:2 (1982): 197–9.

Nash, Walter, 'Puns and Parody', in *Reading Shakespeare's Dramatic Language: A Guide*, Sylvia Adamson, Lynette Hunter, Lynne Magnusson, Ann Thompson and Katie Wales (ed.) (London: Arden Shakespeare, 2001), pp. 71–88.

Naylor, E. W., *Shakespeare and Music* (London: Dent, 1896).

Neely, Carol Thomas, *Distracted Subjects: Madness and Gender in Shakespeare and Early Modern Culture* (Ithaca: Cornell University Press, 2004).

Nevo, Ruth, *Comic Transformations in Shakespeare* (London: Methuen, 1980).

Nixon, Ingeborg, 'Shakespeare in Denmark', *Shakespeare Quarterly* 32:3 (1981): 374–5.

Noble, Richmond Samuel Howe, *Shakespeare's Use of Song* (Oxford: Oxford University Press, 1923).

Norbrook, David, 'The Reformation of the Masque', in *The Court Masque*, (ed.) David Lindley (Manchester: Manchester University Press, 1984), pp. 94–101

Norton, David L. 'On Teaching What Students Already Know', *The School Review* 82:1 (1973): 45–56.

Novak, Peter, ' "Where Lies Your Text?" *Twelfth Night* in American Sign Language Translation', *Shakespeare Survey* 61 (2008): 74–90.

Novy, Marianne, ' "An You Smile Not, He's Gagged": Mutuality in Shakespeare's Comedy', in *Love's Argument: Gender Relations in Shakespeare* (Chapel Hill: University of North Carolina Press, 1984), pp. 21–44.

O'Connor, John (ed.), *New Longman Shakespeare: Twelfth Night* (London: Longman, 1999).

Odell, George C. D., *Shakespeare: From Betterton to Irving*, 2 vols., repr. (New York: Benjamin Blom, 1963).

Orgel, Stephen, *Impersonations: The Performance of Gender in Shakespeare's England* (Cambridge University Press, 1996).

—'Why Did the English Stage Take Boys for Women?', in *Teaching Shakespeare through Performance*, (ed.) Milla Cozart Riggio (New York: Modern Language Association of America, 1999), pp. 102–13.

Osborne, Laurie E., *The Trick of Singularity: Twelfth Night and the Performance Editions* (Iowa City: University of Iowa Press, 1996).

—'Editing Frailty in *Twelfth Night*: "Where Lies Your Text?" ', in *Reading Readings: Essays on Shakespeare Editing in the Eighteenth Century*, (ed.) Joanna Gondris (Madison: Fairleigh Dickinson Press, 1998), pp. 209–23.

—' "The Marriage of True Minds": Amity, Twinning, and Comic Closure in *Twelfth Night*', in *Twelfth Night: New Critical Essays*, (ed.) James Schiffer (London: Routledge, 2011), pp. 99–113.

Otto, Beatrice K., *Fools are Everywhere: The Court Jester Around the World* (Chicago: University of Chicago Press, 2001).

Palfrey, Simon, and Tiffany Stern, *Shakespeare in Parts* (Oxford: Oxford University Press, 2007).

Palmer, Barbara D., 'Early Modern Mobility: Players, Payments, and Patrons', *Shakespeare Quarterly* 56:3 (2005): 259–305.

Palmer, D. J., 'Bottom, St Paul, and Erasmus's *Praise of Folly*', in *KM 80: A Birthday Album for Kenneth Muir*, Philip Edwards, Vincent Newey and Ann Thompson (ed.) (Liverpool: Liverpool University Press, 1987), pp. 112–13.

Parker, Patricia, 'Altering the Letter of *Twelfth Night:* "Some are Born Great" and the Missing Signature', *Shakespeare Survey* 59 (2006): 49–62.

—'Was Illyria as Mysterious and Foreign as We Think?', in *The Mysterious and the Foreign in Early Modern England*, Helen Ostovich, Mary V. Silcox and Graham Roebuck (ed.) (Newark: University of Delaware Press, 2008), pp. 209–33.

—'*Twelfth Night*: Editing Puzzles and Eunuchs of All Kinds', in *Twelfth Night: New Critical Essays*, (ed.) James Schiffer (London: Routledge, 2011), pp. 45–64.

Paster, Gail Kern, *The Body Embarrassed: Drama and the Disciplines of Shame in Early Modern England* (Ithaca: Cornell University Press, 1993).

Patterson, R. F. (ed.), *Ben Jonson's Conversations with William Drummond of Hawthornden* (London: Blackie, 1923).

Pennington, Michael, *Twelfth Night: A User's Guide* (London: Nick Hern, 2000).

Pentland, Elizabeth, 'Beyond the "Lyric" in Illyricum: Some Early Modern Backgrounds to *Twelfth Night*', in *Twelfth Night: New Critical Essays*, (ed.) James Schiffer (London: Continuum, 2011), pp. 149–66.

Penuel, Suzanne, 'Missing Fathers: *Twelfth Night* and the Reformation of Mourning', *Studies in Philology* 107:1 (2010): 74–96.

Pequigney, Joseph, *Such is My Love: A Study of Shakespeare's Sonnets* (Chicago: University of Chicago Press, 1985).

—'The Two Antonios and Same-Sex Love in *Twelfth Night* and *The Merchant of Venice*', *English Literary Renaissance* 22 (1992): 41–54.

Pieri, Marzia, 'Introduzione', in Accademici degli Intronati di Siena, *Gl'Ingannati* (Corazzano: Titivillus, 2009).

Poole, Kristen, *Radical Religion from Shakespeare to Milton* (Cambridge: Cambridge University Press, 2000).

Potter, Lois, *Twelfth Night: Text and Performance* (Basingstoke: Macmillan, 1985).

Poulton, Diana, 'The Favourite Singer of Queen Elizabeth I,' *The Consort* 14 (1957): 24–7.

—*John Dowland* (Berkeley: University of California Press, 1982).

Powers, Alan W., '"What He Wills": Early Modern Rings and Vows in *Twelfth*

Night', in *Twelfth Night: New Critical Essays*, (ed.) James Schiffer (London: Routledge, 2011), pp. 217–28.

Prest, Wilfred (ed.), *The Professions in Early Modern England* (London: Croom Helm, 1987).

Price, David G., *Patrons and Musicians of the English Renaissance* (Cambridge University Press, 1981).

Rackin, Phyllis, 'Androgyny, Mimesis, and the Marriage of the Boy Heroine on the English Renaissance Stages', *Publications of the Modern Language Association* 102 (1987): 29–47.

Reinhard Lupton, Julia, *Citizen-Saints: Shakespeare and Political Theology* (Chicago: University of Chicago Press, 2005).

Riche, Barnaby, *Riche's Farewell to Militarie Profession* (1581).

Rist, Thomas, 'Merry, Marry, Mary: Shakespearian Wordplay and *Twelfth Night*', *Shakespeare Survey* 62 (2009): 81–91.

Ritchie, Fiona, 'Shakespeare and the Eighteenth-Century Actress', *Borrowers and Lenders: The Journal of Shakespeare and Appropriation* 2.2 (2006), http://www.borrowers.uga.edu/7151/toc [accessed 11 February 2013].

Roberts, Jeanne Addison, 'Shakespeare in The Nation's Capital', *Shakespeare Quarterly* 32:2 (1981): 206–10.

Rocklin, Edward L, *Performance Approaches to Teaching Shakespeare* (Urbana: National Council of Teachers of English, 2005).

Rothwell, Kenneth S., and Annabelle Henkin Melzer, *Shakespeare on Screen: An International Filmography and Videography* (New York: Neal-Schuman, 1990).

Rothwell, Kenneth S., *A History of Shakespeare on Screen: A Century of Film and Television*, 2nd edn (Cambridge: Cambridge University Press, 2004).

Rutter, Tom, *Work and Play on the Shakespearean Stage* (Cambridge: Cambridge University Press, 2008).

Salgado, Gamini (ed.), *Eyewitnesses of Shakespeare: First Hand Accounts of Performances 1590–1890* (London: Sussex University Press, 1975).

Salingar, L. G., 'The Design of *Twelfth Night*', *Shakespeare Quarterly* 9 (1958): 117–39.

Salomone, Ronald E. M., and James E. Davis, *Teaching Shakespeare into the Twenty-First Century* (Athens: Ohio University Press, 1997).

Sammons, Eddie, *Shakespeare: A Hundred Years on Film* (Lanham: Scarecrow Press, 2004).

Sands, Kathleen R., *Demon Possession in Elizabethan England* (London: Praeger, 2004).

Sawyer, Paul, 'The Popularity of Shakespeare's Plays, 1720–21 through 1732–33', *Shakespeare Quarterly* 29:3 (1978): 427–30.

Schafer, Elizabeth (ed.), *Shakespeare in Production: Twelfth Night* (Cambridge: Cambridge University Press, 2009).

speare's Comedies', *Hellas: A Journal*
29–37.

Shakespeare: A Selection (Lewiston:

Night', in *Word and Self Estranged in*
lly and L. E. Semler (ed.) (Burlington:

issance Drama (Cambridge: Cambridge

California', *Shakespeare Quarterly* 33:3

* and Text in the Elizabethan Playhouse*
ress, 1987).

oxes', in *The Cambridge Companion to*
son (Cambridge: Cambridge University

welve Years' Study of Plays and Players

Calore (ed.), *Music in Shakespeare: A*
5).

are (Harmondsworth: Penguin Books,

sters: Shakespeare in the Company of
8.

Shadows (New York: Routledge–Taylor

dies of London (1590).
kespeare, Middleton, and the Puritans',
7–86.

—(ed.), *Twelfth Night: Shakespeare in Production* (Cambridge: Cambridge University Press, 2009).

Schalkwyk, David, 'Love and Service in *Twelfth Night* and the *Sonnets*', *Shakespeare Quarterly* 56:1 (2005): 76–100.

—'The Discourses of Friendship and the Structural Imagination of Shakespeare's Theater: Montaigne, *Twelfth Night*, De Gournay', *Renaissance Drama* 38 (2010): 141–71.

—'Music, Food, and Love in the Affective Landscapes of *Twelfth Night*', in *Twelfth Night: New Critical Essays*, (ed.) James Schiffer (London: Routledge, 2011), pp. 81–98.

Schiffer, James (ed.), *Twelfth Night: New Critical Essays* (London: Routledge, 2011).

Scott-Warren, Jason, 'When Theaters Were Bear-Gardens; or, What's at Stake in the Comedy of Humors', *Shakespeare Quarterly* 54:1 (2003): 63–82.

Seng, Peter, *The Vocal Songs in the Plays of Shakespeare: a Critical History* (Cambridge: Harvard University Press, 1967).

Shannon, Laurie J., 'Nature's Bias: Renaissance Homonormativity and Elizabethan Comic Likeness', *Modern Philology* 98 (2000–1): 183–210.

Shepard, Alexandra, 'Manhood, Credit and Patriarchy in Early Modern England, c.1580–1640', *Past and Present* 167.1 (2000): 75–106

Shute, John, *The First and Chief Groundes of Architecture used in all the Auncient and Famous Monymentes* (1563).

Sinfield, Alan, 'Give an account of Shakespeare and Education, showing why you think they are effective and what you have appreciated about them. Support your comments with precise references', in *Political Shakespeare: New Essays in Cultural Materialism*, Jonathan Dollimore and Alan Sinfield (ed.) (Manchester: Manchester University Press, 1985), pp. 134–57.

Smith, Amy L., and Elizabeth Hodgson, ' "A Cypress, Not a Bosom, Hides my Heart": Olivia's Veiled Conversions', *Early Modern Literary Studies*, 15:1 (2009–10), http://purl.oclc.org/emls/15-1/olivveil.htm [accessed 28 April 2012].

Smith, Bruce R. (ed.), *Twelfth Night: Texts and Contexts* (Boston: Bedford/St Martin's, 2001).

—' "His Fancy's Queen": Sensing Sexual Strangeness in *Twelfth Night*', *Twelfth Night: New Critical Essays*, (ed.) James Schiffer (London: Routledge, 2011), pp. 65–80.

Smith, Emma (ed.), *Shakespeare's Comedies* (Malden: Blackwell, 2004).

Speaight, Robert, 'Shakespeare in Britain', *Shakespeare Quarterly* 22:4 (1971): 359–64.

—'Shakespeare in Britain', *Shakespeare Quarterly* 28:2 (1977): 184–90.

Sprague, Arthur Colby, *Shakespeare and the Actors: The Stage Business in H* *Plays (1660–1905)*, repr. (New York: Russell & Russell, 1963).

Sprague, Arthur Colby, and J. C. Trewin, *Shakespeare's Plays Today: Son* *Customs and Conventions of the Stage*, repr. (Columbia: University of Sout Carolina Press, 1971).

St Clare Byrne, M., 'The Shakespeare Season at The Old Vic, 1957–58 an Stratford-upon-Avon, 1958', *Shakespeare Quarterly* 9:4 (1958): 507–30.

Stanivukovic, Goran V., '"What Country, Friends, is This?" The Geographie of Illyria in Early Modern England', *Litteraria Pragensia* 12:23 (2002) 5–20.

—'Illyria Revisited: Shakespeare and the Eastern Adriatic', in *Shakespeare an the Mediterranean: The Selected Proceedings of the International Shakespeare Association World Congress, Valencia, 2001*, Thomas Clayton, Susan Brock and Vincente Forés (ed.) (Newark: University of Delaware Press, 2004), pp. 400–15.

—'Masculine Plots in *Twelfth Night*', in *Twelfth Night: New Critical Essays*, (ed.) James Schiffer (London: Routledge, 2011), pp. 114–30.

Staunton, Howard (ed.), *The Plays of Shakespeare with the Poems*, (ed.) Howard Staunton, 3 vols (London: Routledge, Warnes and Routledge, 1859).

Stern, Tiffany, 'Songs and Masques', in *Documents of Performance in Early Modern England* (Cambridge: Cambridge University Press, 2009).

Stott, Andrew, '"The Fondness, the Filthiness:" Deformity and Laughter in Early-Modern Comedy', *The Upstart Crow* 24, 2004: 15–24

Stredder, James, *The North Face of Shakespeare* (Cambridge: Cambridge University Press, 2009).

Stříbrný, Zdeněk, 'Shakespeare in Czechoslovakia', *Shakespeare Quarterly* 33:4 (1982): 502–5.

Styan, J. L., *The Shakespeare Revolution: Criticism and Performance in the Twentieth Century* (Cambridge: Cambridge University Press, 1977).

Summers, Joseph, 'The Masks of *Twelfth Night*', in *Shakespeare: Modern Essays in Criticism*, (ed.) Leonard F. Dean (New York: Oxford University Press, 1967), pp. 133–43.

Sutherland, John, and Cedric Watts, 'What Happens to Viola's "Eunuch" Plan?' and 'Malvolio: Vengeful or Reconciled?' in *Henry V, War Criminal? And Other Shakespeare Puzzles* (Oxford: Oxford University Press, 2000), pp. 126–36.

Suzuki, Mihoko, 'Gender, Class, and the Ideology of Comic Form: *Much Ado about Nothing* and *Twelfth Night*', *A Feminist Companion to Shakespeare*, (ed.) Dympna C. Callaghan (Oxford: Blackwell, 2000), pp. 121–43.

Taylor, Gary, *Reinventing Shakespeare: A Cultural History from the Restoration to the Present* (New York: Weidenfeld and Nicolson, 1989).

—'Theatrical Proximities: The Stratford Festival 1998', *Shakespeare Quarterly* 50:3 (1999): 334–54.

Whall, Helen M., 'Divining Paul in Shak *of Poetry and the Humanities* 7 (1996):

White, R. S. (ed.), *Hazlitt's Criticism o* Edwin Mellen Press, 1996).

—'Estranging Word and Self in *Twelfth English Texts, 1550–1660*, Philippa Ke Ashgate, 2010), pp. 107–20.

Whitney, Charles, *Early Responses to Ren* University Press, 2006).

Wilds, Lillian, 'Shakespeare in Southern (1982): 380–93.

Wiles, David, *Shakespeare's Clown: Acto* (Cambridge: Cambridge University P

Willems, Michèle, 'Video and its Parad *Shakespeare on Film*, (ed.) Russell Jack Press, 2000), pp. 35–46.

Williamson, Audrey, *Old Vic Drama: A* (London: Rockliff, 1948).

Wilson, Christopher R. and Michela *Dictionary* (London: Continuum, 20

Wilson, Edwin (ed.), *Shaw on Shakesp* 1969).

Wilson, Richard, 'Making Men of Mor Strangers', *Shakespeare* 1 (2005): 8–

—*Shakespeare in French Theory: King of* & Francis, 2007).

Wilson, Robert, *The Three Lords and La*

Yachnin, Paul, 'Reversal of Fortune: Sh *English Literary History* 70 (2003): 7

INDEX

Walker, Timothy 204
Warner, William 209
Warren, Roger 200, 212, 219n. 3,
     225n. 22, 231n. 77, 243n. 13,
     244n. 24, 246n. 5, 249nn. 9,
     11, 250n. 38, 253n. 55
Wayne, Valerie 50, 222n. 66
web resources 212–14
Webster, John 204
Weiss, Alfred 58, 227n. 35
Weiss, John 41
Welles, Orson 59, 227n. 38
Wells, Robin Headlam 74, 233n. 19
Wells, Stanley 4, 198, 200, 212, 216n.
     19, 219nn. 1, 3, 220n. 26,
     233n. 20, 243n. 11, 244n. 24,
     246n. 5, 249nn. 9, 11, 251n.
     13, 253nn. 43, 44, 55, 254n. 74

Welsford, Enid 155, 248n. 32
Werstine, Paul 202, 212, 254n. 61
White, R. S. 1, 12, 16, 98, 219n. 9,
     220n. 19, 239n. 175, 274
Whitehall 120, 167
Williamson, Nicol 66
Wilson, John Dover 42, 186, 251n. 39
Wilson, Richard 81, 91, 235nn. 62,
     80, 237nn. 126, 127, 128
Wilson, Robert, 18
Wolfit, Donald 62
Wollen, Will 211
Woolf, Virginia 48
Wright, Edward 106–7
Wyatt, Thomas 182

Yachnin, Paul 85, 236n. 87, 245n. 31
Young Vic 60